JOURNEYS IN NEW WORLDS

Wisconsin Studies in American Autobiography
William L. Andrews, General Editor

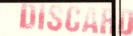
Journeys in New Worlds

Early American Women's Narratives

WILLIAM L. ANDREWS
General Editor

THE UNIVERSITY OF WISCONSIN PRESS

The University of Wisconsin Press
114 North Murray Street
Madison, Wisconsin 53715

3 Henrietta Street
London WC2E 8LU, England

973. 2092
A

5 4 3 2 1

Printed in the United States of America

Library of Congress Cataloging-in-Publication Data
Journeys in new worlds: early American women's narratives / William L. Andrews, editor.
   240 pp.   cm. — (Wisconsin studies in American autobiography)
   Includes bibliographical references.
   1. United States—History—Colonial period, ca. 1600–1775—Biography.
  2. Women—United States—Biography. I. Andrews, William L., 1946–
II. Series.
E187.5.J68   1990
973.2′092′2—dc20
[B]
   ISBN 0-299-12580-7   90-50078
   ISBN 0-299-12584-X (pbk.)   CIP

Contents

Illustrations

Contributors

WILLIAM L. ANDREWS is Joyce and Elizabeth Hall Distinguished Professor of American Literature at the University of Kansas. He is the author and editor of several books on autobiography, including *To Tell a Free Story: The First Century of Afro-American Autobiography, 1760–1865; Sisters of the Spirit: Three Black Women's Autobiographies of the Nineteenth Century,* and *My Bondage and My Freedom,* by Frederick Douglass. He is associate editor of *a/b: auto/biography studies* and general editor of Studies in American Autobiography, published by the University of Wisconsin Press.

SARGENT BUSH, JR., has written on numerous American authors. His work on colonial literature and its intellectual contexts includes his book on all of Thomas Hooker's works, *The Writings of Thomas Hooker: Spiritual Adventure in Two Worlds* (University of Wisconsin Press), and a study, written with Carl J. Rasmussen, of the growth of a major Puritan college library, *The Library of Emmanuel College, Cambridge, 1584–1637* (Cambridge University Press). He is now collecting and editing the correspondence of John Cotton. He is Professor of English and Associate Dean of the College of Letters and Science at the University of Wisconsin–Madison.

ANNETTE KOLODNY is Dean of the Faculty of Humanities and Professor of English at The University of Arizona. Her previous explorations of the cultural mythology of the United States frontiers resulted in numerous articles and two major book-length studies, *The Lay of the Land: Metaphor as Experience and History in American Life and Letters* and *The Land Before Her: Fantasy and Experience of the American Frontiers, 1630–1860.* Equally well known for her contributions to feminist literary criticism, she is currently at work on a book about the impact of feminist literary theory on the American academy, to be entitled *Dancing Through the Minefield.*

AMY SCHRAGER LANG is Associate Professor of the Graduate Institute of Liberal Arts at Emory University. She is the author of *Prophetic Woman: Anne Hutchinson and the Problem of Dissent in the Literature of New England (1987)*. She is currently at work on a book entitled *Negotiating the Border: The Social Vocabulary of American Fiction, 1848–1877* (forthcoming from Princeton University Press).

DANIEL B. SHEA is Professor of English at Washington University. He is the author and editor of several books and articles about early American literature, including *Spiritual Autobiography in Early America,* published by the University of Wisconsin Press.

JOURNEYS IN NEW WORLDS

Introduction

American literature originates, according to long-standing tradition, in the narratives of explorers like Captain John Smith of Virginia and settlers like Governor William Bradford of Massachusetts, men who sought in the New World the fulfillment of Europe's timeless dream of a new beginning. The seventeenth-century Englishmen who first saw and wrote about North America were hardly "literary" in any conventional sense of that word, but their records of their journeys sometimes grow almost rhapsodic about the New World because it seemed to constitute, in the words of one New England enthusiast, "Nature's masterpiece." Thomas Morton, author of *New English Canaan* (1637), spoke for many of his fellows when he wrote of Massachusetts: "The more I looked, the more I liked it. And when I had more seriously considered of the beauty of the place, with all her fair endowments, I did not think that in all the known world it could be paralleled." In language of this sort, the men whose journals of their journeys launched American literature in English endowed the New World with a feminine identity, as Annette Kolodny has argued in *The Lay of the Land*, and then regaled their readers with fantasies of life in America as a "*Paradise* with all her virgin beauties."[1]

In their rush to embrace the land and convert "all her fair endowments" to their own use, the earliest American leaders could scarcely pause to ponder the role of women in the providential mating of Man and Nature in the New World. When William Wood penned his *New England's Prospects* in 1634 as a means of enticing Englishmen to a better life in North America, he addressed himself to "men of good working, and contriving heads"—carpenters, coopers, brickmakers, smiths, gardeners, tailors, and various other tradesmen—but had nothing to say to the women of England. In the first histories of New England—Bradford's *Of Plymouth Plantation* (1630–50) and *The Journal of John Winthrop* (1630–49)—the women of the early Massachusetts colonies receive little distinction unless, like the dissenter Anne Hutchinson, they challenged male leadership and had to be ostracized from the communion of the faithful. On the rare occasions when he mentions women at all, Winthrop speaks of them primarily as curiosities, noting a "distracted" woman who had to be returned to England in 1634, a Boston woman who in desperation over her own salvation threw her child down a well, and the "disorderly" and outlawed practice of women's assembling weekly in Boston in 1637 to discuss,

---

1. *The Lay of the Land* (Chapel Hill: University of North Carolina Press, 1975), 4.

under female leadership, scriptural and doctrinal matters. As a contrast to such women Winthrop offered the example of the wife of John Cotton, who makes a brief appearance in Winthrop's *Journal* in conjunction with the momentous arrival of her husband, a celebrated Puritan preacher, in Boston in 1633. When asked by the Puritan elders to make a public confession of his faith as a condition of admission into the church, Cotton readily consented. He objected, however, to his wife's being required "to make open confession," since such public testimony was "not fit for women's modesty." Agreeing with Cotton, the elders of the Boston church limited themselves to asking his wife "if she did consent in the confession of faith made by her husband." When "she answered affirmatively," she was accepted into the church and faded once again into anonymity in the history of New England.[2]

To answer affirmatively the expectations of a social order dominated by male prerogative was among the chief obligations of women in early America. Although life on the frontier offered women a degree of freedom that many of their Old World sisters did not enjoy, the ultimate purpose and value of woman—as mate and mother—was as much assumed in America as in Europe. Marriage liberated a woman from the power of her father but consigned her to an equally subservient status with regard to her husband. To live as a single woman, in company with another woman or alone, was almost a financial impossibility, to say nothing of the damage to reputation that such nonconformity would incur. Marriage, therefore, became a virtual economic, if not social, necessity for women in early America.

The four women whose autobiographical narratives are reprinted in this book—Mary Rowlandson, Sarah Kemble Knight, Elizabeth Ashbridge, and Elizabeth House Trist—followed the prescribed path of their society by marrying. Their motives, to the extent that we can know them, no doubt typify reasons why women of their time and circumstances entered into matrimony. None of these writers complains of marriage as an institution. Even Elizabeth Ashbridge, the only one who pictures herself in the bonds of a bad marriage, offers no critique of the social and economic exigencies that pushed her into a match with an abusive husband. One of the most striking features of these four narratives, however, given their authors' tacit acceptance of traditional sexual roles and responsibilities in marriage, is the common focus on crucial instances in each woman's life when she had to rely on herself. In only one of these narratives does the husband of the narrator figure prominently, and in that case he functions primarily as an obstacle that his wife (Ashbridge) must overcome on her way to self-realization.

Whatever their attitudes toward their domestic lives, neither Rowlandson,

2. Sarah Cotton's silence in this instance, it should be noted, was not entirely typical of Puritan women. As Patricia Caldwell and other scholars have shown, Puritan women in both the Old and New Worlds sometimes seized the opportunity to speak publicly and eloquently of their spiritual experience when allowed to do so during the course of the membership admission procedures of the Puritan church (see Caldwell, *The Puritan Conversion Narrative* [Cambridge: Cambridge University Press, 1983]).

Knight, Ashbridge, nor Trist saw their experience within the boundaries of instituted roles and traditional behavior as worthy of sustained autobiographical attention. The story that each of these women had to tell was both a tale of exploration beyond the frontiers of woman's sphere and an account of discovery within the uncharted borders of the self. The traditional metaphor of life as a journey enabled Rowlandson, Knight, Ashbridge, and Trist to authorize themselves as women writers whose experience was potentially significant to men as well as women. Rowlandson, for example, spoke to and for an entire community in her captivity narrative, whereas Trist, whose journal is published for the first time in this volume, seems to have written specifically with Thomas Jefferson in mind as her audience. By subscribing to literary models that made possible the transmutation of an individual's journey into a representative quest, these four women risked subsuming the uniqueness of their experience under generic cultural categories that might have robbed their stories of their gender-specific value. Despite their participation in the cultural agenda of their time, however, these four narratives also speak for and to the personal needs and aims of the women who wrote them, giving readers of today a compelling sense of the ways in which early American women writers negotiated the competing priorities of self and social identification.

The *True History of the Captivity and Restoration of Mrs. Mary Rowlandson* (1682) provides a prime example of the tension between obligations to the self and to the social order that underlies all four of these narratives. Well into the story of her Indian captivity, Rowlandson pauses "to mention one principal ground of my setting forth these few Lines, even as the Psalmist says, To declare the works of the Lord, and his wonderful power in carrying us along, preserving us in the Wilderness, while under the Enemies hand, and returning of us in safety again; and his goodness in bringing to my hand so many comfortable and suitable Scriptures in my distress." Such a statement is designed to confirm the faith of the Puritan community in God's decision to chastise his people and yet to preserve them in their chastisement so that they might emerge from it to "safety" in an abiding sense of dependence on the Almighty. Thus the last sentence of Rowlandson's narrative reads, "I have learned to look beyond present and smaller troubles, and to be quieted under them, as *Moses* said, *Exod.* xiv: 13, *Stand still, and see the salvation of the Lord.*"

Yet anyone who reads the account can see almost from the start of her story that Rowlandson was not the sort of person to stand still and passively wait on God's deliverance. She makes a striking contrast to her sister Elizabeth, who died willingly at the onset of the Indian attack on their Lancaster settlement. "I had often before this said, that if the *Indians* should come, I should chuse rather to be killed by them than taken alive," Rowlandson admits, "but when it came to the trial my mind changed." Rather than "end my daies" on that bloody February morning in 1676, "I chose" to go with the Indians. This is the first of many decisions and choices that Rowlandson recounts in her story, all of which testify to her

unrelenting grip on life and the depth of her desire for self-preservation. Rowlandson's recollections of her primal struggle for personal survival are so starkly and
vividly rendered that they tend to overshadow the rather predictable moralizing
that accompanies them. As a result the narrative seems to speak in two voices, the
one eliciting a gut-level response to the corporeal Rowlandson of "wolvish appetite," "feeble knees and aking heart," while the other voice elevates Rowlandson to
symbolic significance by casting her as a type of the spiritually redeemed of God.

Repeatedly in the narratives of Knight, Ashbridge, and Trist a similar tension
between two voices, two different ways of representing the narrator, or two different ways of her perceiving the world emerges. Sometimes, as in Rowlandson's
story, the narrator's strong sense of herself as a subject and her determination to
record her subjective feelings and views are but uneasily reconciled to her sense of
obligation to the social order to picture herself as an object so as to award credit
and praise for her achievements to someone else (in Rowlandson's case to God the
Father) rather than to herself. We find a similar instance of this tension between
woman as subject and as object in the *Life of Elizabeth Ashbridge* (1774). At the beginning of her narrative Ashbridge avows her intention "to make some remarks on
the Dealings of Divine Goodness to me," putting God in the role of protagonist
and herself as simply the object of His actions. Yet Ashbridge's spiritual autobiography cannot be read simply as the story of how God showed a wayward
woman that she was to serve him as a Quaker and a missionary. For this woman
service to God entails a revolutionary self-assessment, the result of which is her
taking control of and responsibility for herself as a spiritual being whose destiny
cannot be dictated from without, only discovered by looking within.

The modesty and self-depreciation of Ashbridge's *Life* is by no means unusual in
male as well as female spiritual autobiography of the time. Yet it is hard to imagine
anyone weathering the perilous journeys that Ashbridge undertook in life without
a buoyant and vital ego. Ashbridge acknowledges that from her youth she had
"great Vivacity in my Natural Disposition," which helps to account for her re-
silience and resourcefulness in the face of many trials, including her immigration
to America, four years of indentured servitude to a mean-spirited master, and a
subsequent marriage to a tyrannical husband. Having little power other than her
wits and her tongue, Ashbridge makes the most of her assets, talking her way out
of a whipping on one occasion by appealing to her master in the name of her father,
thereby effectively pitting patriarchal privilege against itself. Ashbridge resorts to
the power of her eloquence in the climax of her autobiography when she demands
of her husband the right to attend Friends' meeting and live according to Quaker
faith and practice. "As a Dutyfull Wife ought, So I was ready to obey all his Lawfull Commands, but where they Imposed upon my Conscience, I no longer Durst:
For I had already done it too long, & wronged my Self by it." The spiritual evolution of Elizabeth Ashbridge ultimately required her to declare her "Self" as her
most reliable guide to the will of God, much more trustworthy than her husband or

INTRODUCTION 7

the mercenary ministers who become synonyous with hypocrisy and cynicism as Ashbridge grows into a mature sense of her mission. Her narrative concludes with her liberation from her husband, but we are invited to see this not as an end but a means, since Ashbridge had long since decided, whether married or not, "never to leave Searching till I had found the truth."

Unlike the narratives of Rowlandson and Ashbridge, the journals of Knight and Trist record quite literal journeys undertaken for worldly purposes and interpreted, for the most part, in secular ways. Although Knight composed her journal in 1704–1705, just a little more than two decades after Rowlandson's narrative was published, the later writer shares little of the earlier one's spiritual preoccupation. Even when confronted with the fact of her own mortality as she attempts to ford a swollen river on an "exceeding dark" October night, the Boston businesswoman cannot find in her earthly predicament the sort of transcendent religious meaning that readily occurred to her Puritan forebear. "No thoughts but those of the dang'ros River could entertain my Imagination," Knight confesses. Knight's "imagination" offers her an escape from this confrontation with death, but the price of the passage is irony. Warding off "seing my self drowning," her mind offers her but one alternative: the prospect of emerging from the other side of the river "like a holy Sister Just come out of a Spiritual bath in dripping Garments." Knight foresees her fate hovering between the sublime and the ridiculous. Her imagination delivers her from tragedy—a bloated corpse floating in the river— only to plunge her into comedy—a dignified and genteel woman slogging her way to shore in the middle of the night, cold and soaking wet. Thus even when contemplating the "blackest Ideas of my Approching fate," Knight, unlike Rowlandson, cannot seem to take herself seriously for long. Her outlook on life and her view of herself in this scene exemplify New England consciousness in transition.

During the "fifth remove" after her capture Rowlandson recounts crossing the Bacquaug River in late February 1676, summarizing the episode with a quotation from Scripture: "When thou passest through the waters I will be with thee, and through the rivers they shall not overflow thee." No such comforting assurances entered Knight's mind either during the time of her river crossings or afterward when she narrated the events in her journal. A seventeenth-century New Englander might have regarded the river as an apt symbol of baptism, but Knight's likening it to a "Spiritual bath," which yokes something exalted with something homely in a teasing sort of way, betrays her deep-seated ambivalence about otherworldly affairs. She is much more confident making fun of the pretensions of others to extraordinary religious knowledge or piety than she is making pronouncements in this vein for herself. Knight knew she was no "holy Sister" and doubtless looked with skepticism on others (such as Elizabeth Ashbridge) who presumed a high status for themselves simply because they felt they had been transformed by the Spirit within. To Knight, external appearances took precedence over internal ideals, especially on the American frontier, where it was very hard to tell the redeemed from the reprobate, the churchmen from the con men. A lone woman in transit in backwoods New England had little to rely on other than class distinctions, social proprieties, and forms of etiquette when she had to size people up and evaluate their usefulness to her. From today's perspective, Knight's reliance on manners, dress, dialect, and behavior as indices to character may seem superficial, even unfair, though it makes for some excellent broad comedy. We should not forget, however, that behind the joking, some of which is at Knight's own expense, there is a more discerning narrator who uses the bumptious behavior of country folk to emphasize "the great necessity and bennifitt both of Education and Conversation; for these people have as Large a portion of mother witt, and sometimes a Larger, than those who have bin brought up in Citties."

Sara Kemble Knight employed her sense of humor as a defense against her frequent sense of powerlessness and frustration on the road. Elizabeth House Trist, by contract, rarely enlisted humor in the narration of her journey from Philadelphia to Natchez in 1783–84. Trist was trying to record an encounter with America's western frontier which often left her "allmost in extacy at the Magnificence of the display of nature," whereas Knight was recounting a more prosaic experience, her dealings with the backroads people of provincial New England. Humor was a crucial means by which Knight quite literally composed both her journal and herself at the end of each unpredictable, often madcap, day on the road. Knight's sense of what and who are funny let her take control over her experience, restoring order and hierarchy to a world that sometimes daunted but never defeated her powers of wit. To Trist, however, the experience of the West defied virtually all the traditional modes of explanation and evaluation that she traveled with as part of her cultural baggage. The Mississippi River revealed to her a panorama of nature that outstripped in magnitude and wonder anything that Knight saw on her overland travels. It is not surprising, therefore, that instead of Knight's irrepressibly comic outlook on the human drama of her journey, Trist acknowledges at times feelings of "oppression" when surrounded by the soaring western wilderness. Imagining herself "Attlass with the whole World upon my shoulders," Trist labors through the writing of her journal to maintain her sense of her own identity against a perception of nature so vast and imposing that it could "condence to nothing" a less vigorous spirit.

A cultivated and well-connected woman of the urban East, Elizabeth House Trist probably did not expect that her journey west would compel her to unlearn and rethink so many social and moral assumptions basic to a person of her class. She was quite prepared to exercise her "curiossity" on all sorts of intellectual matters, especially those having to do with the marvels of the natural world beyond the Alleghenies. But at the start of her trip she was much less interested in exposing her ideas of social propriety to the stark scrutiny of frontier judgment. In the early pages of her journal Trist repeatedly complains of sleeping arrangements that bedded women and men in the same room, thus infringing on normal (at least in the

East) notions of privacy and decency for ladies. But after she gets on the Ohio River she says nothing else about the matter, though it is likely that the flatboat on which she rode offered no better accommodations than she had encountered during the earlier part of her trip through southern Pennsylvania. Whatever she may have thought about it, Trist seems to have acquiesced to this initiation into the rigors of frontier life.

The journal does not offer a self-conscious account of the process of Trist's initiation, but it does bear witness to the evolution of her consciousness in several revealing ways. For instance, the woman who early in her trip records her racist contempt for a French-Indian halfblood, "a savage in every sense of the word" in her view because of his maternal Indian heritage, writes much less prejudicially at the end of the journal of "a Mullato woman nam'd Nelly." Nelly's generosity and hospitality prevent Trist from indulging in the facile, dismissive assessment of nonwhites of which she was capable at the beginning of her journey. The more Trist learns about Nelly, especially from Nelly's own lips, the less confident the white easterner is about judging the black frontierswoman according to traditional standards. This does not mean that, by the end of her travels, Trist had developed an egalitarian view of humanity. But the comments about Nelly, coupled with other evidence of the narrator's empathy with desperate and miserable people caught up, as she was, "in some great revolution in nature," suggest that Elizabeth House Trist underwent considerable growth of mind and perspective during her journey. What she discovered and reported back to Thomas Jefferson is perhaps less valuable to readers of today than what she learned through her journey and journal writing about herself, her capabilities, and her common humanity with people so apparently different from herself.

Pervading the earliest expressions of the autobiographical impulse in America, we find, according to Patricia Caldwell, "the important alliance between migration and conversion," a consequence of the passage across the ocean that made the first white settlers in New England a unique people.[3] The four narratives collected in this volume testify to the continuing validity of this association between spatial movement and psychological transformation to later generations of American lifewriters. Although the female authorship of these narratives hardly constitutes the sum of their significance to the development of American thought and expression, the view of woman both implicitly and explicitly rendered in all four texts is among the most striking contributions they make to American literature. In the most familiar first-person narratives of early America—William Byrd's *History of the Dividing Line* (written during the 1730s), Jonathan Edwards's *Personal Narrative* (ca. 1740), Benjamin Franklin's *Autobiography* (commenced in 1771), and *The Journal of John Woolman* (1774)—women, even the wives of the narrators, are only bit players with few if any speaking parts. These stories of male social, economic, and political

3. Ibid., 28.

achievement or spiritual enlightenment are not predicated on the idea that women have much to teach men, although in narratives as different as Franklin's and Woolman's, the voice of male experience assumes the privilege of teaching women how best to fulfill their domestic destiny. Yet the narratives of Rowlandson, Knight, Ashbridge, and Trist reveal that a settled and static domestic life was by no means a foregone conclusion for early American women. External circumstances and internal motivation propelled these women into new environments that challenged their traditional sense of social roles and demanded that they find new ways to define themselves as individuals and as women. We are only beginning to reckon with these unprecedented texts of women's social, intellectual, spiritual, and literary conversion. It is the hope of the editors of this collection that readers of today will see evidenced in all these narratives the profound import of Mary Rowlandson's simple assertion—"my mind changed"—to the reevaluation of American, and the restoration of American women's, literary traditions.

WILLIAM L. ANDREWS

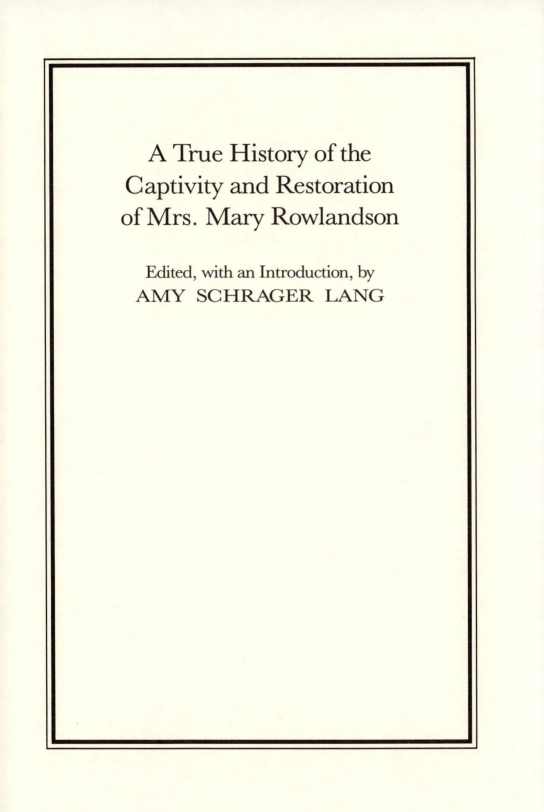

A True History of the Captivity and Restoration of Mrs. Mary Rowlandson

Edited, with an Introduction, by
AMY SCHRAGER LANG

Introduction

At sunrise on February 10, 1676, a band of Indians descended "with great numbers" on the English frontier settlement of Lancaster, Massachusetts. As Mary Rowlandson—the wife of Lancaster's minister and author of the first narrative of Indian captivity—describes it, the attack was launched not by human contestants in a struggle for land and power but by "wolves," "hellhounds," "ravenous bears." For Rowlandson, a well-tutored daughter of the Puritans, the Indians were "black creatures in the night," denizens of a "vast and desolate wilderness" resembling nothing so much as that hell which the saints of New England were destined by God himself to subdue. Rejecting the light of the gospel, the Indians were allied with the forces of Satan; failing to cultivate the land, they were, in the biblical phrase, "not a People." There is nothing extraordinary in Rowlandson's representation of the Indians. If anything, she is in perfect accord with the major spokesmen of the New England colonies.

Not long after the raid on Lancaster, Increase Mather, minister of Boston's Second Church and one of the most prominent political leaders of the Massachusetts Bay Colony, published *A Brief History of the War with the Indians in New-England.* Appearing after the death of "King Philip" of the Wampanoags but before the end of the war that bears his name, *A Brief History* begins with an extraordinary series of assertions about the meaning of the war between the colonists and the Indians:

> That the Heathen People amongst whom we live, and whose Land the Lord God of our Fathers hath given to us for a rightfull Possession, have at sundry times been Plotting mischievous Devices against that part of the English Israel which is seated in these goings down of the Sun, no man that is an Inhabitant of any considerable standing, can be ignorant. . . . And whereas [the Indians] have been quiet untill the last Year, that must be ascribed to the wonderfull Providence of God, who did . . . lay the fear of the *English,* and the dread of them upon all the *Indians.* . . . Nor indeed had [the Indians] such Advantages in former Years as now they have, in respect of Arms and Ammunition. . . . Nor were our sins ripe for so dreadfull a Judgment, untill *the Body of the first Generation* was removed, and another Generation risen up which hath not so pursued . . . the blessed design of their Fathers, in following the Lord into this Wilderness, whilst it was a land not sown.[1]

1. *A Brief History of the War with the Indians in New-England* (1676; Boston: N.p., 1862), 46.

Mather's opening paragraph is something like a map of the Puritan social imagination in the second half of the seventeenth century. Framed in the biblical language that characterized Puritan discourse from the beginning, *A Brief History* recalls the reader to New England's errand. Like Israel of old, the first generation of New England saints understood themselves to have a special covenant with God. In fact, God had "sifted a whole Nation that he might send choice Grain over into this Wilderness." Like the children of Israel, they had crossed a Red Sea, the Atlantic, and come to a wilderness, there to build a new Jerusalem. And just as God spoke to Israel, so he spoke to this new chosen people through the events of their personal and communal life. His hand was to be seen in their every success or failure.

Convinced of their special status as God's chosen, the Puritans wavered between supreme arrogance and utter self-abasement. As a community, they were committed to a view of themselves as a sanctified nation, engaged in God's work in the American "desert." But as individuals, they saw themselves as "poor dependent, nothing-Creatures," relying wholly on God for their "Being, Actions, and the Success of them."

They were certain of one thing, however: that "God's promise to his Plantations" was, as John Cotton put it in 1630, "firme and durable possession" of a "place of their owne." The unfortunate fact that the place they claimed as their own was already inhabited posed no obstacle, for the Puritans believed they had biblical warrant for settlement. One of the ways, they insisted, that God "makes room" for his chosen is by casting out "the enemies of a people before them by lawfull warre with the inhabitants, which God cals them unto: as in Ps 44:2 *Thou didst drive out the heathen before them.*" "Warring against others and driving them out withoute provocation" required, of course, a "speciall Commission from God," but the New England saints were sure they had just such a commission.[2]

Paradoxically, the right to make war on the "heathen" without provocation was paired, from the first, with belief in the redemption of those same heathen. Unlike the Jews, who willfully rejected the saving knowledge of Christ, the native Americans' ignorance of Christianity made them candidates for conversion. Having justified the violent expropriation of Indian land, John Cotton went on: "Offend not the poore Natives, but as you partake in their land, so make them partakers of your precious faith: as you reape their temporalls, so feede them with your spirituals."[3] The Puritans would "feed" the heathen soul with spiritual bread while Indian land would feed the Puritan belly.

God, then, gave New England to the saints as a "rightfull Possession." And to ensure the safety of his chosen people, he stayed the hand of the "heathen" who might otherwise jeopardize the Puritan errand. The relative peace that prevailed between colonists and Indians during the almost forty years separating the end of

2. "God's Promise to His Plantations," *Old South Leaflets* 53 (Boston, 1896), 5–6.
3. Ibid., 14–15.

the war against the Pequots in 1637 from the beginning of King Philip's War was a "wonderfull Providence of God." But the passing of the first settlers marked a change in this cosmic state of affairs. Failing to heed the warning of those like John Cotton who knew the dangers into which biblical Israel had fallen, the saints allowed their children to "degenerate as the Israelites did; after which they were vexed with afflictions." The new generation, having abandoned the "blessed design" of their fathers, faced a "dreadfull" judgment. In reproof of their sinfulness, God let loose the "barbarous Creatures." King Philip's War, in the official Puritan view, was God's rebuke to his people.

Increase Mather's rendering of New England's mythological history thinly masks the political, economic, and social tensions of the twenty years leading up to King Philip's War. Embedded in his account are allusions to dramatic changes in both the external and internal condition of the colonies during this period. The fall of Cromwell in 1658 was a blow to Puritanism, but the restoration of the Stuart monarchy in England in 1660 constituted a direct threat to colonial self-government. Upon his ascension to the throne, Charles II began an effort to revoke the charters that allowed the English colonies the freedom to tax themselves and to regulate their own trade. By 1674, Charles had appointed a royal governor mandated to unite New York and New England under his authority. The period between the restoration of the Stuarts and King Philip's War was one of increasing anxiety over the legal and political status of the colonies.

At the same time that tensions with England were building, the American-born colonists were showing themselves to be a different breed from their English immigrant fathers. Pious though they were, far fewer of this new generation of New World saints felt sufficiently confident of their salvation to attest to their conversion and thus be admitted into full communion, or membership, in the churches. Since political citizenship was tied to church membership, the failure of the first generation of American-born colonists to experience conversion meant that many of their number were effectively disenfranchised. By 1662, membership in the New England churches had declined so dramatically that a ministerial synod met to adopt the Half-Way Covenant providing that the respectable children of converted church members be granted conditional communion and membership in the churches.

The spiritual failings of the new generation were fully matched by their material ambitions. Land hunger led the American-born colonists away from the churches, both spiritually and physically. And it led them as well into contact—and conflict—with the Indians, whose land they coveted as a source of wealth. Competition between the separate colonies of Massachusetts, Plymouth, Rhode Island, and Connecticut for new land and for jurisdiction over the local Indians (both of which the colonial authorities thought would strengthen their individual positions vis-à-vis England), the increasing disruption of traditional Indian life and culture attendant on this competition, the failure of the new generation to keep the covenant and their preoccupation with wealth—all stand behind Mather's cryptic assertion that New England was "ripe for so dreadfull a judgement" as King Philip's War.

In 1664, officers of the Plymouth colony forcibly seized Wamsutta—or "Alexander," as the English called him—the *sachem* (chief) of the Wampanoag Indians, who inhabited Rhode Island's Mount Hope peninsula and the islands of Narragansett Bay. The Wampanoags had a history of friendly relations with the English settlers extending back to the time of Wamsutta's father, Massasoit. And they had, as well, a history of independence from colonial jurisdiction. The Wampanoags were among the so-called free sachems, tribes who pledged their allegiance to the English crown rather than to any one of the more proximate colonial authorities and who thus retained the right to dispose of their land as they chose. In the case of Wampanoags, this status had, in the past, allowed them to divide their loyalties and their alienated lands between Plymouth and Rhode Island.

The authorities at Plymouth seized Wamsutta in an attempt to compel him to grant the colony the sole right to purchase Wampanoag land. While still in colonial custody, however, Wamsutta fell ill and died, leaving leadership of the Wampanoags to his brother Metacom, or "Philip." Still lacking an agreement, the authorities of the colony now arrested Metacom on a charge of inciting Indian rebellion. No doubt fearful of the show of force exhibited in the seizure of Wamsutta, Metacom agreed that his people would not sell their land without the consent of the government at Plymouth.

In the period following 1665, the Plymouth colonists exploited their advantageous position to acquire Wampanoag land, particularly land on the Mount Hope peninsula. But in 1671, after Indian discontent with this encroachment had led to menacing encounters with white settlers, Metacom was once again summoned to Plymouth. Compelled this time to declare his people subject to the Plymouth authorities, Metacom appealed to Massachusetts for support. But the rivalry between the two colonies for land and jurisdiction over the Indians, which Metacom must have hoped would work in his favor, was, on the contrary, set aside. Instead of supporting Metacom in his effort to secure the independence of the Wampanoags, Massachusetts joined its neighbor in forcing him to submit to Plymouth's authority.

Metacom's activities during the next several years are unclear. Some claim that, while maintaining apparently friendly relations with the English, he covertly encouraged and gave voice to Indian grievances; he seems to have organized a loose alliance between the Wampanoags and neighboring Indians. Whatever the case, the incident that precipitated the outbreak of violence known as King Philip's War was the murder of John Sassamon in 1674. According to contemporary accounts, Sassamon, a "Praying Indian"—that is, a convert to Christianity—was one of several Indians who informed the Plymouth authorities that Metacom intended "mischief" to the settlement. When his murder was discovered, it was assumed that he had been killed by Indians as an English spy. Three Wampanoags were arrested and executed.

It may be that Metacom feared for his safety following the executions, as some historians have conjectured. More likely, English encroachment on Indian lands and power had simply reached intolerable levels. On Sunday, June 20, 1675, while the faithful were in church, Metacom led an attack on Swansea, Massachusetts, in the course of which several houses were burned. Ten days later, troops from Massachusetts, Plymouth, and Rhode Island retaliated, driving Metacom from the Mount Hope peninsula and into closer proximity to his allies, the Pocassets, a tribe led by the squaw-sachem Weetamoo, Wamsutta's widow. By August, the historically friendly Nipmucks of eastern and central Massachusetts, one of the most powerful tribes in New England, had allied themselves with Metacom. The confederated colonies of Massachusetts, Rhode Island, Plymouth, and Connecticut declared war against Metacom on September 9, 1675.

As hostilities continued, the tenuous peace between the colonies and the Narragansetts, a tribe equal in power to the Nipmucks, broke down. Early in November, the United Colonies, as they now called themselves, mustered a force of one thousand men to attack the Narragansetts in their winter home in the swamps of central Rhode Island. What followed can only be described as a massacre. Coming upon the palisaded village unexpectedly, the English attacked and, after suffering serious losses, stormed the Narragansett village, killing its inhabitants indiscriminately and setting fire to the camp. As Increase Mather reported it, "There were hundreds of *Wigwams* . . . within the Fort, which our Souldiers set on fire, in the which men, women and Children (no man knoweth how many hundreds of them) were burnt to death."[4] Mather's son, Cotton, noted exultantly in his later history of the war that the Narragansetts were "Berbikew'd." It is estimated that eighty English soldiers and six hundred Narragansett men, women, and children were killed in the Great Swamp Fight. Fleeing their land, the Narragansetts took refuge with the Nipmucks. They remained cut off from their sources of supply for the duration of the war.

The attack on Lancaster in February was part of a continuing Indian offensive begun not long after the Great Swamp Fight. In anticipation of such an attack, the people of Lancaster had organized themselves in six garrisoned houses; only one of these fell in the February raid, although many of the ungarrisoned houses in the town were burned. Of the thirty-seven people occupying the garrison that fell, twelve were killed, one escaped, and twenty-four were taken captive.

Among the captured were "God's precious servant and hand-maid," Mary Rowlandson, and her three children. "Thus," points out the "Friend" whose preface introduces Rowlandson's narrative, "all things come alike to all." That affliction levels social distinctions was, indeed, amply demonstrated by Rowlandson's capture, for she was no ordinary citizen of Lancaster. Born to John and Joan White in Somerset, England, around 1637, the sixth of their ten children, Mary White was raised from infancy in New England, living first in Salem, then in the frontier town of Wenham, Massachusetts. The Whites were among the original settlers of

4. *A Brief History,* 107.

Lancaster, arriving there in 1653 when the still unincorporated town numbered nine families. At that time, John White was the settlement's single wealthiest land-holder. In 1656, Mary White married the English-born, Harvard-educated Joseph Rowlandson, Lancaster's first minister. It was this "near relation to a *Man of God*" that set Mary Rowlandson apart from her neighbors.

Because she was the wife of a minister, Mary Rowlandson's captivity was widely regarded as an especially forceful sign of God's displeasure with his people. Like-wise, as a well-known minister's wife, Rowlandson was of special value as a cap-tive, a fact recognized by the Indians fully as well as by the colonists. As a casualty of the Lancaster raid, however, Rowlandson's relationship to Lancaster's minister was anything but distinctive. At the time of the attack, Joseph Rowlandson and his brother-in-law, Henry Kerley, were en route to Boston to plead with the colonial government for Lancaster's protection. They returned to find their family deci-mated. Mary Rowlandson's sister, Elizabeth Kerley, and two of her children had been killed in the Rowlandson garrison, as had Mary's sister Hannah's husband and son and a Rowlandson nephew. Of those captured, thirteen were members of the Rowlandson family.

Taken with Mary Rowlandson were her daughters—six-year-old Sarah, who was wounded in the raid and died a week later, and ten-year-old Mary—and her son Joseph, then fourteen. She was separated from the two older children immedi-ately, she herself having been captured by Narragansetts, her son by Nipmucks, and her daughter by an unidentified tribe. Captives ordinarily became the posses-sion of the particular Indian by whom they were taken, though they could, as Rowlandson's narrative indicates, be purchased or traded.

For eleven weeks and five days, Rowlandson lived and travelled with the Nar-ragansetts. Her "master" and "mistress," as she calls them, were a Narragansett sachem, Quanopen, and Weetamoo, the squaw-sachem of the Pocassets, who by 1675 had joined the Narragansetts in Nipmuck territory. On May 3, 1676, after "much prayer had been particularly made before the Lord on her behalf," Rowlandson was released to the English in exchange for goods valued at £20. In late June, Joseph was released by the Nipmucks and Mary was brought to Provi-dence by an unnamed Indian woman.

Lancaster had by then been destroyed, and the Rowlandsons spent the follow-ing year in Boston, supported by their friends. In the spring of 1677 they moved to Wethersfield, Connecticut, where Joseph Rowlandson was recalled to the minis-try. He died the following year at the age of forty-seven. Until very recently, histo-rians believed that Mary Rowlandson died shortly after her husband. It now appears, however, that Rowlandson was lost to view because, a year after Row-landson's death, she remarried, this time to one of the leaders of Connecticut, Cap-tain Samuel Talcott. Mary White Rowlandson Talcott died on January 5, 1711, at the age of seventy-three.

Our new knowledge of Rowlandson's life after her captivity sets the historical

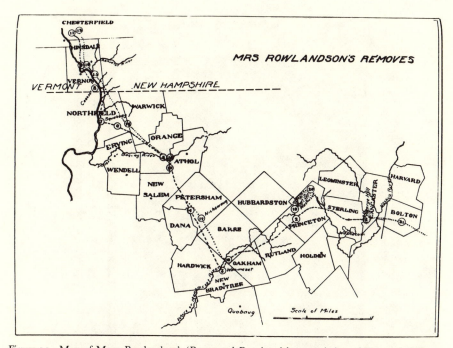

Figure 1.1 Map of Mary Rowlandson's 'Removes.' Reprinted by permission of Harvard College Library from *The Narrative of the Captivity and restoration of Mrs. Mary Rowlandson,* facsimile, 1682 Cambridge, Mass., ed. (Cambridge 1903).

record straight but, more important, it clarifies two quite different problems that have absorbed readers of her narrative. The first of these concerns the publication of Rowlandson's work. *A True History of the Captivity and Restoration of Mrs. Mary Rowlandson* was apparently written shortly after the Rowlandsons' arrival in Wethersfield in 1677, but the first edition of the narrative did not appear until 1682. The assumption that both Rowlandson and her husband died in the late 1670s, shortly after her release from captivity, left the means of publication of her narrative a mystery. Likewise, this assumption encouraged the melodramatic view of a languishing Rowlandson, unable to resume a normal life after the Lancaster tragedy. This image of Rowlandson's death dovetails neatly with the popular view of the captive Rowlandson as a passive victim, equally unwilling to risk an escape and unable to return victorious with the scalps of her captors as at least one other female captive did. But our impatience with Rowlandson's passivity has more to do with expectations set by later and far more sensational tales of pioneers and Indians than it has with the original form of the captivity narrative.

First published in New England in 1682 under the apt if somewhat uninformative title *The Sovereignty and Goodness of God*, Rowlandson's account of her captivity was an instant success, numbering four editions in its first year in print and

Figure 1.2   Frontispiece, *A Narrative of the Captivity, Sufferings and Removes of Mrs. Mary Rowlandson,* Boston, 1770. Reprinted by permission of the Houghton Library, Harvard University.

20

twenty-three editions by 1828. (To date, at least forty editions of the narrative have appeared.) Although Rowlandson was not the first white taken captive by Indians, her narrative originated what scholars regard as the first distinctively American literary genre. Following Rowlandson, the captivity narrative became a staple of American letters. As *A True History* amply demonstrates, the early narratives were vehicles for religious expression; they at once confirmed the election of God's people, the piety of the captive, and the rightness of the Indian's removal.

By the middle of the eighteenth century, however, the religious concerns of the captivity narrative had been overtaken by propagandistic ones. The highly sensational narratives of this period were explicitly intended to incite hatred of the Indians (and of the French as well) and to generate support for the war against them by recounting the horrors of captivity in graphic detail. By the 1790s, Indian captivity—particularly the captivity of white women—was being exploited by novelists like Charles Brockden Brown and, later, James Fenimore Cooper. Popular demand for gruesome tales of life among the "heathen" remained great enough in the nineteenth century to encourage the production of fictionalized captivity narratives.

Despite her chronic resort to the rhetoric of Indian-hating, Rowlandson's narrative is anything but the tale of a hapless pioneer beset by exotic savages. Her story is meant not to thrill but to instruct. It is a story not of Indian atrocities but of Christian affliction. In fact, it is a story about Indians only in the most limited sense, for our attention is held throughout by Rowlandson herself. *A True History* carefully records the physical and social details of her 150-mile trek with the Narragansetts, but Rowlandson's real journey is an interior one. From the outset, we move through a landscape at once literal and symbolic: physical suffering mirrors spiritual affliction; time is marked in space as "Removes" from white civilization and from the light of the gospel; the darkness of the thicket is indistinguishable from the darkness of the soul when God has turned away his face; redemption is both release from captivity and assurance of salvation.

Like many colonial spiritual autobiographies, *A True History* begins with the rupture of ordinary life, with a violent end to the daily rounds of the Puritan wife and mother. "All was gone," Rowlandson tells us, "my husband gone . . . my children gone, my relations and friends gone, our house and home . . . all was gone (except my life)." Stripped of affectionate relationships, social identity, and familiar surroundings, Rowlandson is forced to re-create herself. As a woman, a wife, and a mother, she must define her "life" in the absence of everything that once constituted life. As a faithful Puritan, she must find meaning in her affliction, uncover the spiritual failings that prompted her punishment, and submit to God's will. Captive to an alien people on whom she cannot depend for even the barest necessities of life, she must learn to provide for herself. In making a new life—or, more accurately, a new self—she moves simultaneously toward submission and self-sufficiency.

A

NARRATIVE

OF THE

CAPTIVITY, SUFFERINGS AND REMOVES

OF

Mrs. Mary Rowlandson,

Who was taken Prisoner by the INDIANS, with several others; and treated in the most barbarous and cruel Manner by the Savages : With many other remarkable Events during her Travels.

Written by her own Hand, for her private Use, and since made public at the earnest Desire of some Friends, and for the Benefit of the Afflicted.

BOSTON:

PRINTED & SOLD by THOMAS FLEET, 1805.

Figure 1.3   Frontispiece, *A Narrative of the Captivity, Sufferings and Removes of Mrs. Mary Rowlandson,* Boston, 1805. Reprinted by permission of the Houghton Library, Harvard University.

These two movements are closely related in Rowlandson's narrative, yet we can trace them by attending to the two different voices that speak to us in *A True History:* the voice of the Christian crying out to her God from the wilderness, and the voice of the survivor obsessively recording the details of Indian diet, ritual, garb, and social organization.

The wilderness itself, as Rowlandson describes it, symbolizes this doubleness. It is, on the one hand, an untracked, menacing place in which she is unable to travel one mile without getting lost, in which she is unable to find food or shelter without assistance. On the other hand, it is a spiritual and psychological "condition" carrying both personal and corporate significance. The spiritual darkness to which Mary Rowlandson has been relegated by God and from which she can be redeemed only when she has repudiated the "vanity of this world" and acknowledged her "whole dependence" on God is also a Babylon in which the American Israel is captive. Intimacy with the wilderness—even the intimacy of aesthetic appreciation—is, then, to be resisted. Traveling through the pristine woodland of New England, Rowlandson makes no mention of the scenery. She finds no beauty in untamed nature, only terror.

But Rowlandson's failure to learn the ways of the wilderness—her inability to find food or shelter or her way—attests not to her feminine frailty but to her spiritual strength. The very image of *Judea capta,* Israel in bondage, she understands that her part in the cosmic drama called King Philip's War is, as she tells us again and again, to "wait upon the Lord." In this character, Rowlandson acts as spiritual interpreter and guide; the literal wilderness continually thwarts her efforts, but she is mistress of the symbolic one. She may lose her way in the woods, but she plots her course unerringly through the wilderness of Christian exegesis.

The process of spiritual fulfillment requires patience and passivity, but survival makes different demands. The prisoner of a people she regards as "heathens" and "barbarians," Rowlandson must nonetheless make her place among them. The Christian who continually reminds herself to "Be still," who believes that her salvation rests in a Joblike submission to affliction, is at the same time a woman faced with the problem of negotiating a foreign culture from a position of powerlessness. Of necessity, Rowlandson's progress toward passive acceptance of God's will goes hand in hand with a movement toward active accommodation to the Indian world.

The difficulties posed by this accommodation are perhaps best illustrated by Rowlandson's attitude toward food, a subject that necessarily receives great attention in *A True History.* Cut off from their winter stores, the Narragansetts were starving. As Rowlandson herself makes clear, they were reduced to eating whatever they could find, from acorns and bark to bear, beaver, and "horse's guts." For Rowlandson, the eating of the Indians' "filthy trash," although essential to her survival, signifies capitulation to the "howling wilderness." The first week of her captivity she fasts; the second week she overcomes her revulsion, but only barely.

By the third week, however, she finds, to her amazement, that food that would once have turned her stomach tastes "pleasant and savory."

Just as she learns to eat Indian food, so Rowlandson learns to distinguish between her various captors. Gradually, the "wild beasts of the forest" reveal themselves as distinct individuals—some, like Metacom, generous, others cruel. By the middle of the narrative, she speaks of Quanopen as "the best friend that I had of an Indian," whereas the "proud gossip" Weetamoo's vanity and imperiousness become more and more pronounced as the weeks go by. Although the Narragansetts figure more often as agents of God than as independent actors in Rowlandson's narrative, she scrupulously records their acts of kindness as well as those of gratuitous violence. She acquits her captors of drunkenness and of the sexual abuse of female captives and describes Narragansett rituals with genuine interest, if considerable disdain.

This change in Rowlandson's view of the Narragansetts is paired with a gradual change in her status. Faced with the need to find food and sometimes shelter, Rowlandson carves out a place for herself in the Indian economy. Knitting and sewing in exchange for food, she describes herself as sufficiently secure to negotiate the terms of barter and, on one occasion, to try to refuse an offer of work. In fact, as her time with the Narragansetts lengthens, Rowlandson's willingness to assert herself increases.

On the one hand, then, A True History offers us Rowlandson as a meticulous and not altogether unsympathetic observer of Indian life. This Rowlandson manages, despite her repugnance, to negotiate the wilderness condition into which she is thrust. But like the stories of other survivors, her story is fraught with unspoken ambivalence. Rowlandson indicates, though rarely explores, her worries about whether her accommodation to the "enemy" is a form of complicity, about the morality of taking food from a captive child, about what it is that enables her son to grieve for his father when she cannot, and, most important, about why her life has been spared when so many others have died.

Nonetheless the survivor, the Rowlandson who argues with Weetamoo, who manages to find enough to eat and a place to sleep in the "vast and howling wilderness," remains always secondary to the pious woman who moves from desolation and affliction to faith and dependence. The first Rowlandson acts while the second, in good Puritan fashion, keeps "a memorandum of God's dealing with her." This pious Rowlandson understands, retrospectively if not immediately, the twofold lesson of her captivity: that suffering and adversity are God's way of chastising his disobedient children, and that his "overruling" providence governs even "the most unruly" of heathen. At each juncture, this Rowlandson finds the appropriate public meaning in private experience. She normalizes the extraordinary experience of captivity by finding in it the familiar patterns of her own culture.

Rowlandson's remarkable capacity to bring her experience and emotions as a captive into perfect accord with the meanings offered by official Puritan culture is, of course, what enables her, as a woman, to speak publicly. She can, as the writer of the preface suggests, "come . . . into the publick" to tell her story because she has learned through her affliction "how . . . to talk of God's acts and to speak of and publish his wonderful works." She can, without loss of modesty, "thrust" her story "into the press" because the story she tells is, paradoxically, a story of not telling, a story of being "still" and awaiting the Lord.

"I can remember the time," Rowlandson muses at the close of her narrative, "when I used to sleep quietly without workings in my thoughts, whole nights together; but now it is otherwise with me." This allusion to insomnia is the only indication Rowlandson gives us of the lingering personal effects of her captivity. But even here, her private distress, her weeping in the night, is meaningful only as it is linked to "the wonderful power of God" that has brought her safely out of the wilderness. She has, as she says, "learned to look beyond the present and smaller troubles, and to be quieted under them." Rowlandson's tragic encounter with the Indians is tragic only from the vantage point of the present, of the survivor. Seen rightly, as part of God's design, Rowlandson insists, her captivity is her salvation.

One would like to introduce the story of Mary Rowlandson's captivity with images of normalcy—with images of kitchen gardens and houses, of women in community, among their children, and alone—with a portrait of Rowlandson as Puritan wife, mother, citizen. But Rowlandson writes only one brief moment of her life, a moment that has neither prelude nor aftermath. We have no picture of Rowlandson's life prior to the raid on Lancaster and no picture of her life as she reconstructed it after her release from captivity. Rowlandson's narrative is, in this sense, reminiscent of spiritual autobiography. And in this sense, too, it is most typical of the stories of colonial women's lives which come to us, more often than not, as fragments—glimpses from letters, diaries, jottings—or as records of heightened experiences of such great social significance that the strictures against women's public speech are briefly lifted.

Rowlandson was saved both physically and spiritually, and her words were saved as well. Her captors were less fortunate. On August 6, 1676, a party of Indians was captured near Taunton, Massachusetts. Shortly thereafter, the body of an Indian woman was found in the same vicinity. The English, according to Increase Mather, "cut off her head, and it hapned to be *Weetamoo*." "When it was set upon a pole in *Taunton*," Mather went on, "the Indians who were prisoners there, knew it presently, and made a mosst horrid and diabolical Lamentation, crying out it was their Queens head."[5] On August 12, shortly after his wife and nine-year-old son were captured, to be sold into slavery in the West Indies along with innumerable other captive Indians, Metacom himself was killed while trying to escape the English on the Mount Hope peninsula. The officer in charge ordered him decapitated and quartered. The quarters were hung on trees, the head sent to Plymouth, one

5. Ibid., 191.

hand to Boston, the other awarded to the Indian who shot him. On August 24, Quanopen was executed in Newport, Rhode Island, along with two of his brothers.

A   NOTE   ON   THE   TEXT

The text of *A True History* follows the London edition of 1682. Like the three editions of Rowlandson's narrative that appeared in New England in the same year, the London edition appears to be based on a lost first edition printed in Cambridge, Massachusetts. The variation in the existing texts is slight, but the London edition corrects the minor omissions and errors of the Cambridge "Addition" printed by Samuel Green with the assistance of James the Printer, a minor character in Rowlandson's tale. Original punctuation, spelling, and use of italics have been retained. I am indebted to the work of Robert K. Diebold, who collated the various seventeenth-century editions of *A True History.*

ACKNOWLEDGMENT

I would like to thank my student Catherine M. Dionne for her invaluable assistance.

BIBLIOGRAPHY

Diebold, Robert K. "A Critical Edition of Mrs. Mary Rowlandson's Captivity Narrative." Ph.D. diss., Yale University, 1972.

Greene, David L. "New Light on Mary Rowlandson." *Early American Literature* 20 (Spring 1985): 24–38.

Kolodny, Annette. *The Land Before Her: Fantasy and Experience of the American Frontiers, 1630–1860.* Chapel Hill: University of North Carolina Press, 1984.

Leach, Douglas E. *Flintlock and Tomahawk.* New York: Norton, 1958.

Pearce, Roy Harvey. "The Significance of the Captivity Narrative." American Literature 19 (March 1947): 1–21.

Slotkin, Richard, and James K. Folsom, eds. *So Dreadful a Judgement: Puritan Response to King Philip's War, 1676–1677.* Middletown, Conn.: Wesleyan University Press, 1978.

A True History of the Captivity and Restoration of Mrs. Mary Rowlandson,

A Minister's Wife in *New-England:* Wherein is set forth,
The Cruel and Inhumane Usage she underwent amongst the
Heathens for Eleven Weeks time: And her Deliverance from
them. Written by her own Hand, for her Private Use: and now
made Public at the earnest Desire of some Friends, for the
Benefit of the Afflicted.

Printed first at *New-England: And Re-printed at London;* and sold by *Joseph Poole,* at the *Blue Bowl* in the *Long-Walk,* by *Christ's-Church* Hospital. 1682.

PREFACE TO THE READER

It was on Tuesday, Feb. 1, 1675,[1] in the afternoon, when the *Narrhagansets'* Quarters (in or toward the *Nipmug* Country, whither they were now retired for fear of the *English* Army, lying in their own Country) were the second time beaten up by the Forces of the United Colonies,[2] who thereupon soon betook themselves to flight, and were all the next day pursued by the *English,* some overtaken and destroyed. But on Thursday, Feb. 3, the *English,* having now been six days' on their March from their Headquarters in Wickford, in the Narrhaganset Country, toward and after the enemy, and Provision grown exceeding short; insomuch that they were fain to kill some Horses for the supply, especially of their *Indian* Friends, they were necessitated to consider what was best to be done; and about noon (having hitherto followed the Chase as hard as they might) a Council was called, and though some few were of another mind, yet it was concluded, by far the greater part of the Council of War, that the Army should desist the pursuit, and retire; the forces of Plimouth and the Bay to the next town of the Bay, and Connecticut forces to their

---

1. *Feb. 1, 1675:* Using the modern calendar, this date would be February 11, 1676.
2. *United Colonies:* That is, Massachusetts, Connecticut, and Plymouth.

27

own next towns, which determination was immediately put in execution: The consequent whereof, as it was not difficult to be foreseen by those that knew the causeless enmity of these *Barbarians* against the *English,* and the malicious and revengeful spirit of these Heathen; so it soon proved dismal.

The *Narrhagansets* were now driven quite from their own Country, and all their Provisions there hoarded up, to which they durst not at present return, and being so numerous as they were, soon devoured those to whom they went, whereby both the one and the other were now reduced to extreme straits, and so necessitated to take the first and best opportunity for supply, and very glad no doubt of such an opportunity as this, to provide for themselves, and make spoile of the *English* at once; and seeing themselves thus discharged of their pursuers, and a little refreshed after their flight, the very next week, on Thursday, Feb. 10, they fell with a mighty force and fury upon Lancaster: which small Town, remote from aid of others, and not being Garrison'd as it might, the Army being now come in, and as the time indeed required (the design of the *Indians* against that place being known to the English some time before) was not able to make effectual resistance; but notwithstanding the utmost endeavour of the Inhabitants, most of the buildings were turned into ashes, many People (Men, Women, and Children) slain, and others captivated. The most solemn and remarkable part of this Tragedy may that justly be reputed which fell upon the Family of that Reverend Servant of God, Mr Joseph Rowlandson, the faithful Pastor of the Church of Christ in that place, who, being gone down to the Council of the Massachusets, to seek aid for the defence of the place, at his return found the Town in flames or smoke, his own house being set on fire by the Enemy, through the disadvantage of a defective Fortification, and all in it consumed; his precious yoke-fellow, and dear Children, wounded and captivated (as the issue evidenced, and the following Narrative declares) by these cruel and barbarous Salvages. A sad Catastrophe! Thus all things come alike to all: None knows either love or hatred by all that is before him. 'Tis no new thing for God's precious ones to drink as deep as others, of the Cup of common Calamity: take just *Lot* (yet captivated) for instance, beside others. But it is not my business to dilate on these things, but only in few words introductively to preface to the following script, which is a Narrative of the wonderfully awful, wise, holy, powerful, and gracious providence of God, toward that worthy and precious Gentlewoman, the dear Consort of the said Reverend Mr Rowlandson, and her Children with her, as in casting of her into such a waterless pit, so in preserving, supporting, and carrying through so many such extream hazards, unspeakable difficulties and disconsolateness, and at last delivering her out of them all, and her surviving Children also. It was a strange and amazing dispensation that the Lord should so afflict his precious Servant, and Hand-maid: It was as strange, if not more, that he should so bear up the spirits of his Servant under such bereavements, and of his Hand-maid under such Captivity, travels, and hardships (much too hard for flesh and blood) as he did, and at length deliver and restore. But he was their Saviour, who hath said, *When thou passes through the Waters, I will be with thee, and through the Rivers, they shall not overflow thee: when thou walkest through the Fire, thou shalt not be burnt, nor shall the flame kindle upon thee,* Isai. xliii ver. 3; and again, *He woundeth, and his hands make whole; he shall deliver thee in six troubles, yea, in seven there shall no evil touch thee: In Famine he shall redeem thee from death; and in War from the power of the sword,* Job v. 18, 19, 20. Methinks this dispensation doth bear some resemblance to those of *Joseph, David,* and *Daniel,* [3] yea, and of the three children [4] too, the stories whereof do represent us with the excellent textures of divine providence, curious pieces of divine work: And truly so doth this, and therefore not to be forgotten, but worthy to be exhibited to, and viewed and pondered by all, that disdain not to consider the operation of his hands.

The works of the Lord (not only of Creation, but of Providence also, especially those that do more peculiarly concern his dear ones, that are as the apple of his eye, as the signet upon his hand, the delight of his eyes, and the object of his tenderest care) are great, sought out of all those that have pleasure therein; and of these, verily, this is none of the least.

This Narrative was Penned by this Gentlewoman her self, to be to her a *Memorandum* of God's dealing with her, that she might never forget, but remember the same, and the several circumstances thereof, all the daies of her life. A pious scope, which deserves both commendation and imitation. Some Friends having obtained a sight of it, could not but be so much affected with the many passages of working providence discovered therein, as to judge it worthy of publick view, and altogether unmeet that such works of God should be hid from present and future Generations; and therefore though this Gentlewoman's modesty would not thrust it into the Press, yet her gratitude unto God, made her not hardly perswadable to let it pass, that God might have his due glory, and others benefit by it as well as her selfe.

I hope by this time none will cast any reflection upon this Gentlewoman, on the score of this publication of her Affliction and Deliverance. If any should, doubtless they may be reckoned with the nine Lepers, of whom it is said, *Were there not ten cleansed? where are the nine?* [5] but one returning to give God thanks. Let such further know, that this was a dispensation of publick note and of Universal concernment; and so much the more, by how much the nearer this Gentlewoman stood related to that faithful Servant of God, whose capacity and employment was publick, in the House of God, and his Name on that account of a very sweet savour in the Churches of Christ. Who is there of a true Christian spirit, that did not look upon himself much concerned in this bereavement, this Captivity in the time thereof,

---

3. God enabled Joseph to interpret the Pharaoh's dream, thus securing his release from prison in Genesis 39–41; David, in 1 Samuel 17, is delivered by God's intervention from the Philistine, Goliath; the prophet Daniels' faith saves him from the lions in Daniel 6.

4. *the three children:* See Daniel 3.

5. *"Were there not . . . nine?":* Luke 17:17.

and in this deliverance when it came, yea, more than in many others? And how many are there to whom, so concerned, it will doubtless be a very acceptable thing, to see the way of God with this Gentlewoman in the aforesaid dispensation, thus laid out and pourtrayed before their eyes.

To conclude, Whatever any coy phantasies may deem, yet it highly concerns those that have so deeply tasted how good the Lord is, to enquire with *David, What shall I render to the Lord for all his benefits to me?* Psal. cxvi. 12. He things nothing too great: yea, being sensible of his own disproportion to the due praises of God, he calls in help: *O magnifie the Lord with me, let us exalt his Name together, Psal.* xxxiv. 3. And it is but reason that our praises should hold proportion with our prayers; and that as many have helped together by prayer for the obtaining of this mercy, so praises should be returned by many on this behalf; and forasmuch as not the general but particular knowledge of things makes deepest impression upon the affections, this Narrative particularizing the several passages of this providence, will not a little conduce thereunto: and therefore holy David, in order to the attainment of that end, accounts himself concerned to declare what God had done for his Soul, *Psal.* lxvi. 16. *Come and hear, all ye that fear God, and I will declare what God hath done for my Soul,* i.e. *for his Life.* See ver. 9, 10. *He holdeth our soul in life, and suffers not our feet to be moved; for thou our God hast proved us: thou hast tried us, as silver is tried.* Life-mercies are heart-affecting mercies; of great impression and force, to enlarge pious hearts in the praises of God, so that such know not how but to talk of God's acts, and to speak of and publish his wonderful works. Deep troubles, when the waters come in unto the Soul, are wont to produce vows: Vows must be paid: *It is better not vow, than to vow and not pay.* I may say, that as none knows what it is to fight and pursue such an enemy as this, but they that have fought and pursued them: so none can imagine, what it is to be captivated, and enslaved to such Atheistical, proud, wild, cruel, barbarous, brutish, (in one word,) diabolical Creatures as these, the worst of the heathen; nor what difficulties, hardships, hazards, sorrows, anxieties, and perplexities, do unavoidably wait upon such a condition, but those that have tried it. No serious spirit then (especially knowing any thing of this Gentlewoman's Piety) can imagine but that the vows of God are upon her. Excuse her then if she come thus into the publick, to pay those Vows. Come and hear what she hath to say.

I am confident that no Friend of divine Providence, will ever repent his time and pains spent in reading over these sheets, but will judge them worth perusing again and again.

Here *Reader,* you may see an instance of the Sovereignty of God, who doth what he will with his own as well as others; and who may say to him, *what dost thou?* here you may see an instance of the Faith and Patience of the Saints, under the most heart-sinking Tryals; here you may see, the Promises are breasts full of Consolation, when all the World besides is empty, and gives nothing but sorrow. That God is indeed the supream Lord of the World: ruling the most unruly, weakening the most cruel and salvage: granting his People mercy in the sight of the most unmerciful: curbing the lusts of the most filthy, holding the hands of the violent, delivering the prey from the mighty, and gathering together the out-casts of Israel. Once and again, you have heard, but here you may see, that power belongeth unto God: that our God is the God of Salvation: and to him belong the issues from Death. That our God is in the Heavens, and doth whatever pleases him. Here you have *Samson's* riddle exemplified, and that great promise, *Rom.* viii. 28, verified: *Out of the Eater comes forth meat, and sweetness out of the strong;* The worst of evils working together for the best good. How evident is it that the Lord hath made this Gentlewoman a gainer by all this Affliction, that she can say, 'tis good for her, yea better that she hath been, than she should not have been, thus afflicted.

Oh how doth God shine forth in such things as these!

Reader, if thou gettest no good by such a Declaration as this, the fault must needs be thine own. Read, therefore, peruse, ponder, and from hence lay up something from the experience of another, against thine own turn comes: that so thou also through patience and consolation of the Scripture mayest have hope,

PER AMICUM[6]

A NARRATIVE OF THE CAPTIVITY AND RESTORATION OF MRS MARY ROWLANDSON

On the tenth of February, 1675, came the *Indians* with great number upon Lancaster. Their first coming was about Sun-rising. Hearing the noise of some guns, we looked out; several Houses were burning, and the smoke ascending to Heaven. There were five persons taken in one House, the Father and the Mother, and a sucking Child, they knock'd on the head; the other two they took, and carried away alive. There were two others, who, being out of their Garrison upon some occasion, were set upon; one was knock'd on the head, the other escaped. Another there was, who, running along, was shot and wounded, and fell down; he begged of them his Life, promising them Money, (as they told me;) but they would not hearken to him, but knock'd him on the head, stripped him naked, and split open his Bowels. Another, seeing many of the *Indians* about his Barn, ventured and went out, but was quickly shot down. There were three others belonging to the same Garrison who were killed. The *Indians,* getting up upon the Roof of the Barn, had advantage to shoot down upon them over their Fortification. Thus these murtherous Wretches went on, burning and destroying before them.

At length they came and beset our own House, and quickly it was the dolefullest

---

6. *Per Amicum:* Literally, "by a friend." The preface is usually attributed to Increase Mather, but at least one scholar has proposed the minister Gershom Bulkeley as its author.

day that ever mine eyes saw. The House stood upon the edge of a Hill; some of the *Indians* got behind the Hill, others into the Barn, and others behind any thing that would shelter them; from all which Places they shot against the House, so that the Bullets seemed to fly like Hail; and quickly they wounded one Man among us, then another, and then a third. About two Hours (according to my observation in that amazing time) they had been about the House before they could prevail to fire it, (which they did with flax and Hemp, which they brought out of the Barn, and there being no Defence about the House, only two Flankers,[7] at two opposite Corners, and one of them not finished). They fired it once, and one ventured out and quenched it; but they quickly fired it again, and that took. Now is that dreadful Hour come that I have often heard of, (in the time of the War, as it was the Case of others,) but now mine Eyes see it. Some in our House were fighting for their Lives, others wallowing in their Blood; the House on fire over our Heads, and the bloody Heathen ready to knock us on the Head if we stirred out. Now might we hear Mothers and Children crying out for themselves and one another, *Lord, what shall we do?* Then I took my Children (and one of my Sisters, hers) to go forth and leave the House; but as soon as we came to the Door and appeared, the *Indians* shot so thick that the Bullets rattled against the House as if one had taken an handful of Stones and threw them; so that we were fain to give back. We had six stout Dogs belonging to our Garrison, but none of them would stir, though another time, if an *Indian* had come to the Door, they were ready to fly upon him, and tear him down. The Lord hereby would make us the more to acknowledge his Hand, and to see that our Help is always in him. But out we must go, the Fire increasing and coming along behind us roaring, and the *Indians* gaping before us with their Guns, Spears, and Hatchets to devour us. No sooner were we out of the House but my Brother-in-Law[8] (being before wounded, in defending the House, in or near the Throat) fell down dead, whereat the *Indians* scornfully shouted and hallowed, and were presently upon him, stripping off his Clothes. The Bullets flying thick, one went thorow my side, and the same (as would seem) thorow the Bowels and Hand of my dear Child in my Arms.[9] One of my eldest Sister's Children (named William) had then his Leg broken, which the *Indians* perceiving, they knock'd him on the head. Thus were we butchered by those merciless Heathen, standing amazed, with the Blood running down to our Heels. My elder sister,[10] being yet in the House, and seeing those woful Sights, the Infidels hauling Mothers one way and Children another, and some wallowing in their Blood, and her elder son telling her that (her Son) William was dead, and myself was wounded; she said, *And, Lord, let me die with them!* which was no sooner said but she was struck with a Bullet, and fell down

---

7. *flankers:* Projecting fortifications.

8. *my brother-in-law:* Ensign John Divoll, husband of Rowlandson's youngest sister, Hannah.

9. *my dear child in my arms:* Sarah, age six.

10. *my elder sister:* Elizabeth, wife of Henry Kerley. Kerley was en route to Boston with Joseph Rowlandson at the time of the raid.

dead over the Threshold. I hope she is reaping the Fruit of her good Labours, being faithful to the Service of God in her Place. In her younger years she lay under much trouble upon Spiritual accounts, till it pleased God to make that precious Scripture take hold of her Heart, 2 *Cor.* xii. 9, *And he said unto me, My grace is sufficient for thee.* More than twenty years after, I have heard her tell how sweet and comfortable that Place was to her. But to return: the *Indians* laid hold of us, pulling me one way and the Children another, and said, *Come, go along with us.* I told them they would kill me. They answered, *If I were willing to go along with them, they would not hurt me.*

O the doleful Sight that now was to behold at this House! *Come, behold the works of the Lord, what desolation he has made in the earth.* [11] Of thirty seven Persons who were in this one House, none escaped either present Death or a bitter Captivity, save only one, who might say as he, *Job* i. 15, *And I only am escaped alone to tell the news.* There were twelve killed, some shot, some stabb'd with their Spears, some knock'd down with their Hatchets. When we are in prosperity, oh the Little that we think of such dreadful Sights; and to see our dear Friends and Relations lie bleeding out their Heart-blood upon the Ground! There was one who was chopped into the Head with a Hatchet, and stripp'd naked, and yet was crawling up and down. It was a solemn Sight to see so many Christians lying in their Blood, some here and some there, like a company of Sheep torn by Wolves; all of them stript naked by a company of hell-hounds, roaring, singing, ranting, and insulting, as if they would have torn our very hearts out; yet the Lord, by his Almighty power, preserved a number of us from death, for there were twenty-four of us taken alive; and carried Captive.

I had often before this said, that if the *Indians* should come, I should chuse rather to be killed by them than taken alive; but when it came to the trial my mind changed; their glittering Weapons so daunted my Spirit, that I chose rather to go along with those (as I may say) ravenous Bears, than that moment to end my daies. And that I may the better declare what happened to me during that grievous Captivity, I shall particularly speak of the several Removes we had up and down the Wilderness.

The first Remove. —Now away we must go with those Barbarous Creatures, with our bodies wounded and bleeding, and our hearts no less than our bodies. About a mile we went that night; up upon a hill, within sight of the Town, where they intended to lodge. There was hard by a vacant house; (deserted by the English before for fear of the *Indians;*) I asked them whether I might not lodge in the house that night? to which they answered, What, will you love *English-men* still? This was the dolefullest night that ever my eyes saw: oh the roaring, and singing, and dancing, and yelling of those black creatures in the night, which made the place a lively

11. *"Come, behold . . . in the earth":* Psalm 46:8. Like many of the biblical passages Rowlandson quotes, this one alludes to God's conquest of the heathen and closes with the injunction "Be still, and know that I am God: I will be exalted among the heathen, I will be exalted in the earth."

resemblance of hell! And as miserable was the waste that was there made of Horses, Cattle, Sheep, Swine, Calves, Lambs, Roasting Pigs, and Fowls, (which they had plundered in the Town,) some roasting, some lying and burning, and some boyling, to feed our merciless Enemies; who were joyful enough, though we were disconsolate. To add to the dolefulness of the former day, and the dismalness of the present night, my thoughts ran upon my losses and sad bereaved condition. All was gone; my Husband gone, (at least separated from me, he being in the Bay; and, to add to my grief, the *Indians* told me they would kill him as he came homeward,) my Children gone, my Relations and Friends gone, our house and home, and all our comforts within door and without, all was gone, (except my life,) and I knew not but the next moment that might go too.

There remained nothing to me but one poor wounded Babe, and it seemed at present worse than death that it was in such a pitiful condition, bespeaking Compassion, and I had no refreshing for it, nor suitable things to revive it. Little do many think what is the savageness and brutishness of this barbarous Enemy, even those that seem to profess[12] more than others among them, when the *English* have fallen into their hands.

Those seven that were killed at Lancaster the summer before, upon a Sabbath-day, and the one that was afterward killed upon a week day, were slain and mangled in a barbarous manner by one-eyed John, and Marlberough's Praying *Indians,*[13] which Capt. Mosely[14] brought to Boston, as the *Indians* told me.

The second Remove. —But now (the next morning) I must turn my back upon the Town, and travel with them into the vast and desolate Wilderness, I know not whither. It is not my tongue or pen can express the sorrows of my heart and bitterness of my spirit that I had at this departure: but God was with me in a wonderful manner, carrying me along, and bearing up my Spirit, that it did not quite fail. One of the *Indians* carried my poor wounded Babe upon a horse: it went moaning all along, I shall die, I shall die! I went on foot after it, with sorrow that cannot be exprest. At length I took it off the horse, and carried it in my arms, till my strength failed, and I fell down with it. Then they set me upon a horse, with my wounded Child in my lap; and there being no Furniture upon the horse back; as we were going down a steep hill, we both fell over the horse's head, at which they, like inhuman creatures, laught, and rejoiced to see it, though I thought we should there have ended our dayes, as overcome with so many difficulties. But the Lord

12. *profess:* That is, profess Christianity.

13. *one-eyed John, and Marlberough's Praying Indians:* Rowlandson refers here to a raid on the outskirts of Lancaster the previous August led by "One-eyed" John Monoco, chief of the Nashaway Indians, and involving the Christian Indians who owned 150 acres in the town of Marlborough, ten miles from Lancaster.

14. *Capt. Mosely:* An ex-Jamaica privateer and a notorious Indian-hater, Samuel Mosely was one of the most popular and cruelest officers in the English army.

renewed my strength still, and carried me along, that I might see more of his power, yea, so much that I could never have thought of had I not experienced it.

After this it quickly began to Snow; and when night came on they stopt; and now down I must sit in the Snow, (by a little fire and a few boughs behind me,) with my sick Child in my lap; and calling much for water, being now (thorough the wound) fallen into a violent Fever; (my own wound also growing so stiff that I could scarce sit down or rise up;) yet so it must be, that I must sit all this cold winter night upon the cold snowy ground, with my sick Child in my arms, looking that every hour would be the last of its life; and having no Christian Friend near me, either to comfort or help me. Oh I may see the wonderful power of God, that my Spirit did not utterly sink under my affliction!—still the Lord upheld me with his gracious and merciful Spirit, and we were both alive to see the light of the next morning.

The third Remove.—The morning being come, they prepared to go on their way. One of the Indians got up upon a horse, and they set me up behind him, with my poor sick Babe in my lap. A very wearisome and tedious day I had of it; what with my own wound, and my Child's being so exceeding sick, and in a lamentable Condition with her wound. It may easily be judged what a poor feeble condition we were in, there being not the least crumb of refreshing that came within either of our mouths from Wednesday night to Saturday night, except only a little cold water. This day in the afternoon, about an hour by Sun, we came to the place where they intended, *viz.* an *Indian town* called Wenimesset,[15] Northward of Quabaug. When we were come, Oh the number of Pagans (now merciless Enemies) that there came about me, that I may say as *David,* Psal. xxvii. 13. *I had fainted, unless I had believed,*[16] &c. The next day was the Sabbath: I then remembered how careless I had been of God's holy time; how many Sabbaths I had lost and mispent, and how evilly I had walked in God's sight; which lay so close upon my Spirit, that it was easie for me to see how righteous it was with God to cut off the thread of my life, and cast me out of his presence for ever. Yet the Lord still shewed mercy to me, and upheld me; and as he wounded me with one hand, so he healed me with the other. This day there came to me one Robert Pepper, (a Man belonging to Roxbury,) who was taken in Capt. Beers his fight;[17] and had been now a considerable time with

15. *Wenimesset:* The swamp stronghold of the Quabaug Indians, near New Braintree, Massachusetts.

16. *"I had fainted . . . believed":* Once again the psalm enjoins patience: "I had fainted, unless I had believed to see the goodness of the Lord in the land of the living. Wait on the Lord: be of good courage, and he shall strengthen thine heart: wait, I say, on the Lord."

17. *Robert Pepper . . . Capt. Beers his fight:* Captain Richard Beers of Watertown was waylaid by Indians on September 3, 1675, while leading a party of thirty-six reinforcements to the garrison at Northfield. Beers and nineteen others were killed, Robert Pepper was taken captive, and the remainder escaped.

the *Indians;* and up with them almost as far as Albany, to see King Philip, as he told me, and was now very lately come with them into these parts. Hearing, I say, that I was in this *Indian* Town, he obtained leave to come and see me. He told me he himself was wounded in the Leg, at Capt. Beers his fight; and was not able sometime to go, but as they carried him, and that he took oaken leaves and laid to his wound, and through the blessing of God he was able to travel again. Then I took oaken leaves and laid to my side, and with the blessing of God it cured me also; yet before the cure was wrought, I may say as it is in *Psal.* xxxviii. 5, 6, *My wounds stink and are corrupt, I am troubled, I am bowed down greatly, I go mourning all the day long.* I sate much alone with a poor wounded Child in my lap, which mourned night and day, having nothing to revive the body or chear the Spirits of her; but, instead of that, sometimes one Indian would come and tell me one hour, And your Master will knock your Child in the head, and then a second, and then a third, Your Master will quickly knock your Child in the head.

This was the Comfort I had from them; miserable comforters are ye all, as he said. Thus nine dayes I sat upon my knees, with my babe in my lap, till my flesh was raw again. My child, being even ready to depart this sorrowful world, they bad me carry it out to another Wigwam; (I suppose because they would not be troubled with such spectacles;) whither I went with a very heavy heart, and down I sate with the picture of death in my lap. About two hours in the Night, my sweet Babe, like a Lamb, departed this life, on Feb. 18, 1675 [1676] it being about six years and five months old. It was nine dayes (from the first wounding) in this Miserable condition, without any refreshing of one nature or other, except a little cold water. I cannot but take notice how, at another time, I could not bear to be in the room where any dead person was; but now the case is changed; I must and could lye down by my dead Babe, side by side, all the night after. I have thought since of the wonderful goodness of God to me, in preserving me so in the use of my reason and senses in that distressed time, that I did not use wicked and violent means to end my own miserable life. In the morning, when they understood that my child was dead, they sent for me home to my Master's Wigwam; (by my Master, in this writing, must be understood Quannopin, who was a Saggamore, and married King Philip's wife's Sister; not that he first took me, but I was sold to him by another *Narrhaganset Indian,* who took me when first I came out of the Garrison). I went to take up my dead Child in my arms to carry it with me, but they bid me let it alone; there was no resisting, but go I must and leave it. When I had been a while at my Master's wigwam, I took the first opportunity I could get to go look after my dead child. When I came, I asked them what they had done with it. They told me it was upon the hill; then they went and shewed me where it was, where I saw the ground was newly digged, and there they told me they had buried it; there I left that child in the Wilderness, and must commit it, and myself also, in this wilderness condition, to Him who is above all. God having taken away this dear child, I went to see my daughter Mary, who was at the same *Indian Town,* at a Wigwam not very far off, though we had little liberty or opportunity to see one another: she was about ten years old, and taken from the door at first by a Praying *Indian,* and afterward sold for a gun. When I came in sight she would fall a-weeping; at which they were provoked, and would not let me come near her, but bade me be gone, which was a heart-cutting word to me. I had one child dead, another in the wilderness I knew not where, the third they would not let me come near to: *Me* (as he said) *have ye bereaved of my children; Joseph is not, and Simeon is not, and ye will take Benjamin also, all these things are against me.* [18] I could not sit still in this condition, but kept walking from one place to another: and as I was going along, my heart was even overwhelmed with the thoughts of my condition, and that I should have Children and a Nation which I knew not ruled over them; whereupon I earnestly intreated the Lord that he would consider my low estate, and shew me a token for good, and, if it were his blessed will, some sign and hope of some relief: and indeed quickly the Lord answered, in some measure, my poor Prayer; for, as I was going up and down, mourning and lamenting my condition, my Son came to me, and asked me how I did. I had not seen him before since the destruction of the Town; and I knew not where he was till I was informed by himself, that he was amongst a smaller parcel of *Indians,* whose place was about six miles off. With tears in his eyes, he asked me whether his sister Sarah was dead, and told me he had seen his Sister Mary; and prayed me that I would not be troubled in reference to himself. The occasion of his coming to see me at this time was this: There was, as I said, about six miles from us a small Plantation of *Indians,* where it seems he had been during his Captivity; and at this time there were some Forces of the *Indians* gathered out of our company, and some also from them, (amongst whom was my Son's Master,) to go to assault and burn Medfield: in this time of the absence of his Master, his Dame brought him to see me. I took this to be some gracious Answer to my earnest and unfeigned desire. The next day, *viz.* to this, the *Indians* returned from Medfield, (all the Company, for those that belonged to the other smaller company came thorow the Town that now we were at). But before they came to us, Oh the outragious roaring and hooping that there was! They began their din about a mile before they came to us. By their noise and hooping, they signified how many they had destroyed; (which was at that time twenty-three). Those that were with us at home were gathered together as soon as they heard the hooping, and every time that the other went over their number, these at home gave a shout, that the very Earth rang again; and thus they continued till those that had been upon the expedition were come up to the Saggamore's Wigwam; and then, Oh the hideous insulting and triumphing that there was over some *English-men's* Scalps that they had taken (as their manner is) and brought with them! I cannot but take notice of the wonderful mercy of God to me in those afflictions, in sending me a Bible: one of the *Indians* that came from Medfield fight, and had brought some plunder; came to

18. *"Me have ye . . . against me":* Genesis 42:36.

me, and asked me if I would have a Bible, he had got one in his Basket. I was glad of it, and asked him whether he thought the *Indians* would let me read. He answered, yes. So I took the Bible, and in that melancholy time it came into my mind to read first the 28th *Chapter* of *Deuteronomie,* which I did; and when I had read it, my dark heart wrought on this manner, that there was no mercy for me; that the blessings were gone, and the curses came in their room, and that I had lost my opportunity. But the Lord helped me to go on reading till I came to *Chap.* xxx, the seven first verses;[19] where I found there was mercy promised again, if we would return to him by repentance; and though we were scattered from one end of the earth to the other, yet the Lord would gather us together, and turn all those curses upon our Enemies. I do not desire to live to forget this Scripture, and what comfort it was to me.

Now the *Indians* began to talk of removing from this place, some one way and some another. There were now, besides myself, nine *English* Captives in this place, (all of them Children, except one Woman). I got an opportunity to go and take my leave of them; they being to go one way and I another. I asked them whether they were earnest with God for deliverance; they all told me they did as they were able; and it was some comfort to me that the Lord stirred up Children to look to him. The Woman, *viz.* Good wife Joslin, told me she should never see me again, and that she could find in her heart to run away. I wisht her not to run away by any means, for we were near thirty miles from any *English* Town, and she very big with Child, and had but one week to reckon; and another Child in her arms two years old; and bad rivers there were to go over, and we were feeble with our poor and coarse entertainment. I had my Bible with me; I pulled it out; and asked her whether she would read; we opened the Bible, and lighted on *Psal.* xxvii, in which Psalm we especially took notice of that, *ver. ult. Wait on the Lord, be of good courage, and he shall strengthen thine heart; wait, I say, on the Lord.*

The fourth Remove. —And now must I part with that little company that I had. Here I parted from my daughter Mary, (whom I never saw again till I saw her in Dorchester, returned from Captivity,) and from four little Cousins and Neighbors, some of which I never saw afterward; the Lord only knows the end of them.

---

19. *the seven first verses:* "And it shall come to pass, when all these things are come upon thee, the blessing and the curse, which I have set before thee, and thou shalt call them to mind among all the nations, whither the Lord thy God hath driven thee, and shalt return unto the Lord thy God, and shalt obey his voice according to all that I command thee this day, thou and thy children, with all thine heart, and with all thy soul; that then the Lord thy God will turn thy captivity, and have compassion upon thee, and will return and gather thee from all the nations, whither the Lord thy God hath scattered thee. If any of thine be driven out unto the outmost parts of heaven, from thence will the Lord thy God gather thee, and from thence will he fetch thee: and the Lord thy God will bring thee into the land which thy fathers possessed, and thou shalt possess it; and he will do thee good, and multiply thee above thy fathers. And the Lord thy God will circumcise thine heart, and the heart of thy seed, to love the Lord thy God with all thine heart, and with all thy soul, that thou mayest live. And the Lord thy God will put all these curses upon thine enemies, and on them that hate thee, which persecuted thee" (Deuteronomy 30:1–7).

Amongst them also was that poor woman beforementioned,[20] who came to a sad end, as some of the company told me in my travel: she having much grief upon her Spirit about her miserable condition, being so near her time, she would be often asking the Indians to let her go home; they, not being willing to that, and yet vexed with her importunity, gathered a great company together about her, and stript her naked, and set her in the midst of them; and when they had sung and danced about her (in their hellish manner) as long as they pleased; they knockt her on the head, and the child in her arms with her. When they had done that they made a fire, and put them both into it; and told the other Children that were with them, that if they attempted to go home, they would serve them in like manner. The Children said she did not shed one tear, but prayed all the while. But, to return to my own Journey,—we travelled about half a day, or a little more, and came to a desolate place in the Wilderness; where there were no Wigwams or Inhabitants before; we came about the middle of the afternoon to this place; cold, and wet, and snowy, and hungry, and weary, and no refreshing (for man) but the cold ground to sit on, and our poor *Indian cheer.*

Heart-aking thoughts here I had about my poor Children, who were scattered up and down amongst the wild Beasts of the Forest: my head was light and dizzy, (either through hunger, or hard lodging, or trouble, or all together,) my knees feeble, my body raw by sitting double night and day, that I cannot express to man the affliction that lay upon my Spirit; but the Lord helped me at that time to express it to himself. I opened my Bible to read, and the Lord brought that precious Scripture to me, *Jer.* xxxi. 16, *Thus saith the Lord, refrain thy voice from weeping, and thine eyes from tears, for thy work shall be rewarded, and they shall come again from the land of the enemy.*[21] This was a sweet Cordial to me when I was ready to faint; many and many a time have I sate down and wept sweetly over this Scripture. At this place we continued about four days.

The fifth Remove. —The occasion (as I thought) of their moving at this time was the *English Army,* its being near and following them; for they went as if they had gone for their lives for some considerable way; and then they made a stop, and chose out some of their stoutest men, and sent them back to hold the *English Army* in play whilst the rest escaped; and then, like Jehu,[22] they marched on furiously, with their old and with their young: some carried their old decrepit Mothers, some carried one and some another. Four of them carried a great *Indian* upon a bier; but going through a thick Wood with him they were hindered, and could make no haste; whereupon they took him upon their backs, and carried him, one at a time, till we came to Bacquaug River. Upon a Friday, a little after noon, we came to this River. When all the Company was come up, and were gathered together, I thought

20. *that poor woman:* That is, Goodwife Joslin.
21. *"Thus saith . . . enemy":* These words are spoken to Rachel, who is mourning her lost children.
22. *like Jehu:* See 2 Kings 9:20.

to count the number of them; but they were so many, and being somewhat in motion, it was beyond my skill. In this travel, because of my wound, I was somewhat favoured in my load; I carried only my knitting-work, and two quarts of parched Meal. Being very faint, I asked my Mistress to give me one spoonful of the meal, but she would not give me a taste. They quickly fell to cutting dry trees, to make rafts to carry them over the River; and soon my turn came to go over. By the advantage of some brush, which they had laid upon the Raft to sit on; I did not wet my foot, (when many of themselves at the other end were mid-leg deep,) which cannot but be acknowledged as a favour of God to my weakened body, it being a very cold time. I was not before acquainted with such kind of doings or dangers.— *When thou passest through the waters I will be with thee, and through the rivers they shall not overflow thee.* Isai. xliii. 2. A certain number of us got over the river that night, but it was the night after the Sabbath before all the company was got over. On the Saturday they boyled an old Horse's leg, (which they had got,) and so we drank of the broth; as soon as they thought it was ready, and when it was almost all gone, they filled it up again.

The first week of my being among them I hardly eat any thing; the second week I found my stomach grow very faint for want of something; and yet 'twas very hard to get down their filthy trash; but the third week (though I could think how formerly my stomach would turn against this or that, and I could starve and die before I could eat such things, yet) they were pleasant and savoury to my taste. I was at this time knitting a pair of white Cotton Stockings for my Mistress; and I had not yet wrought upon the Sabbath-day: when the Sabbath came, they bade me go to work; I told them it was Sabbath-day, and desired them to let me rest, and told them I would do as much more to-morrow; to which they answered me, they would break my face. And here I cannot but take notice of the strange providence of God in preserving the Heathen: They were many hundreds, old and young, some sick and some lame; many had *Papooses* at their backs, the greatest number (at this time with us) were *Squaws;* and they travelled with all they had, bag and baggage, and yet they got over this River aforesaid; and on Monday they set their Wigwams on fire, and away they went: on that very day came the *English* Army after them to this River, and saw the smoke of their Wigwams; and yet this River put a stop to them. God did not give them courage or activity to go after us; we were not ready for so great a mercy as victory and deliverance; if we had been, God would have found out a way for the *English* to have passed this River, as well as for the *Indians,* with their *Squaws* and *Children,* and all their *Luggage.—Oh that my people had hearkened to me, and Israel had walked in my wayes, I should soon have subdued their Enemies, and turned my hand against their Adversaries,* Psal. lxxxi. 13, 14.

The sixth Remove. —On Monday (as I said) they set their Wigwams on fire and went away. It was a cold morning; and before us was a great Brook with Ice on it; some waded through it up to the knees and higher; but others went till they came to a Beaver-Dam, and I amongst them, where, thorough the good providence of

God, I did not wet my foot. I went along that day mourning and lamenting, leaving farther my own Countrey, and travelling into the vast and howling Wilderness; and I understood something of Lot's Wife's Temptation,[23] when she looked back. We came that day to a great Swamp; by the side of which we took up our lodging that night. When I came to the brow of the hill that looked toward the Swamp, I thought we had been come to a great *Indian Town,* (though there were none but our own Company,) the *Indians* were as thick as the Trees; it seemed as if there had been a thousand Hatchets going at once: if one looked before one there was nothing but *Indians,* and behind one nothing but *Indians;* and so on either hand; I myself in the midst, and no Christian Soul near me, and yet how hath the Lord preserved me in safety! Oh the experience that I have had of the goodness of God to me and mine!

The seventh Remove.—After a restless and hungry night there, we had a wearisome time of it the next day. The Swamp by which we lay was, as it were, a deep Dungeon, and an exceeding high and steep hill before it. Before I got to the top of the hill, I thought my heart and legs and all would have broken and failed me; what through faintness and soreness of Body, it was a grievous day of Travel to me. As we went along, I saw a place where *English* Cattle had been; that was a comfort to me, such as it was. Quickly after that we came to an *English* path, which so took with me that I thought I could there have freely lyen down and died. That day, a little after noon, we came to Squaukheag; where the *Indians* quickly spread themselves over the deserted *English* Fields, gleaning what they could find; some pickt up Ears of Wheat that were crickled down; some found ears of *Indian Corn;* some found Ground-nuts, and others sheaves of wheat, that were frozen together in the Shock, and went to threshing of them out. Myself got two Ears of *Indian Corn;* and whilst I did but turn my back, one of them was stollen from me, which much troubled me. There came an *Indian* to them at that time with a Basket of *Horse-liver.* I asked him to give me a piece. What, (says he) can you eat Horse-liver? I told him I would try, if he would give me a piece; which he did; and I laid it on the coals to roast; but before it was half ready, they got half of it away from me; so that I was fain to take the rest, and eat it as it was, with the blood about my mouth, and yet a savory bit it was to me; for to the hungry soul every bitter thing is sweet. A solemn sight me thought it was to see whole fields of Wheat and *Indian Corn* forsaken and spoiled; and the remainders of them to be food for our merciless Enemies. That night we had a mess of Wheat for our supper.

The eighth Remove.—On the morrow morning we must go over the River, *i.e.* Connecticut, to meet with King Philip. Two Cannoos full they had carried over, the next turn I myself was to go; but as my foot was upon the Cannoo to step in, there was a sudden outcry among them, and I must step back; and, instead of going over the River, I must go four or five miles up the River farther northward.

23. *Lot's wife:* Lot's wife is turned into a pillar of salt when she disobeys God's command and looks back at the destruction of Sodom and Gomorrah (see Genesis 19).

Some of the *Indians* ran one way, and some another. The cause of this rout was, as I thought, their espying some *English* Scouts who were thereabout.

In this travel up the River, about noon the Company made a stop, and sat down; some to eat, and others to rest them. As I sate amongst them, musing of things past, my Son Joseph unexpectedly came to me; we asked of each others welfare; bemoaning our doleful condition, and the change that had come upon us: we had Husband and Father, and Children and Sisters, and Friends and Relations, and House and Home, and many Comforts of this life; but now we might say as *Job, Naked came I out of my mother's womb, and naked shall I return; the Lord gave, and the Lord hath taken away, blessed be the name of the Lord.* I asked him, whether he would read? he told me he earnestly desired it. I gave him my Bible, and he lighted upon that comfortable Scripture, *Psal.* cxviii. 17, 18, *I shall not die, but live, and declare the works of the Lord: the Lord hath chastened me sore, yet he hath not given me over to death.* Look here, *Mother,* (says he) did you read this? And here I may take occasion to mention one principal ground of my setting forth these few Lines; even as the Psalmist says, To declare the works of the Lord, and his wonderful power in carrying us along, preserving us in the Wilderness, while under the Enemies hand, and returning of us in safety again; and his goodness in bringing to my hand so many comfortable and suitable Scriptures in my distress. But, to Return: we travelled on till night, and, in the morning, we must go over the River to Philip's Crew. When I was in the Cannoo, I could not but be amazed at the numerous Crew of Pagans that were on the Bank on the other side. When I came ashore, they gathered all about me, I sitting alone in the midst; I observed they asked one another Questions, and laughed, and rejoyced over their Gains and Victories; then my heart began to faile; and I fell a-weeping; which was the first time, to my remembrance, that I wept before them. Although I had met with so much Affliction, and my heart was many times ready to break, yet could I not shed one tear in their sight; but rather had been all this while in a maze, and like one astonished; but now I may say, as *Psal.* cxxxvii. 1, *By the rivers of* Babylon, *there we sate down, yea we wept when we remembered Zion.* There one of them asked me, why I wept? I could hardly tell what to say; yet I answered, they would kill me: No, said he, none will hurt you. Then came one of them and gave me two spoonfuls of Meal to comfort me, and another gave me half a pint of Pease, which was more worth than many Bushels at another time. Then I went to see King Philip; he bade me come in and sit down, and asked me, whether I would smoak it? (an usual Compliment now-a-days amongst Saints and Sinners.) But this no way suited me; for though I had formerly used Tobacco, yet I had left it ever since I was first taken. *It seems to be a Bait the Devil layes to make men lose their precious time.* I remember with shame, how, formerly, when I had taken two or three Pipes, I was presently ready for another, such a bewitching thing it is; but I thank God he has now given me power over it; surely there are many who may be better imployed than to lye sucking a stinking Tobacco-pipe.

Now the *Indians* gather their Forces to go against North-hampton; over night one went about yelling and hooting to give notice of the design; whereupon they fell to boyling of Ground Nuts, and parching of Corn, (as many as had it) for their Provision; and, in the morning, away they went. During my abode in this place Philip spake to me to make a shirt for his Boy, which I did; for which he gave me a shilling; I offered the money to my Master, but he bade me keep it; and with it I bought a piece of Horse flesh. Afterwards I made a Cap for his Boy, for which he invited me to Dinner; I went, and he gave me a Pancake about as big as two fingers; it was made of parched Wheat, beaten and fryed in Bears grease, but I thought I never tasted pleasanter meat in my life. There was a Squaw who spake to me to make a shirt for her Sannup;[24] for which she gave me a piece of Bear. Another asked me to knit a pair of Stockings, for which she gave me a quart of Pease. I boyled my Pease and Bear together, and invited my Master and Mistress to Dinner; but the proud Gossip,[25] because I served them both in one Dish, would eat nothing, except one bit that he gave her upon the point of his Knife. Hearing that my Son was come to this place, I went to see him, and found him lying flat upon the ground; I asked him how he could sleep so? he answered me, that he was not asleep, but at Prayer; and lay so, that they might not observe what he was doing. I pray God he may remember these things, now he is returned in safety. At this place (the Sun now getting higher) what with the beams and heat of the Sun, and the smoak of the Wigwams, I thought I should have been blind: I could scarce discern one Wigwam from another. There was here one Mary Thurston of Med-field, who, seeing how it was with me, lent me a Hat to wear; but as soon as I was gone, the Squaw (who owned that Mary Thurston) came running after me, and got it away again. Here there was a Squaw who gave me one spoonful of Meal; I put it in my Pocket to keep it safe; yet, notwithstanding, somebody stole it, but put five *Indian Corns* in the room of it; which Corns were the greatest Provision I had in my travel for one day.

The *Indians* returning from North-hampton, brought with them some Horses and Sheep, and other things which they had taken; I desired them that they would carry me to Albany upon one of those Horses, and sell me for Powder; for so they had sometimes discoursed. I was utterly hopeless of getting home on foot the way that I came. I could hardly bear to think of the many weary steps I had taken to come to this place.

The ninth Remove. —But instead of going either to Albany or homeward, we must go five miles up the River, and then go over it. Here we abode a while. Here lived a sorry *Indian,* who spake to me to make him a shirt; when I had done it, he would pay me nothing. But he living by the River side, where I often went to fetch water, I would often be putting him in mind, and calling for my pay; at last, he told me, if I would make another shirt, for a Papoos not yet born, he would give me a knife,

24. *Sannup:* Algonquin for "husband."
25. *Gossip:* A person, usually a woman, of light and trifling character.

which he did, when I had done it. I carried the knife in, and my Master asked me to give it him, and I was not a little glad that I had any thing that they would accept of, and be pleased with. When we were at this place, my Master's Maid came home; she had been gone three Weeks into the *Narrhaganset country* to fetch Corn, where they had stored up some in the ground; she brought home about a peck and half of Corn. This was about the time that their great Captain (Naananto)[26] was killed in the *Narrhaganset* Country.

My son being now about a mile from me, I asked liberty to go and see him; they bade me go, and away I went; but quickly lost myself, travelling over Hills and through Swamps, and could not find the way to him. And I cannot but admire at the wonderful power and goodness of God to me, in that though I was gone from home, and met with all sorts of *Indians,* and those I had no knowledge of, and there being no *Christian Soul* near me; yet not one of them offered the least imaginable miscarriage to me. I turned homeward again, and met with my Master; he shewed me the way to my Son: when I came to him I found him not well; and withal he had a Boyl on his side, which much troubled him; we bemoaned one another a while, as the Lord helped us, and then I returned again. When I was returned, I found myself as unsatisfied as I was before. I went up and down moaning and lamenting; and my spirit was ready to sink with the thoughts of my poor Children; my Son was ill, and I could not but think of his mournful looks; and no *Christian Friend* was near him to do any office of love for him, either for Soul or Body. And my poor Girl, I knew not where she was, nor whether she was sick or well, or alive or dead. I repaired under these thoughts to my Bible (my great comforter in that time) and that scripture came to my hand, *Cast thy burden upon the Lord, and he shall sustain thee.* Psal. lv. 22.

But I was fain to go and look after something to satisfie my hunger; and going among the Wigwams, I went into one, and there found a Squaw who shewed herself very kind to me, and gave me a piece of Bear. I put it into my pocket, and came home; but could not find an opportunity to broil it, for fear they would get it from me, and there it lay all that day and night in my stinking pocket. In the morning I went again to the same Squaw, who had a Kettle of Ground nuts boyling; I asked her to let me boyle my piece of Bear in her Kettle, which she did, and gave me some Ground nuts to eat with it, and I cannot but think how pleasant it was to me. I have seen Bear baked very handsomely amongst the *English,* and some liked it, but the thoughts that it was Bear made me tremble: but now that was savoury to me that one would think was enough to turn the stomach of a bruit Creature.

One bitter cold day I could find no room to sit down before the fire; I went out, and could not tell what to do, but I went into another Wigwam where they were

---

26. *Naananto:* Better known as Canonchet, the "king" of the Narragansetts, Naananto was captured by the English on April 2, 1676.

also sitting round the fire; but the Squaw laid a skin for me, and bid me sit down; and gave me some Ground nuts, and bade me come again; and told me they would buy me if they were able; and yet these were Strangers to me that I never knew before.

The tenth Remove. —That day a small part of the Company removed about three quarters of a mile, intending farther the next day. When they came to the place where they intended to lodge, and had pitched their Wigwams; being hungry, I went again back to the place we were before at, to get something to eat, being incouraged by the Squaw's kindness who bade me come again; when I was there, there came an *Indian* to look after me; who, when he had found me, kickt me all along; I went home, and found Venison roasting that night, but they would not give me one bit of it. Sometimes I met with Favour, and sometimes with nothing but Frowns.

The eleventh Remove. —The next day in the morning they took their Travel, intending a dayes journey up the River; I took my load at my back, and quickly we came to wade over a River, and passed over tiresome and wearisome Hills. One Hill was so steep, that I was fain to creep up upon my knees; and to hold by the twigs and bushes to keep myself from falling backward. My head also was so light, that I usually reeled as I went, but I hope all those wearisome steps that I have taken are but a forwarding of me to the Heavenly rest. *I know, O Lord, that thy judgments are right, and that thou in faithfulness hast afflicted me.* Psal. cxix. 75.

The twelfth Remove. —It was upon a Sabbath-day morning that they prepared for their Travel. This morning, I asked my Master, whether he would sell me to my Husband? he answered, *Nux,*[27] which did much rejoyce my spirit. My Mistress, before we went, was gone to the burial of a *Papoos;* and returning, she found me sitting and reading in my Bible; she snatched it hastily out of my hand, and threw it out of doors; I ran out and catcht it up, and put it into my pocket, and never let her see it afterward. Then they packed up their things to be gone, and gave me my load; I complained it was too heavy, whereupon she gave me a slap in the face, and bade me go; I lifted up my heart to God, hoping the Redemption was not far off; and the rather, because their insolency grew worse and worse.

But the thoughts of my going homeward (for so we bent our course) much cheared my Spirit, and made my burden seem light, and almost nothing at all. But (to my amazement and great perplexity) the scale was soon turned; for, when we had gone a little way, on a sudden my Mistress gives out she would go no further, but turn back again, and said I must go back again with her, and she called her Sannup, and would have had him gone back also, but he would not, but said, he would go on, and come to us again in three dayes. My Spirit was upon his (I confess) very impatient and almost outragious. I thought I could as well have died as went back. I cannot declare the trouble that I was in about it; but yet back again

27. *nux:* That is, yes.

I must go. As soon as I had an opportunity, I took my Bible to read, and that quieting Scripture came to my hand, *Psal.* xlvi. 10, *Be still, and know that I am God,* which stilled my spirit for the present; but a sore time of trial I concluded I had to go through. My Master being gone, who seemed to me the best Friend that I had of an *Indian,* both in cold and hunger, and quickly so it proved; down I sat, with my Heart as full as it could hold, and yet so hungry, that I could not sit neither; but going out to see what I could find, and walking among the Trees, I found six Acorns and two Chesnuts, which were some refreshment to me. Towards night I gathered me some sticks for my own comfort, that I might not lye a Cold; but when we came to lye down, they bade me go out and lye somewhere else, for they had company (they said) come in more than their own; I told them I could not tell where to go, they bade me go look; I told them, if I went to another *Wigwam* they would be angry, and send me home again. Then one of the company drew his Sword, and told me he would run me through if I did not go presently. Then was I fain to stoop to this rude Fellow, and to go out in the Night, I knew not whither. Mine eyes have seen that fellow afterwards walking up and down in Boston, under the appearance of a *Friend-Indian,* and several others of the like Cut. I went to one *Wigwam,* and they told me they had no room; then I went to another, and they said the same: at last an old *Indian* bade me come to him, and his squaw gave me some Ground nuts, she gave me also something to lay under my head, and a good fire we had; and, through the good Providence of God, I had a comfortable lodging that Night. In the morning, another *Indian* bade me come at night, and he would give me six Ground nuts, which I did. We were at this place and time about two miles from Connecticut river. We went in the morning (to gather Ground nuts) to the River, and went back again at Night. I went with a great load at my back (for they, when they went, though but a little way, would carry all their trumpery with them) I told them the skin was off my back, but I had no other comforting answer from them than this, that it would be no matter if my Head were off too.

The thirteenth Remove. —Instead of going toward the Bay[28] (which was that I desired) I must go with them five or six miles down the River, into a mighty Thicket of Brush; where we abode almost a fortnight. Here one asked me to make a shirt for her Papoos, for which she gave me a mess of Broth, which was thickened with meal made of the Bark of a Tree; and to make it the better, she had put into it about a handful of Pease, and a few roasted Ground nuts. I had not seen my Son a pretty while, and here was an *Indian* of whom I made inquiry after him, and asked him when he saw him? he answered me, that such a time his Master roasted him; and that himself did eat a piece of him as big as his two fingers, and that he was very good meat: but the Lord upheld my Spirit under his discouragement; and I considered their horrible addictedness to lying, and that there is not one of them that makes the least conscience of speaking the truth. In this place, on a cold night,

---

28. *Bay:* Massachusetts Bay Colony.

as I lay by the fire, I removed a stick which kept the heat from me; a Squaw moved it down again, at which I lookt up, and she threw an handful of ashes in my eyes; I thought I should have been quite blinded and have never seen more; but lying down, the Water run out of my eyes, and carried the dirt with it, that, by the morning, I recovered my sight again. Yet upon this, and the like occasions, I hope it is not too much to say with *Job, Have pity upon me, have pity upon me, Oh ye my Friends, for the hand of the Lord has touched me.*[29] And here I cannot but remember how many times, sitting in their Wigwams, and musing on things past, I should suddenly leap up and run out, as if I had been at home, forgetting where I was, and what my condition was: but, when I was without, and saw nothing but Wilderness and Woods, and a company of barbarous Heathen; my mind quickly returned to me, which made me think of that spoken concerning *Sampson,* who said, *I will go out and shake myself as at other times, but he wist not that the Lord was departed from him.*[30] About this time I began to think that all my hope of Restoration would come to nothing; I thought of the *English* Army, and hoped for their coming, and being retaken by them, but that failed. I hoped to be carried to Albany, as the *Indians* had discoursed, but that failed also. I thought of being sold to my Husband, as my Master spake; but, instead of that, my Master himself was gone, and I left behind; so that my spirit was now quite ready to sink. I asked them to let me go out and pick up some sticks, that I might get alone, and pour out my heart unto the Lord. Then also I took my Bible to read, but I found no comfort here neither; yet I can say, that in all my sorrows and afflictions, God did not leave me to have my impatience work towards himself, as if his ways were unrighteous; but I knew that he laid upon me less than I deserved. Afterward, before this doleful time ended with me, I was turning the leaves of my Bible, and the Lord brought to me some Scriptures which did a little revive me, as that, *Isaiah* lv. 8, *For my thoughts are not your thoughts, neither are your ways my ways, saith the Lord.* And also that, *Psal.* xxxvii. 5, *Commit thy way unto the Lord, trust also in him, and he shall bring it to pass.*

About this time they came yelping from Hadly, having there killed three *English-men,* and brought one Captive with them, *viz.* Thomas Read.[31] They all gathered about the poor Man, asking him many Questions. I desired also to go and see him; and when I came, he was crying bitterly; supposing they would quickly kill him; whereupon I asked one of them, whether they intended to kill him? he answered me, they would not: he being a little cheared with that, I asked him about the welfare of my Husband; by which I certainly understood (though I suspected it before) that whatsoever the *Indians* told me respecting him was vanity and lies. Some of them told me he was dead, and they had killed him; some said he

29. *"Have pity . . . touched me":* Interestingly, the passage continues, "Oh that my words were now written! oh that they were printed in a book! that they were graven with an iron pen and lead in the rock forever! For I know that my redeemer liveth ..." (Job 19:23–25).

30. *"I will go out . . . from him":* Judges 16:20.

31. *Thomas Read:* The soldier Thomas Read, captured at Hadley, escaped on May 15, 1676.

was Married again, and that the Governour wished him to Marry; and told him he should have his choice, and that all perswaded him I was dead. So like were these barbarous creatures to him who was a liar from the beginning.[32]

As I was sitting once in the Wigwam here, Philip's Maid came in with the Child in her arms, and asked me to give her a piece of my Apron to make a flap[33] for it; I told her I would not: then my Mistress bade me give it, but still I said no. The Maid told me, if I would not give her a piece, she would tear a piece off it; I told her I would tear her Coat then: with that my Mistress rises up; and takes up a stick big enough to have killed me, and struck at me with it, but I stept out, and she struck the stick into the Mat of the Wigwam. But while she was pulling of it out, I ran to the Maid and gave her all my Apron, and so that storm went over.

Hearing that my Son was come to this place, I went to see him, and told him his Father was well, but very melancholy; he told me he was as much grieved for his Father as for himself; I wondred at his speech, for I thought I had enough upon my spirit in reference to myself, to make me mindless of my Husband and every one else; they being safe among their Friends. He told me also, that a while before, his Master (together with other *Indians*) were going to the *French* for Powder, but by the way the *Mohawks* met with them, and killed four of their Company, which made the rest turn back again; for which I desire that myself and he may bless the Lord; for it might have been worse with him, had he been sold to the *French,* than it proved to be in his remaining with the *Indians.*

I went to see an *English* Youth in this place, one John Gilberd,[34] of Springfield. I found him lying without doors, upon the ground; I asked him how he did? he told me he was very sick of a flux,[35] with eating so much blood. They had turned him out of the Wigwam, and with him an *Indian Papoos,* almost dead, (whose parents had been killed) in a bitter cold day, without fire or clothes: the young man himself had nothing on but his shirt and waistcoat; this sight was enough to melt a heart of flint. There they lay quivering in the Cold, the youth round like a dog; the *Papoos* stretcht out, with his eyes and nose and mouth full of dirt, and yet alive and groaning. I advised John to go and get to some fire; he told me he could not stand, but I perswaded him still, lest he should ly there and die; and with much ado I got him to a fire, and went myself home. As soon as I was got home, his Master's Daughter came after me, to know what I had done with the *English-man?* I told her I had got him to a fire in such a place. Now had I need to pray *Paul's* prayer, 2 *Thess.* iii. 2, *That we may be delivered from unreasonable and wicked men.* For her satisfaction I went along with her, and brought her to him; but, before I got home again, it was noised about that I was running away, and getting the *English* youth along with me; that,

32. *a liar from the beginning:* That is, Satan.
33. *flap:* Any piece of cloth fastened on only one side, hanging broad and loose; in this case, perhaps a bib.
34. *John Gilberd:* John Gilbert, a seventeen-year-old captive who later escaped.
35. *flux:* Dysentery.

as soon as I came in, they began to rant and domineer; asking me where I had been? and what I had been doing? and saying they would knock me in the head; I told them I had been seeing the *English Youth;* and that I would not run away; they told me I lied, and taking up a Hatchet, they came to me, and said they would knock me down if I stirred out again; and so confined me to the Wigwam. Now may I say with *David,* 2 *Sam.* xxiv. 14, *I am in a great strait.* If I keep in, I must dye with hunger, and if I go out, I must be knockt in the head. This distressed condition held that day and half the next; and then the Lord remembered me, whose mercies are great. Then came an *Indian* to me with a pair of Stockings which were too big for him, and he would have me ravel them out, and knit them fit for him. I shewed myself willing, and bid him ask my Mistress if I might go along with him a little way; she said yes, I might, but I was not a little refresht with that news, that I had my liberty again. Then I went along with him, and he gave me some roasted Ground nuts, which did again revive my feeble stomach.

Being got out of her sight, I had time and liberty again to look into my Bible, which was my guide by day, and my Pillow by night. Now that comfortable Scripture presented itself to me, *Isaiah* liv. 7, *For a small moment have I forsaken thee; but with great mercies will I gather thee.* Thus the Lord carried me along from one time to another; and made good to me this precious promise, and many others. Then my Son came to see me, and I asked his Master to let him stay a while with me, that I might comb his head, and look over him, for he was almost overcome with lice. He told me, when I had done, that he was very hungry, but I had nothing to relieve him; but bid him go into the Wigwams as he went along, and see if he could get any thing among them, which he did, and (it seems) tarried a little too long; for his Master was angry with him, and beat him, and then sold him. Then he came running to tell me he had a new Master, and that he had given him some Ground nuts already. Then I went along with him to his new Master, who told me he loved him; and he should not want. So his Master carried him away, and I never saw him afterward: till I saw him at Pascataqua, in Portsmouth.

That night they bade me go out of the Wigwam again; my Mistress's *Papoos* was sick, and it died that night; and there was one benefit in it, that there was more room. I went to a Wigwam, and they bade me come in, and gave me a skin to lye upon, and a mess of Venison and Ground nuts; which was a choice Dish among them. On the morrow they buried the *Papoos;* and afterward, both morning and evening, there came a company to mourn and howl with her; though I confess I could not much condole with them. Many sorrowful days I had in this place; often getting alone; *Like a Crane or a Swallow so did I chatter; I did mourn as a Dove, mine eyes fail with looking upward. Oh Lord, I am oppressed, undertake for me.* Isaiah xxxviii. 14. I could tell the Lord, as *Hezechiah,* ver. 3, *Remember now, O Lord, I beseech thee, how I have walked before thee in truth.* [36] Now had I time to examine all my wayes; my Conscience did not

---

36.　*"Remember now . . . in truth":* Isaiah 37:3.

accuse me of unrighteousness toward one or other, yet I saw how in my walk with God I had been a careless creature. As *David* said, *Against thee, thee only have I sinned:*[37] and I might say, with the poor Publican, *God be merciful unto me a sinner.*[38] On the Sabbath days I could look upon the Sun, and think how People were going to the house of God to have their Souls refresht; and then home, and their bodies also; but I was destitute of both; and might say, as the poor Prodigal, *he would fain have filled his belly with the husks that the Swine did eat, and no man gave unto him.* Luke xv. 16. For I must say with him, *Father, I have sinned against Heaven, and in thy sight,* ver. 21. I remember how, on the night before and after the Sabbath, when my Family was about me, and Relations and Neighbours with us, we could pray and sing, and then refresh our bodies with the good creatures of God, and then have a comfortable Bed to ly down on; but, instead of all this, I had only a little Swill for the body, and then, like a Swine, must ly down on the Ground; I cannot express to man the sorrow that lay upon my Spirit, the Lord knows it. Yet that comfortable Scripture would often come to my mind, *For a small moment have I forsaken thee, but with great mercies I will gather thee.*[39]

The fourteenth Remove.—Now must we pack up and be gone from this Thicket, bending our course towards the Bay-Towns. I having nothing to eat by the way this day, but a few crumbs of Cake, that an *Indian* gave my Girl the same day we were taken. She gave it me, and I put it into my pocket; there it lay till it was so mouldy (for want of good baking) that one could not tell what it was made of; it fell all to crumbs, and grew so dry and hard, that it was like little flints; and this refreshed me many times when I was ready to faint. It was in my thoughts when I put it into my mouth; that if ever I returned, I would tell the world what a blessing the Lord gave to such mean food. As we went along, they killed a *Deer,* with a young one in her; they gave me a piece of the fawn, and it was so young and tender, that one might eat the bones as well as the flesh, and yet I thought it very good. When night came on we sate down; it rained, but they quickly got up a Bark Wigwam, where I lay dry that night. I looked out in the morning, and many of them had lain in the rain all night. I saw by their Reeking. Thus the Lord dealt mercifully with me many times; and I fared better than many of them. In the morning they took the blood of the *Deer* and put it into the Paunch, and so boiled it; I could eat nothing of that; though they ate it sweetly; and yet they were so nice[40] in other things, that when I had fetcht water, and had put the Dish I dipt the water with into the Kettle of water which I brought, they would say they would knock me down; for they said it was a sluttish trick.

The fifteenth Remove.—We went on our travel, I having got one handful of

<hr>

37. *"Against thee . . . sinned":* Psalm 51:4.
38. *"God be merciful . . . sinner":* Luke 18:13.
39. *"For a small moment . . . gather thee":* Isaiah 54:7.
40. *nice:* Fastidious, dainty.

Ground nuts for my support that day: they gave me my load, and I went on cheerfully, (with the thoughts of going homeward) having my burden more on my back than my spirit; we came to Baquaug River again that day, near which we abode a few days. Sometimes one of them would give me a Pipe, another a little Tobacco, another a little Salt; which I would change for a little Victuals. I cannot but think what a Wolvish appetite persons have in a starving condition; for many times, when they gave me that which was hot, I was so greedy, that I should burn my mouth, that it would trouble me hours after; and yet I should quickly do the same again. And after I was thoroughly hungry, I was never again satisfied; for though sometimes it fell out that I got enough, and did eat till I could eat no more, yet I was as unsatisfied as I was when I began. And now could I see that Scripture verified, (there being many Scriptures which we do not take notice of, or understand, till we are afflicted,) *Mic.* vi. 14, *Thou shalt eat and not be satisfied.* Now might I see more than ever before, the miseries that sin hath brought upon us. Many times I should be ready to run out against the Heathen, but that Scripture would quiet me again, *Amos* iii. 6, *Shall there be evil in the City and the Lord hath not done it?* The Lord help me to make a right improvement of his word, and that I might learn that great lesson, *Mic.* vi. 8, 9, *He hath shewed thee, O Man, what is good; and what doth the Lord require of thee but to do justly, and love mercy, and walk humbly with thy God? Hear ye the rod, and who hath appointed it.*

The sixteenth Remove. —We began this Remove with wading over Baquaug River. The Water was up to the knees, and the stream very swift, and so cold that I thought it would have cut me in sunder. I was so weak and feeble, that I reeled as I went along, and thought there I must end my days at last, after my bearing and getting through so many difficulties. The *Indians* stood laughing to see me staggering along; but in my distress the Lord gave me experience of the truth and goodness of that promise, *Isai.* xliii. 2, *When thou passest thorough the waters, I will be with thee, and thorough the Rivers, they shall not overflow thee.* Then I sate down to put on my stockings and shoes, with the tears running down my eyes, and many sorrowful thoughts in my heart, but I gat up to go along with them. Quickly there came up to us an *Indian,* who informed them that I must go to Wachuset to my Master; for there was a Letter come from the Council[41] to the *Saggamores,*[42] about redeeming the Captives, and that there would be another in fourteen days, and that I must be there ready. My heart was so heavy before that I could scarce speak, or go in the path, and yet now so light that I could run. My strength seemed to come again, and to recruit my feeble knees and aking heart; yet it pleased them to go but one mile that night, and there we stayed two days. In that time came a company of *Indians* to us, near thirty, all on Horse back. My heart skipt within me, thinking they had been *English-men* at the first sight of them; for they were dressed in *English*

41. *the Council:* The Massachusetts Council.
42. *Saggamores:* The heads or chiefs of the tribe.

Apparel, with Hats, white Neckcloths, and Sashes about their waists, and Ribbons upon their shoulders; but, when they came near, there was a vast difference between the lovely Faces of *Christians,* and the foul looks of those *Heathens;* which much damped my spirit again.

The seventeenth Remove. —A comfortable Remove it was to me, because of my hopes. They gave me my pack, and along we went cheerfully; but quickly my Will proved more than my strength; having little or no refreshing, my strength failed, and my spirits were almost quite gone. Now may I say as *David,* Psal. cix. 22, 23, 24, *I am poor and needy, and my heart is wounded within me. I am gone like the shadow when it declineth: I am tossed up and down like the Locust: my knees are weak through fasting, and my flesh faileth of fatness.* At night we came to an *Indian Town,* and the *Indians* sate down by a Wigwam discoursing, but I was almost spent, and could scarce speak. I laid down my load, and went into the Wigwam, and there sate an *Indian* boiling of *Horses feet:* (they being wont to eat the flesh first, and when the feet were old and dried, and they had nothing else, they would cut off the feet and use them.) I asked him to give me a little of his Broth, or Water they were boiling in: he took a Dish, and gave me one spoonful of Samp,[43] and bid me take as much of the Broth as I would. Then I put some of the hot water to the Samp, and drank it up, and my spirit came again. He gave me also a piece of the Ruffe or Ridding[44] of the small Guts, and I broiled it on the coals; and now may I say with *Jonathan, See, I pray you, how mine eyes have been enlightened, because I tasted a little of this honey,* 1 Sam. xiv. 29. Now is my Spirit revived again: though means be never so inconsiderable, yet if the Lord bestow his blessing upon them, they shall refresh both Soul and Body.

The eighteenth Remove. —We took up our packs, and along we went; but a wearisome day I had of it. As we went along I saw an *English-man* stript naked, and lying dead upon the ground, but knew not who it was. Then we came to another Indian Town, where we stayed all night: In this Town there were four *English Children,* Captives: and one of them my own Sister's: I went to see how she did, and she was well, considering her Captive condition. I would have tarried that night with her, but they that owned her would not suffer it. Then I went to another Wigwam, where they were boiling Corn and Beans, which was a lovely sight to see; but I could not get a taste thereof. Then I went into another Wigwam, where there were two of the *English Children:* The Squaw was boiling horses feet; then she cut me off a little piece, and gave one of the *English Children* a piece also: Being very hungry, I had quickly eat up mine; but the Child could not bite it, it was so tough and sinewy, but lay sucking, gnawing, chewing, and slobbering it in the mouth and hand; then I took it of the Child, and eat it myself; and savoury it was to my taste.

That I may say as *Job,* chap. vi. 7, *The things that my Soul refused to touch are as my sorrowful meat.* Thus the Lord made that pleasant and refreshing which another time

43. *Samp:* Porridge made from coarsely ground Indian corn.
44. *Ruffe or Ridding:* The refuse or waste portion.

would have been an Abomination. Then I went home to my Mistress's Wigwam; and they told me I disgraced my Master with begging; and if I did so any more they would knock me on the head: I told them, they had as good knock me on the head as starve me to death.

The nineteenth Remove.—They said when we went out, that we must travel to Wachuset this day. But a bitter weary day I had of it; travelling now three dayes together, without resting any day between. At last, after many weary steps, I saw Wachusets hills, but many miles off. Then we came to a great Swamp; through which we travelled up to the knees in mud and water; which was heavy going to one tired before: Being almost spent, I thought I should have sunk down at last, and never got out; but I may say, as in *Psal.* xciv. 18, *When my foot slipped, thy mercy, O Lord, held me up.* Going along, having indeed my life, but little spirit, Philip, (who was in the Company) came up, and took me by the hand, and said, *Two weeks more, and you shall be Mistress again.* I asked him if he spake true? he answered, Yes, and quickly you shall come to your Master again; who had been gone from us three weeks. After many weary steps we came to Wachuset, where he was; and glad I was to see him. He asked me, when I washt me? I told him not this moneth; then he fetch me some water himself, and bid me wash, and gave me the Glass to see how I lookt, and bid his Squaw give me something to eat: So she gave me a mess of Beans and meat, and a little Ground-nut Cake. I was wonderfully revived with this favour shewed me, *Psal.* cvi. 46, *He made them also to be pitied of all those that carried them Captives.*

My Master had three Squaws; living sometimes with one, and sometimes with another: One, this old Squaw at whose Wigwam I was, and with whom my Master had been those three weeks: Another was Wettimore, with whom I had lived and served all this while: A severe and proud Dame she was; bestowing every day in dressing herself near as much time as any of the Gentry of the land; powdering her hair and painting her face, going with her Neck-laces, with Jewels in her ears, and bracelets upon her hands: When she had dressed herself, her Work was to make Girdles of Wampom[45] and Beads. The third Squaw was a younger one, by whom he had two Papooses. By that time I was refresht by the old Squaw, with whom my Master was, Wettimore's Maid came to call me home, at which I fell a weeping; then the old Squaw told me, to encourage me, that if I wanted victuals I should come to her, and that I should lye there in her Wigwam. Then I went with the Maid, and quickly came again and lodged there. The Squaw laid a Mat under me and a good Rugg over me; the first time I had any such Kindness shewed me. I understood that Wettimore thought, that if she should let me go and serve with the old Squaw she would be in danger to lose not only my service, but the redemption-pay also: And I was not a little glad to hear this; being by it raised in my hopes, that in God's due time there would be an end of this sorrowful hour. Then came an

---

45. *Wampom:* That is, wampum, cylindrical beads made from shells and used as currency.

Indian, and asked me to knit him three pair of Stockings for which I had a Hat and a silk Handkerchief. Then another asked me to make her a shift, for which she gave me an Apron.

Then came Tom and Peter,[46] with the second Letter from the Council about the Captives. Though they were *Indians,* I gat them by the hand, and burst out into tears; my heart was so full that I could not speak to them: But recovering myself, I asked them how my Husband did, and all my Friends and Acquaintance? they said, they were well, but very Melancholy. They brought me two Biskets and a pound of Tobacco; the Tobacco I quickly gave away; when it was all gone, one asked me to give him a pipe of Tobacco; I told him all was gone; then began he to rant and to threaten; I told him when my Husband came I would give him some: Hang him, Rogue, (says he) I will knock out his brains if he comes here. And then again, in the same breath, they would say, that if there should come an hundred without Guns they would do them no hurt. So unstable and like madmen they were: So that, fearing the worst, I durst not send to my Husband, though there were some thoughts of his coming to Redeem and fetch me, not knowing what might follow; for there was little more to trust them than to the Master they served. When the Letter was come, the Saggamores met to consult about the Captives; and called me to them to enquire how much my Husband would give to redeem me: When I came, I sate down among them, as I was wont to do, as their manner is: Then they bade me stand up, and said, they were the *General Court:* They bid me speak what I thought he would give. Now, knowing that all we had was destroyed by the *Indians,* I was in a great strait. I thought if I should speak of but little it would be slighted, and hinder the matter; if of a great Sum, I knew not where it would be procured; yet at a venture, I said *Twenty pounds,* yet desired them to take less; but they would not hear of that, but sent that message to Boston, that for *twenty pounds* I should be redeemed. It was a Praying *Indian* that wrote their Letter for them. There was another Praying *Indian,* who told me, that he had a Brother that would not eat Horse; his Conscience was so tender and scrupulous, (though as large as Hell for the destruction of poor *Christians.*) Then he said, he read that Scripture to him, 2 *King.* vi. 25, *There was a famine in* Samaria, *and behold they besieged it, until an Ass's head was sold for four-score pieces of silver, and the fourth part of a Kab of Doves dung for five pieces of silver.* He expounded this place to his Brother, and shewed him that it was lawful to eat that in a Famine, which is not at another time. And now, says he, he will eat Horse with any *Indian* of them all. There was another Praying *Indian,* who, when he had done all the Mischief that he could, betrayed his own Father into the *Englishes* hands, thereby to purchase his own Life. Another Praying *Indian* was at Sudbury Fight, though, as he deserved, he was afterward hanged for it. There was another

---

46. *Tom and Peter:* Tom Dublet (Nepanet) and Peter Conway (Tataquinea), Christian Indians of Nashoba village, were persuaded by Joseph Rowlandson and other clergymen to serve as messengers to the hostile sachems to ask about terms for the release of captives.

Praying *Indian,* so wicked and cruel, as to wear a string about his neck strung with *Christian* Fingers. Another Praying *Indian,* when they went to Sudbury Fight,[47] went with them, and his Squaw also with him, with her Papoos at her back: Before they went to that Fight, they got a company together to *Powaw:*[48] the manner was as followeth: There was one that kneeled upon a *Deer-skin,* with the Company round him in a Ring, who kneeled, striking upon the Ground with their hands and with sticks, and muttering or humming with their Mouths. Besides him who kneeled in the Ring, there also stood one with a Gun in his hand: Then he on the Deer-skin made a speech, and all manifested assent to it; and so they did many times together. Then they bade him with the Gun go out of the Ring, which he did; but when he was out they called him in again; but he seemed to make a stand; then they called the more earnestly, till he returned again. Then they all sang. Then they gave him two Guns, in either hand one. And so he on the Deer-skin began again; and at the end of every Sentence in his speaking they all assented, humming or muttering with their Mouths, and striking upon the Ground with their Hands. Then they bade him with the two Guns go out of the Ring again; which he did a little way. Then they called him in again, but he made a stand, so they called him with greater earnestness; but he stood reeling and wavering, as if he knew not whether he should stand or fall, or which way to go. Then they called him with exceeding great vehemency, all of them, one and another: after a little while, he turned in, staggering as he went, with his Arms stretched out; in either hand a Gun. As soon as he came in, they all sang and rejoyced exceedingly a while. And then he upon the Deer-skin made another speech, unto which they all assented in a rejoycing manner: And so they ended their business, and forthwith went to Sudbury Fight. To my thinking, they went without any scruple but that they should prosper and gain the Victory; and they went out not so rejoycing, but that they came home with as great a Victory. For they said they had killed two Captains and almost an hundred men. One *Englishman* they brought alive with them; and he said it was too true, for they had made sad work at Sudbury; as indeed it proved. Yet they came home without that rejoycing and triumphing over their Victory which they were wont to shew at other times; but rather like Dogs (as they say) which have lost their Ears: Yet I could not perceive that it was for their own loss of Men: they said they had not lost above five or six; and I missed none, except in one Wigwam. When they went, they acted as if the Devil had told them that they should gain the Victory; and now they acted as if the Devil had told them that they should have a fall: Whether it were so or no, I cannot tell, but so it proved; for quickly they began to fall, and so held on that Summer, till they came to utter

47. *Sudbury Fight:* On April 18, 1676, Captain Samuel Wadsworth of Milton, Samuel Brockle-bank of Rowley, and thirty other men were ambushed and slain at Sudbury.

48. *Powaw:* That is, *powwow,* the term used by the English settlers to describe a feast, dance, or other event preliminary to a hunt or war expedition. By extention, the term was used to identify a native priest or shaman.

ruine. They came home on a Sabbath day; and the Powaw that kneeled upon the
Deer-skin came home (I may say without any abuse) as black as the Devil. When
my Master came home, he came to me and bid me make a shirt for his Papoos of a
Hollandlaced Pillowbeer.[49] About that time there came an *Indian* to me, and bade
me come to his *Wigwam* at night, and he would give me some Pork and Ground-
nuts; which I did, and as I was eating, another *Indian* said to me, he seems to be
your good Friend, but he killed two *English-men* at Sudbury, and there lye their
Cloaths behind you: I looked behind me, and there I saw bloody Cloaths, with
Bullet-holes in them: yet the Lord suffered not this Wretch to do me any hurt. Yea,
instead of that, he many times refresht me: five or six times did he and his Squaw
refresh my feeble Carcass. If I went to their *Wigwam* at any time, they would
always give me something; and yet they were strangers that I never saw before.
Another *Squaw* gave me a piece of fresh Pork and a little Salt with it; and lent me
her Frying pan to fry it in: and I cannot but remember what a sweet, pleasant, and
delightful relish that bit had to me, to this day. So little do we prize common
mercies when we have them to the full.

 The twentieth Remove. —It was their usual manner to remove when they had done
any mischief, lest they should be found out; and so they did at this time. We went
about three or four miles, and there they built a great *Wigwam,* big enough to hold
an hundred *Indians;* which they did in preparation to a great day of Dancing. They
would say now amongst themselves, that the *Governour* would be so angry for his loss
at Sudbury, that he would send no more about the Captives; which made me grieve
and tremble. My Sister being not far from the place where we now were, and
hearing that I was here, desired her Master let her come and see me, and he was
willing to it, and would go with her; but she being ready before him, told him she
would go before, and was come within a Mile or two of the place: Then he overtook
her, and began to rant as if he had been mad, and made her go back again in the
Rain; so that I never saw her till I saw her in Charlstown. But the Lord requited
many of their ill-doings; for this *Indian,* her Master, was hanged after at Boston.
The *Indians* now began to come from all quarters against the merry dancing day.
Amongst some of them came one Goodwife Kettle:[50] I told her that my Heart was
so heavy that it was ready to break: so is mine too, said she; but yet said, I hope we
shall hear some good news shortly. I could hear how earnestly my Sister desired to
see me, and I as earnestly desired to see her; and yet neither of us could get an
opportunity. My Daughter was also now but about a Mile off; and I had not seen
her in nine or ten Weeks, as I had not seen my Sister since our first taking. I
earnestly desired them to let me go and see them: yea, I intreated, begged, and
perswaded them but to let me see my Daughter; and yet so hard-hearted were they,

 49. *Pillowbeer:* Pillowcase.
 50. *Goodwife Kettle:* Elizabeth Kettle and her three children were taken captive from the
Rowlandson garrison.

that they would not suffer it. They made use of their Tyrannical Power whilst they had it: but through the Lord's wonderful mercy, their time now was but short.

On a Sabbath day, the Sun being about an hour high, in the Afternoon, came Mr John Hoar,[51] (the Council permitting him, and his own forward spirit inclining him) together with the two forementioned *Indians,* Tom and Peter, with the third letter from the Council. When they came near, I was abroad; though I saw them not, they presently called me in, and bade me sit down, and not stir. Then they catched up their Guns, and away they ran, as if an Enemy had been at hand; and the Guns went off apace. I manifested some great trouble, and they asked me what was the matter? I told them I thought they had killed the *English-man,* (for they had in the meantime informed me that an *English-man* was come;) they said No; they shot over his Horse, and under, and before his horse, and they pusht him this way and that way at their pleasure, shewing what they could do: Then they let them come to their Wigwams. I begged of them to let me see the *English-man,* but they would not; but there was I fain to sit their pleasure. When they had talked their fill with him, they suffered me to go to him. We asked each other of our welfare, and how my Husband did, and all my Friends? he told me they were all well, and would be glad to see me. Amongst other things which my Husband sent me, there came a pound of *Tobacco;* which I sold for nine shillings in Money: for many of the *Indians,* for want of *Tobacco,* smoaked *Hemlock* and *Ground-ivy.* It was a great mistake in any who thought I sent for *Tobacco:* for, through the favour of God, that desire was overcome. I now asked them, whether I should go home with Mr Hoar? they answered, No, one and another of them: and it being Night, we lay down with that Answer: in the Morning Mr Hoar invited the *Saggamores* to Dinner: but when we went to get it ready, we found that they had stollen the greatest part of the Provision Mr Hoar had brought out of the Bags in the Night. And we may see the wonderful power of God, in that one passage, in that when there was such a great number of the *Indians* together, and so greedy of a little good Food; and no *English* there, but Mr Hoar and myself; that there they did not knock us in the Head, and take what we had; there being, not only some Provision, but also Trading Cloth, a part of the twenty pounds agreed upon: But instead of doing us any mischief, they seemed to be ashamed of the Fact, and said, it were some *Matchit Indians*[52] that did it. O that we could believe that there is nothing too hard for God! God shewed his power over the Heathen in this, as he did over the hungry Lions when *Daniel* was cast into the Den. Mr Hoar called them betime to Dinner; but they ate very little, they being so busie in dressing themselves, and getting ready for their Dance; which was carried on by eight of them; four Men and four Squaws; my Master and Mistress being two. He was dressed in his Holland

51. *John Hoar:* John Hoar was a Concord lawyer who aided Rowlandson in finding Nashobas willing to asist in the ransom negotiations.

52. *Matchit Indians:* Bad Indians.

Shirt,[53] with great Laces sewed at the tail of it; he had his silver Buttons, his white Stockings, his Garters were hung round with shillings; and he had Girdles of *Wampom* upon his Head and Shoulders. She had a Kersey Coat,[54] and covered with Girdles of Wampom from the Loins and upward; her Arms, from her elbows to her Hands, were covered with Bracelets; there were handfuls of Neck-laces about her Neck, and several sorts of Jewels in her Ears: She had fine red Stockings and white Shoes, her Hair powdered, and her face painted Red, that was always before Black; and all the Dancers were after the same manner. There were two other singing and knocking on a Kettle for their Musick. They kept hopping up and down one after another, with a Kettle of Water in the midst, standing warm upon some Embers, to drink of when they were a-dry. They held on till it was almost night, throwing out Wampom to the standers-by. At night I asked them again if I should go home? they all as one said, No, except my Husband would come for me. When we were lain down, my Master went out of the Wigwam, and by and by sent in an *Indian,* called James, the PRINTER,[55] who told Mr Hoar, that my Master would let me go home to-morrow, if he would let him have one pint of Liquors. Then Mr Hoar called his own *Indians,* Tom and Peter; and bid them all go and see whether he would promise it before them three; and if he would, he should have it; which he did, and had it. Then Philip smelling the business, called me to him, and asked me what I would give him to tell me some good news, and to speak a good word for me, that I might go home to-morrow? I told him I could not tell what to give him: I would give any thing I had, and asked him what he would have? He said, two Coats and twenty shillings in Money, and half a bushel of Seed-Corn and some Tobacco: I thanked him for his love; but I knew the good news as well as that crafty Fox. My Master, after he had had his Drink, quickly came ranting into the Wigwam again, and called for Mr Hoar, drinking to him, and saying he was a good man; and then again he would say, Hang him, Rogue. Being almost drunk, he would drink to him, and yet presently say he should be hanged. Then he called for me; I trembled to hear him, yet I was fain to go to him; and he drunk to me, shewing no incivility. He was the first *Indian* I saw drunk all the while that I was amongst them. At last his Squaw ran out, and he after her, round the Wigwam, with his money gingling at his knees: but she escaped him; but, having an old Squaw, he ran to her; and so, through the Lord's mercy, we were no more troubled with him that night: Yet I had not a comfortable night's rest; for I think I can say, I did not sleep for three nights together. The night before the Letter came from the Council, I could not rest, I was so full of fears and troubles, (God many times leaving us most in the dark when deliverance is nearest) yea, at this time I could

---

53. *Holland Shirt:* A shirt made of linen from the Netherlands.

54. *Kersey Coat:* A coat made of coarse, narrow cloth, usually ribbed.

55. *James, the PRINTER:* James the Printer (Wowaus) was a Christian Indian who was apprenticed to the Cambridge printer Samuel Green.

not rest night nor day. The next night I was over-joyed, Mr Hoar being come, and that with such good Tydings. The third night I was even swallowed up with the thoughts of things; *viz.* that ever I should go home again; and that I must go, leaving my Children behind me in the Wilderness; so that sleep was now almost departed from mine eyes.

On Tuesday morning they called their General Court (as they stiled it) to consult and determine whether I should go home or no: And they all as one man did seemingly consent to it, that I should go home; except Philip, who would not come among them.

But before I go any further, I would take leave to mention a few remarkable passages of Providence; which I took special notice of in my afflicted time.

1. Of the fair opportunity lost in the long March, a little after the Fort-fight, when our *English* Army was so numerous, and in pursuit of the Enemy; and so near as to overtake several and destroy them; and the Enemy in such distress for Food, that our men might track them by their rooting in the Earth for Groundnuts, whilst they were flying for their lives: I say, that then our Army should want Provision, and be forced to leave their pursuit, and return homeward; and the very next week the Enemy came upon our Town like Bears bereft of their whelps, or so many ravenous Wolves, rending us and our Lambs to death. But what shall I say? God seemed to leave his People to themselves, and ordered all things for his own holy ends. *Shall there be evil in the City and the Lord hath not done it? They are not grieved for the affliction of Joseph, therefore they shall go captive with the first that go Captive. It is the Lord's doing, and it should be marvellous in our Eyes.*[56]

2. I cannot but remember how the *Indians* derided the slowness and dulness of the *English* Army in its setting out: For, after the desolations at Lancaster and Medfield, as I went along with them, they asked me when I thought the *English* Army would come after them? I told them I could not tell: it may be they will come in May, said they. Thus did they scoffe at us, as if the *English* would be a quarter of a Year getting ready.

3. Which also I have hinted before; when the *English* Army with new supplies were sent forth to pursue after the Enemy, and they understanding it; fled before them till they came to Baquaug River, where they forthwith went over safely: that that River should be impassable to the *English,* I cannot but admire to see the wonderful providence of God in preserving the Heathen for farther affliction to our poor Country. They could go in great numbers over, but the *English* must stop: God had an overruling hand in all those things.

4. It was thought, if their Corn were cut down, they would starve and die with hunger: and all their Corn that could be found was destroyed, and they driven from that little they had in store into the Woods in the midst of Winter; and yet how to admiration did the Lord preserve them for his holy ends, and the destruction of

56.   *"Shall there be evil . . . our eyes":* A fusion of Amos 3:6, Amos 6:6–7, and Psalm 118:23.

many still amongst the *English*! strangely did the Lord provide for them, that I did not see (all the time I was among them) one Man, or Woman, or Child, die with Hunger.

Though many times they would eat that that a hog or a dog would hardly touch, yet by that God strengthened them to be a scourge to his people.

Their chief and commonest food was Ground-nuts; they eat also Nuts and Acorns, Hartychoaks, Lilly-roots, Ground-beans, and several other weeds and roots that I know not.

They would pick up old bones, and cut them in pieces at the joynts, and if they were full of worms and magots, they would scald them over the fire to make the vermine come out; and then boyle them, and drink up the Liquor, and then beat the great ends of them in a Mortar, and so eat them. They would eat Horses guts and ears, and all sorts of wild birds which they could catch; also Bear, Venison, Beavers, Tortois, Frogs, Squirrels, Dogs, Skunks, Rattle-snakes; yea, the very Barks of Trees; besides all sorts of creatures and provision which they plundered from the *English*. I cannot but stand in admiration to see the wonderful power of God, in providing for such a vast number of our Enemies in the Wilderness, where there was nothing to be seen but from hand to mouth. Many times in the morning the generality of them would eat up all they had, and yet have some farther supply against they wanted. It is said, *Psal.* lxxxi. 13, 14, *Oh that my people had hearkened to me, and Israel had walked in my wayes, I should soon have subdued their Enemies, and turned my hand against their adversaries.* But now our perverse and evil carriages in the sight of the Lord have so offended him; that, instead of turning his hand against them, the Lord feeds and nourishes them up to be a scourge to the whole land.

5. Another thing that I would observe is, the strange providence of God in turning things about when the *Indians were at the highest,* and the *English at the lowest.* I was with the Enemy eleven weeks and five days; and not one Week passed without the fury of the Enemy, and some desolation by fire and sword upon one place or other. They mourned (with their black faces) for their own losses; yet triumphed and rejoyced in their inhumane (and many times devilish cruelty) to the *English.* They would boast much of their Victories; saying, that in two hours time, they had destroyed such a Captain and his Company in such a place; and such a Captain and his Company in such a place; and such a Captain and his Company in such a place: and boast how many Towns they had destroyed, and then scoff, and say, they had done them a good turn to send them to Heaven so soon. Again they would say, this Summer they would knock all the Rogues in the head, or drive them into the Sea, or make them flie the Country: thinking surely, *Agag-like, The bitterness of death is past.*[57] Now the *Heathen* begin to think that all is their own, and the poor *Christians* hopes to fail (as to man) and now their eyes are more to God, and their hearts sigh heaven-ward; and to say in good earnest, *Help, Lord, or we perish;* when

57. *Agag-like:* See 1 Samuel 15:32.

the Lord had brought his People to this, that they saw no help in any thing but himself; then he takes the quarrel into his own hand; and though they had made a pit (in their own imaginations) as deep as hell for the *Christians* that Summer; yet the Lord hurl'd themselves into it. And the Lord had not so many wayes before to preserve them, but now he hath as many to destroy them.

But to return again to my going home; where we may see a remarkable change of Providence: At first they were all against it, except my Husband would come for me; but afterwards they assented to it, and seemed much to rejoyce in it; some asking me to send them some Bread, others some Tobacco, others shaking me by the hand, offering me a Hood and Scarf to ride in; not one moving hand or tongue against it. Thus hath the Lord answered my poor desires, and the many requests of others put up unto God for me. In my Travels an *Indian* came to me, and told me, if I were willing, he and his Squaw would run away, and go home along with me. I told him, No, I was not willing to run away, but desired to wait God's time, that I might go home quietly, and without fear. And now God hath granted me my desire. O the wonderful power of God that I have seen, and the experiences that I have had! I have been in the midst of those roaring Lions and Savage Bears, that feared neither God nor Man, nor the Devil, by night and day, alone and in company, sleeping all sorts together; and yet not one of them ever offered the least abuse or unchastity to me in word or action. Though some are ready to say I speak it for my own credit; but I speak it in the presence of God, and to his Glory. God's power is as great now, and as sufficient to save, as when he preserved *Daniel* in the Lions Den, or the three Children in the Fiery Furnace. I may well say, as he, *Psal.* cvii. 1, 2, *Oh give thanks unto the Lord, for he is good, for his mercy endureth for ever. Let the Redeemed of the Lord say so, whom he hath redeemed from the hand of the Enemy;* especially that I should come away in the midst of so many hundreds of Enemies quietly and peaceably, and not a Dog moving his tongue. So I took leave of them, and in coming along my heart melted into Tears, more than all the while I was with them, and I was almost swallowed up with the thoughts that ever I should go home again. About the Sun's going down, Mr Hoar and myself, and the two *Indians,* came to Lancaster; and a solemn sight it was to me. There had I lived many comfortable years amongst my Relations and Neighbours; and now not one *Christian* to be seen, nor one House left standing. We went on to a Farm-house that was yet standing, where we lay all night; and a comfortable lodging we had, though nothing but straw to lye on. The Lord preserved us in safety that night, and raised us again in the morning, and carried us along, that before noon we came to Concord. Now was I full of joy, and yet not without sorrow: joy to see such a lovely sight, so many *Christians* together, and some of them my Neighbours: There I met with my Brother, and my Brother-in-Law, who asked me, if I knew where his Wife was? Poor heart! he had helped to bury her, and knew it not; she being shot down by the house, was partly burnt: so that those who were at Boston at the desolation of the Town, and came back afterward, and buried the dead, did not know her. Yet I was

not without sorrow, to think how many were looking and longing, and my own
Children amongst the rest, to enjoy that deliverance that I had now received; and I
did not know whether ever I should see them again. Being recruited with Food and
Raiment, we went to Boston that day, where I met with my dear Husband; but the
thoughts of our dear Children, one being dead, and the other we could not tell
where, abated our comfort each in other. I was not before so much hemm'd in with
the merciless and cruel *Heathen,* but now as much with pitiful, tender-hearted, and
compassionate *Christians.* In that poor, and distressed, and beggarly condition, I
was received in, I was kindly entertained in several houses; so much love I received
from several, (some of whom I knew, and others I knew not,) that I am not capable
to declare it. But the Lord knows them all by name: the Lord reward them seven-
fold into their bosoms of his spirituals for their temporals. The twenty pounds, the
price of my Redemption, was raised by some Boston Gentlewomen, and M.
Usher,[58] whose bounty and religious charity I would not forget to make mention
of. Then Mr Thomas Shepherd[59] of Charlstown received us into his House, where
we continued eleven weeks; and a Father and Mother they were unto us. And
many more tender-hearted Friends we met with in that place. We were now in the
midst of love, yet not without much and frequent heaviness of heart for our poor
Children and other Relations who were still in affliction.

The week following, after my coming in, the Governour and Council sent forth
to the *Indians* again, and that not without success; for they brought in my Sister and
Goodwife Kettle; their not knowing where our Children were was a sore trial to us
still, and yet we were not without secret hopes that we should see them again. That
which was dead lay heavier upon my spirit than those which were alive amongst
the *Heathen;* thinking how it suffered with its wounds, and I was no way able to
relieve it; and how it was buried by the *Heathen* in the Wilderness, from amongst all
Christians. We were hurried up and down in our thoughts; sometimes we should
hear a report that they were gone this way and sometimes that; and that they were
come in in this place or that; we kept inquiring and listning to hear concerning
them, but no certain news as yet. About this time the Council had ordered a day of
publick *Thanksgiving;* though I thought I had still cause of mourning; and being
unsettled in our minds, we thought we would ride toward the Eastward, to see if we
could hear any thing concerning our Children. And as we were riding along (God
is the wise disposer of all things) between Ipswich and Rowly we met with Mr
William Hubbard,[60] who told us our Son Joseph was come in to Major Wal-

58. *M. Usher:* Probably Hezekiah Usher, a wealthy Boston bookseller and selectman, who died
two weeks after Rowlandson's ransom.

59. *Thomas Shepherd:* Son of the more famous Reverend Thomas Shepard (1605–1649), pastor of
the church at Cambridge and one of the most prominent religious and intellectual leaders of New
England.

60. *William Hubbard:* The Reverend William Hubbard of Ipswich was the author of *A Narrative of
the Troubles with the Indians* (1677).

drens,[61] and another with him, which was my Sister's Son. I asked him how he knew it? he said, the Major himself told me so. So along we went till we came to Newbury; and their Minister being absent, they desired my Husband to Preach the *Thanksgiving* for them; but he was not willing to stay there that night, but would go over to Salisbury to hear farther, and come again in the morning; which he did, and Preached there that day. At night, when he had done, one came and told him that his Daughter was come in at Providence: here was mercy on both hands. Now hath God fulfilled that precious Scripture, which was such a comfort to me in my distressed condition. When my heart was ready to sink into the Earth, (my Children being gone I could not tell whither) and my knees trembled under me, and I was walking through the valley of the shadow of death; then the Lord brought, and now has fulfilled that reviving word unto me; *Thus saith the Lord, Refrain thy voice from weeping, and thy eyes from tears, for thy work shall be rewarded, saith the Lord, and they shall come again from the Land of the Enemy.*[62] Now we were between them, the one on the East, and the other on the West; our Son being nearest we went to him first, to Portsmouth; where we met with him, and with the Major also; who told us he had done what he could, but could not redeem him under seven pounds, which the good People thereabouts were pleased to pay. The Lord reward the Major and all the rest, though unknown to me, for their labour of love. My Sister's Son was redeemed for four pounds, which the Council gave order for the payment of. Having now received one of our Children, we hastened towards the other; going back through Newbury, my Husband preached there on the Sabbath day; for which they rewarded him manifold.

On Monday we came to Charlstown; where we heard that the Governour of Road-Island had sent over for our Daughter to take care of her, being now within his Jurisdiction; which should not pass without our acknowledgments. But she being nearer Rehoboth than Road-Island, Mr. Newman[63] went over and took care of her, and brought her to his own house. And the goodness of God was admirable to us in our estate; in that he raised up compassionate Friends on every side to us; when we had nothing to recompence any for their love. The *Indians* were now gone that way, that it was apprehended dangerous to go to her; but the Carts which carried Provision to the *English* Army being guarded, brought her with them to Dorchester, where we received her safe; blessed be the Lord for it, *for great is his power, and he can do whatsoever seemeth him good.* Her coming in was after this manner: She was travelling one day with the *Indians* with her basket at her back; the company of *Indians* were got before her, and gone out of sight, all except one Squaw; she followed the Squaw till night, and then both of them lay down; having

61. *Major Waldrens:* Actually Major Richard Waldron of Dover, New Hampshire, notorious for the severity of his dealings with the Indians.

62. *"Thus saith the Lord . . . enemy":* Jeremiah 31:16.

63. *Mr Newman:* Noah Newman of Rehoboth.

nothing over them but the Heavens, nor under them but the Earth. Thus she travelled three days together, not knowing whither she was going; having nothing to eat or drink but water and green *Hirtleberries*. At last they came into Providence, where she was kindly entertained by several of that Town. The *Indians* often said that I should never have her under twenty pounds; but now the Lord hath brought her in upon free cost, and given her to me the second time. The Lord make us a blessing indeed each to others. Now have I seen that Scripture also fulfilled, *Deut.* xxx. 4, 7, *If any of thine be driven out to the utmost parts of heaven, from thence will the Lord thy God gather thee, and from thence will he fetch thee. And the Lord thy God will put all these curses upon thine enemies, and on them which hate thee, which persecuted thee.* Thus hath the Lord brought me and mine out of that horrible pit, and hath set us in the midst of tender-hearted and compassionate Christians. 'Tis the desire of my soul that we may walk worthy of the mercies received, and which we are receiving.

Our Family being now gathered together, (those of us that were living) the South Church in Boston hired an house for us; then we removed from Mr. Shepards (those cordial Friends) and went to Boston, where we continued about three quarters of a year; Still the Lord went along with us, and provided graciously for us. I thought it somewhat strange to set up house-keeping with bare walls; but, as *Solomon* says, *Money answers all things,*[64] and that we had, through the benevolence of *Christian* Friends, some in this Town and some in that, and others, and some from England, that in a little time we might look and see the house furnished with love. The Lord hath been exceeding good to us in our low estate, in that when we had neither house nor home, nor other necessaries, the Lord so moved the hearts of these and those towards us; that we wanted neither food nor rayment for ourselves or ours, Prov. xviii. 24. *There is a Friend that sticketh closer than a Brother.* And how many such Friends have we found, and now living amongst! and truly such a Friend have we found him to be unto us, in whose house we lived, *viz.* Mr James Whitcomb,[65] a Friend unto us near hand and afar off.

I can remember the time, when I used to sleep quietly without workings in my thoughts, whole nights together; but now it is otherwise with me. When all are fast about me, and no eye open but His who ever waketh, my thoughts are upon things past, upon the awful dispensations of the Lord towards us; upon his wonderful power and might in carrying us through so many difficulties, in returning us in safety, and suffering none to hurt us. I remember in the night season, how the other day I was in the midst of thousands of enemies, and nothing but death before me; it was then hard work to persuade myself that ever I should be satisfied with bread again. But now we are fed with the finest of the Wheat, and (as I may so say) with honey out of the rock; instead of the husks, we have the fatted Calf; the thoughts of

---

64. *"Money answers all things":* Ecclesiastes 10:19.

65. *Mr James Whitcomb:* James Whitcomb was a wealthy Bostonian, apparently active in the Indian slave trade.

these things in the particulars of them, and of the love and goodness of God towards us, make it true of me, what *David* said of himself, *Psal.* vi. 6, *I water my couch with my tears.* Oh the wonderful power of God that mine eyes have seen, affording matter enough for my thoughts to run in, that when others are sleeping mine eyes are weeping.

I have seen the extreme vanity of this World; one hour I have been in health and wealth, wanting nothing; but the next hour in sickness, and wounds, and death, having nothing but sorrow and affliction.

Before I knew what affliction meant I was ready sometimes to wish for it. When I lived in prosperity; having the comforts of this World about me, my Relations by me, and my heart chearful; and taking little care for any thing; and yet seeing many (whom I preferred before myself) under many trials and afflictions, in sickness, weakness, poverty, losses, crosses, and cares of the World, I should be sometimes jealous least I should have my portion in this life; and that Scripture would come to my mind, *Heb.* xii 6, *For whom the Lord loveth he chasteneth, and scourgeth every Son whom he receiveth;* but now I see the Lord had his time to scourge and chasten me. The portion of some is to have their Affliction by drops, now one drop and then another; but the dregs of the Cup, the wine of astonishment, like a sweeping rain that leaveth no food, did the Lord prepare to be my portion. Affliction I wanted, and Affliction I had, full measure, (I thought) pressed down and running over; yet I see when God calls a person to any thing, and through never so many difficulties, yet he is fully able to carry them through,and make them see and say they have been gainers thereby. And I hope I can say in some measure as *David* did, *It is good for me that I have been afflicted.* [66] The Lord hath shewed me the vanity of these outward things, that they are the *vanity of vanities, and vexation of spirit;*[67] that they are but a shadow, a blast, a bubble, and things of no continuance; that we must rely on God himself, and our whole dependence must be upon him. If trouble from smaller matters begin to arise in me, I have something at hand to check myself with, and say when I am troubled, it was but the other day, that if I had had the world, I would have given it for my Freedom, or to have been a Servant to a *Christian.* I have learned to look beyond present and smaller troubles, and to be quieted under them, as *Moses* said, *Exod.* xiv. 13, *Stand still, and see the salvation of the Lord.* [68]

FINIS

66. *"It is good . . . afflicted"*: Psalm 119:71.
67. *"vanity of vanities, and vexation of spirit"*: Ecclesiastes 1:2, 14.
68. *"Stand still . . . Lord"*: The complete verse from Exodus reads: "And Moses said unto the people, Fear ye not, stand still, and see the salvation of the Lord, which he will show to you today; for the Egyptians whom ye have seen today, ye shall see them again no more forever."

The Journal of Madam Knight

Edited, with an Introduction, by
SARGENT BUSH, JR.

Introduction

When Sarah Kemble Knight set forth from her Moon Street home in Boston on the afternoon of October 2, 1704, to begin an arduous journey to New Haven, her act made a very clear statement. She was declaring a self-confidence and an indifference to convention that was, if not unique, certainly noteworthy. The road from Boston to New Haven, though increasingly well traveled, was still rustic at best. Madam Knight—as she is traditionally called, in the early eighteenth-century manner of address for a middle-aged matron—had received news about the settlement of the estate of a New Haven relative, Caleb Trowbridge, whose widow may have been her sister.[1] She decided she needed to attend and set off forthwith, in her initial determination making light of the rigors and actual dangers of such a journey. She left behind a fifteen-year-old daughter, whose father was apparently traveling on business abroad, and an elderly mother. Her departure was hastily decisive; her progress during the next five days would be alternately arduous, amusing, trying, and frightening. The road she took was the established one between Boston and New Haven; just three months earlier Connecticut's governor, Fitz-John Winthrop, and his son and daughter had taken the same road from Connecticut to Boston.[2] But it must have been the rare woman who undertook the journey alone.

No other account like Madam Knight's *Journal,* by man or woman, survives. In the course of her journey Sarah Knight was a persistent diarist, resorting to her pen at the end of each day's travel "to enter my mind in my Jornal," sometimes in pungent prose, occasionally in clever verse, but always with engaging directness and concreteness. She repeatedly reveals the striking force of character which enabled her to overcome both external obstacles and internal fears in a rigorous round-trip that extended, with an enjoyable two-week excursion to New York and

---

1. William R. Deane identified Trowbridge in the introuction to his edition of Knight's *Journal* published in *The Living Age* (New York), June 26, 1858, 966.

2. The one-paragraph "Memoir of a Journey from New London to Boston" (Massachusetts Historical Society *Proceedings* 13 (1873–75), 249–50) was written in July 1704 by the governor's son, John Winthrop, who was then twenty-two years old. He made the journey with his father and a sister on hearing of an aunt's death in Boston. Despite the brevity of the account, it is clear the Winthrop party took the same route, from the opposite direction, that Madam Knight would take three months later, making their last night's stop at Billings's Inn, where Madam Knight stopped briefly her first day out.

a winter spent among relatives in Connecticut, exactly five months, though the journal itself is concerned only with her experiences while on the road. The resulting work, besides vividly presenting a dynamic personality, is also a valuable record of conditions in provincial America at the time, written just halfway between the settlement of the Massachusetts Bay Colony in 1630 and the beginning of the revolutionary war in 1775. As scholars have begun to notice, it is also an important contribution to the tradition of American humor, the first known substantial contribution to that tradition by a woman.

Who was Sarah Kemble Knight? In the Boston Public Library a document survives bearing the signatures of her father, Thomas Kemble, and her husband-to-be, Richard Knight, dated April 17, 1688, and indicating the intention that Knight would marry Kemble's "Spinster Daughter," Sarah, then two days short of her twenty-second birthday.[3] The marriage presumably occurred sometime shortly thereafter. The Knights' only child, Elizabeth, arrived on May 8, 1689. Richard Knight seems to have been a shipmaster and was apparently significantly older than Sarah; there is no record of his living past 1706. Even before her husband's death, Madam Knight kept a shop in Boston, and it is often written that she taught writing, which is to say handwriting, to local children, though the town's records do not list her as an official schoolteacher. The popular claim that the young Benjamin Franklin was among her pupils has never been proven. He was born in 1706, and Madam Knight left Boston sometime in the period 1713–15, so it is at least possible. But her claim to our attention does not rest on this sketchy detail.

Recalling that she made her journey in the same decade as Franklin's birth, however, helps us place her in relation to her historical context. She was born, grew up, and married in the Boston dominated by those Puritan patriarchs, the Reverend Increase Mather, longtime minister of the Second Church, and his son and associate, Cotton Mather, though increasingly in the early eighteenth century the Mathers' commanding influence on the region's intellectual and religious life showed signs of erosion. But the decade of Madam Knight's journey was an eventful one in colonial America. At the turn of the century, Judge Samuel Sewall, the most famous American diarist of the era, wrote the first antislavery tract, *The Selling of Joseph* (1700), and John Saffin answered with the first published defense of slavery in America. Cotton Mather published his famous history of New England, the *Magnalia Christi Americana,* in 1702. The map of New England published in that work shows the route Sarah Knight would follow just two years later (see Figure 2.1). In 1704 the road was already the route of postal riders, as Knight often reminds us. It later became known as the Post Road and is, more or less, the way followed at

---

3. This document is MS. Ch. M. 2.3.105, which I cite here with the courtesy of the Trustees of the Boston Public Library. Thomas Kemble, a merchant, had lived in Charlestown, near Boston, at least as early as 1651 (Deane, "The Journal of Madam Knight," 964).

later stages by U.S. Route 1, the Boston and Maine Railroad, and the New England Turnpike. Madam Knight would not be the last to experience hardships and frustrations along that highway.

Still, what Sarah Knight makes obvious is that travel, though still daunting, was by the first decade of the eighteenth century becoming a more common feature of the lives of American colonists. Arduous travel had long had a figural significance in the minds of New Englanders. For many years, even before John Bunyan's *Pilgrim's Progress* made the idea popular, Puritans had used the metaphor of travel as a way of picturing their spiritual journey from corruption to salvation. Many in New England in the first decade of the eighteenth century continued this literary-spiritual tradition. On the western side of the Connecticut River Valley in frontier Westfield, Massachusetts, the Puritan minister-poet Edward Taylor in 1703 gave a theological turn to the very real fears wilderness travel still involved in his part of the world:

> Then lead me, Lord, through all this Wilderness
>   By this Choice shining Pillar Cloud and Fire.
> By Day, and Night I shall not then digress.
>   If thou wilt lead, I shall not lag nor tire
> But as to Cana'n I am journeying
> I shall thy praise under this Shadow sing.[4]

But whereas the devout minister of Westfield wended his way to a spiritual haven, or "Canaan," Madam Knight's wilderness encounters with places of darkness and danger were decidedly secular, taking her toward New Haven, Connecticut. It is a feature of New England's changing character at the turn of the century that two such very different treatments of travel as Taylor's and Knight's could be written within a year of each other.[5]

Madam Knight's fears, misgivings, and loneliness, forthrightly expressed, originated in her immediate sensory experience. She traveled alone but was never entirely solitary. She hired guides as she proceeded and met up with other travelers, including a French doctor and later a widower named Polly and his daughter Jemima, who accompanied her part of the way. As she describes them, her travels seem to have had more in common with those of Ebenezer Cook's protagonist in

4. From "Preparatory Meditation 39," second series, *The Poems of Edward Taylor,* ed. Donald E. Stanford (New Haven: Yale University Press, 1960), 187.

5. John Seelye has pointed out that the year 1704 saw two other journeys, each very different, which also produced memorable accounts of travel: John Williams's Indian captivity narrative, *The Redeemed Captive Returning to Zion* (1707), and Benjamin Church's *Entertaining Passages Relating to King Philip's War* (1716). See Seelye's *Prophetic Waters: the River in Early American Life and Literature* (New York: Oxford University Press, 1977), 292–309, which concludes with an excellent discussion of Madam Knight's *Journal.*

his nearly contemporary *Sot-Weed Factor* (1708) than with Taylor's archetypal spiritual wayfarer. Cook's narrative of rambunctious adventures on the back roads and city streets of Maryland also capitalizes humorously on encounters with rural and rustic America.

It might be objected that Madam Knight's record of her thoughts is not entirely lacking a spiritual aspect. In fact, Knight suddenly recognizes the absence of a centrally spiritual approach in her life when, agonizing in her fear of an imposing river crossing, she acknowledges that she has not been concerned enough about her soul's redemption in the course of her lifetime, or, as she puts it, the experience of being "encompased with Terrifying darkness" is compounded by "the Reflections . . . that my Call was very Questionable, wch till then I had not so Prudently as I ought considered." Yet rather than leading to a fuller assurance of grace, as similar reflections in many a Puritan spiritual autobiography or journal had done, these reflections are followed by the account of her conquering the next hill and being rewarded with a view of the moon, which she proceeds to praise in neoclassical heroic couplets. The sharp juxtaposition of momentary musing on the problem of vocation, her spiritual "Call," with much fuller concentration on her familiarity with pagan personifications of the moon speaks eloquently of the increasing secularization of the lives of many early eighteenth-century New Englanders, not to mention their increasing interest in European belles lettres.

We know relatively little about the personal life of Madam Knight. At the time of her journey she was living in Boston, where she kept a shop and apparently also took in boarders. Her role as a businesswoman is an important one in understanding her own view of her social status, an issue that frequently arises, at least implicitly, in the *Journal*. At the "vendue," or auction sale, she visited in New York she "made a great many acquaintances amongst the good women of the town" and was accordingly invited to their homes and "generously entertained." But she also kept an eye open for a good buy there, carefully recording her purchase of one hundred reams of paper from Holland, purchased "very Reasonably" at ten or even as low as eight shillings a ream. She clearly expected to turn a nice profit back in Boston. Confident of her own middling economic and social standing, she is condescending in her comical descriptions of country people encountered on her route, from the hostesses at various inns who give themselves airs to illiterate bumpkins, Indians, and blacks, for whom she shows even less respect. Knight accepts her society's hierarchical layering, including the existence of slavery. She criticizes the residents along Connecticut's shoreline, "especially the farmers," for being "too Indulgent . . . to their slaves," allowing them to "sit at Table and eat with them." Yet when she arrived in New London, where she encountered members of higher ranks of society than her own, she showed decided respect for their manners and position. The Reverend Gurdon Saltonstall, for instance, who later became the governor of Connecticut and who was already known to her by reputation as "the most affable, courteous, Genero's and best of men," treated her considerately and hospitably, entirely bearing out her assumptions about him. She also makes a point near the end of her *Journal* of remarking the attentions paid to her by "the present Govenor in Conecticott": "I stayed a day here Longer than I intended by the Commands of the Honble Govenor Winthrop to stay and take a supper with him whose wonderful civility I may not omitt." She adds that "the next morning I Crossed the ferry to Groton, having had the Honor of the Company, of Madam Livingston (who is the Govenors Daughter) and Mary Christophers and divers others to the boat."

Her care in taking note of these social niceties is all the more interesting when we recall that some eight years later, after this "Madam [Mary Winthrop] Livingston" had died of breast cancer on January 8, 1713,[6] and her widower, John, sought a new wife, he turned to none other than Elizabeth Knight, Sarah's daughter, marrying her on October 1, 1713. The Livingstons were a wealthy and powerful family, particularly in New York. The picture of Madam Knight's social status is somewhat more fully rounded out, therefore, when we note that John Livingston's two sisters disapproved of the Knights. Joanna complained that Elizabeth Knight had "a very Stend [i.e., stained] Cerraceter," saying that her brother had lowered their family's status "to make it Equell with Mis^t. Kniets." Joanna's married sister, Margaret Vieth, repeats the charge that Elizabeth possessed "a staind charracter," suggesting that she had a "verry indifferent reputation" in Boston. These charges were partly based on reports that Elizabeth had indulged in "unlawfull familiarityes" with John while his wife was still alive.[7] John, however, urged his father to verify Elizabeth's good character by writing to Increase and Cotton Mather in Boston. The upshot was that Increase Mather performed the wedding ceremony, though some of the Livingstons continued to see their family as compromised by this alliance with their social inferiors. After the marriage, Madam Knight followed her daughter to the New London area and engaged there in business and land dealings, coming into trouble with the law at least once "for selling strong drink to the Indians." Though a working woman, she was a successful one, a fact she may have meant to declare by presenting a silver cup to the Norwich, Connecticut, church;[8] when she died,

6. Letters from Mary Livingston's husband, John, to his father, Robert Livingston, in the Livingston Family Papers at the Franklin D. Roosevelt Library, Hyde Park, New York, refer periodically in 1712 to Mary's illness; his letter of January 19, 1713, tells of her death and burial.

7. See Joanna Livingston to Robert Livingston, June 22, 29, 1713; Margaret Vieth to Robert Livingston, June 29, 1713, Livingston Papers, quoted here with the kind permission of the Franklin D. Roosevelt Library. Lawrence H. Leder quotes some of these passages (modifying the spelling somewhat) in his *Robert Livingston, 1654–1728, and the Politics of Colonial New York* (Chapel Hill: University of North Carolina Press, Institute of Early American History and Culture, 1961), 229–30. Malcolm Freiburg takes note of some of these details in his introduction to *The Journal of Madam Knight* (Boston: Godine, 1972).

8. The cup is inscribed with the date April 20, 1722. Information on Madam Knight's later

in 1727, she left her daughter property valued at over £1,800.[9]

It is clear from the little we know about Madam Knight that her approach to life was robust. She was not the typical woman of her day, but she was by no means the rare exception in her stalwart independence. She seems to have enjoyed the advantages that an emerging civilization afforded an enterprising individual. Her writing-instructor's handwriting was careful and clear, with occasional elegant flourishes,[10] and she made some of her family's income by copying legal documents, doubtless picking up a certain amount of legal knowledge in the process. Scholars have suggested that this acquaintance with the law may explain her desire to be present at the settlement of her relative's estate in Connecticut.[11] Like Herman Melville's imagined copier of legal documents, Bartleby the scrivener, Sarah Knight's writing—and not writing—has given her a character in readers' minds well beyond her own time. Although we remember her because she wrote this journal, we are also aware that most of her life is not contained in it. Did she, like Bartleby, usually prefer *not* to write? Either she became a journal writer specifically to record this exceptional journey, or—as seems more likely—other writings have failed to survive. In any event, we must be content with her brief *Journal,* a richly suggestive remnant of a life well worth recording.

Her motivation for writing this portion of her life was probably similar to that of another travel journalist two decades later, Virginia's William Byrd, whose *History of the Dividing Line,* written in 1728, like his briefer *Voyage to the Land of Eden* and *A Progress to the Mines,* was written not for publication but for the amusement of a private circle of relatives and friends. For Sarah Knight surely wrote for an audience other than herself. She is not the self-analytical, probingly reflective believer aiming at spiritual growth in the manner of many writers of private autobiographies in early New England. Nor is she a heroic quester, though one reader has observed mythological qualities in the *Journal.*[12] Rather, she is often, when she makes herself the subject of her comments, the victim of circumstances of the journey, forced to deal with inconsiderate or ignorant local people or simply suffering from the rigors of her

---

career in Connecticut is from Frances Manwaring Caulkins, *History of New London, Connecticut* (New London, Conn.: N.p., 1852), 371–73.

9. Deane, "The Journal of Madam Knight," 965.

10. Though the manuscript of the *Journal* has been lost, three letters in her hand are in the Livingston Papers, two written in her own right and another as scribe for her daughter.

11. George Parker Winship, introductory note to *The Journal of Madam Knight* (1920; rpt. New York: Smith, 1935), vi. Ann Stanford reiterates the suggestion in "Images of Women in Early American Literature," in *What Manner of Woman: Essays on English and American Life and Literature,* ed. Marlene Springer (New York: New York University Press, 1977), 198.

12. Robert O. Stephens, "The Odyssey of Sarah Kemble Knight," *CLA Journal* 7 (March 1964): 247–55. Peter Thorpe sees her not as an epic heroine but as a female picaro ("Sarah Kemble Knight and the Picaresque Tradition," *CLA Journal* 10 [December 1966]: 114–21), as does Seelye, who observes that the *Journal* "resembles a picaresque narrative by Smollett, taking its tension from the essential disparity between town and country life" (*Prophetic Waters,* 303).

journey, which involved traveling along unlighted roads at night, taking her chances with the menu of the day at every inn she encountered, or finding the bedding too lumpy or the pub-crawlers too noisy. In such scenes, which recur throughout the account, the innocent protagonist becomes a ready object of amusement. Such treatment of self would have appealed to an intimate circle of friends who already knew the bumptious good humor and superior physical stamina as well as mental readiness for the unforeseen which Madam Knight clearly possessed. It seems very likely that her anticipation of such an appreciative audience of listeners or readers prompted her to write her lively narrative. The life of a shopkeeper and housewife did not allow for much time away from home, so she took advantage of the opportunity to record what probably seemed a unique experience. While the occasion made her an author, the author wonderfully seized the occasion.

Sarah Knight was a woman who loved a good story. Several times in the *Journal* she records stories told to her by tale-spinners she encountered in her travels. At New Haven, she pauses to make some observations about "the manners and customs of the place," taking a special interest in the typically zealous punishment for acts considered crimes by their laws, "even to a harmless Kiss or Innocent merriment among Young people." Having broached this subject with local residents, she says, "They told mee a pleasant story about a pair of Justices," a story in which the pretensions to dignity of farmer-judges who must have a bench before they can execute justice is amply satirized by the justices' impromptu manufacture of a "bench" out of pumpkins in a field; from that eminence they hear the case of an Indian accused of stealing a hogshead, a case that ends in uproarious laughter, as Madam Knight says in retelling it for her own audience's amusement. Again, when she called on a Mr. and Mrs. Burroughs on her way from New Haven to New York, she was diverted by the old merchant and his wife, "who were now both Deaf but very agreeable in their Conversation." They told "pleasant stories of their knowledge in Brittan from whence they both come, one of which was above the rest very pleasant to me." This anecdote concerns a young man whose fortune was left in charge of a widowed aunt and who in her presence prays (in rhymed verse) for her death so that he might unburden himself of his father's debts. Madam Knight does justice to an amusing story a third time when telling of the inhabitants of Fairfield, Connecticut, where there was no great love lost between their minister and the congregation: "They have aboundance of sheep, whose very Dung brings them great gain, with part of which they pay their Parsons sallery, And they Grudg that, prefering their Dung before their minister." She also repeats a funny story involving singing Quakers and another, only partially overheard, of an old man whose children disapproved of his remarrying. Her ability to recognize a good story when she heard one no doubt contributed to her ability to relate an original one. If read by or to friends and relatives at the conclusion of her journey, perhaps after she had made revisions at home,[13]

13. The work's first editor, Theodore Dwight, the only one who had the use of the manuscript,

it surely would have had a great success with such an audience.

Madam Knight's *Journal,* with its numerous assertions of the entertaining quality of experience in the life of its female author-protagonist, serves as a counterexample to Patricia Meyer Spacks's claim that for women in eighteenth-century autobiography, "adulthood—marriage or spinsterhood—implied relative loss of self."[14] There is surely no such loss here, but rather a very strong assertion of self. Madam Knight begins her narrative as a decidedly Bostonian lady who is, for example, offended at the presumptions of the female innkeeper who demands too high a price for the services of her son, John, as a guide. The country folk she encountered, from the woman who put on extra rings and then insisted on "showing the way to Reding," which is to say, flourishing her hands in the air, to the indigent "Indian-like Animal," scratching the dirt with his shoe in "one of the wretchedest" hovels she had ever seen, all become the objects of this socially self-assured woman's satire. She is at the beginning of a traditional convention of American travel literature in which genteel, greenhorn innocents make excursions into rough territories—travelers such as Washington Irving in *A Tour on the Prairie,* Francis Parkman in *The Oregon Trail,* and Mark Twain in *Roughing It.*[15] William Spengemann points to Madam Knight's self-consciously civilized attitude when she speaks as a "disengaged Bostonian," one of her two chief "voices" in the *Journal.* This condescending or "judging voice" gives way in the narrative, Spengemann argues, to an "experiencing voice" that reflects her tendency to react to her travels by adjusting her attitudes and knowledge.[16] The latter claim implies that the *Journal* functions as an incipient bildungsroman, a fictional mode often compared to autobiography. It is useful to think about Madam Knight's *Journal*—or any autobiographical work—in this context, though many readers will find too little evidence of a clear pattern of growth from ignorance to knowledge in so short a work as this brief narrative. However that may be, her awareness of social difference between herself and the many local people she encountered along her way does create a humorous satirical dimension in the work.

But Madam Knight's role as a humorist is much broader than merely making satirical observations on social contrasts. It extends to the fundamental use of lan-

---

wrote in his introduction (which is reprinted in the present volume) that his edition "is a faithful copy from a diary in the author's own hand-writing, compiled soon after her return home, as it appears, from notes recorded daily, while on the road." Dwight's edition was published in *The Journals of Madam Knight, and Rev. Mr. Buckingham, from the Original Manuscripts, written in 1704 and 1710* (New York: Wilder and Campbell, 1825).

14. "Stages of Self: Notes on Autobiography and the Life Cycle," 1977, rpt. in *The American Autobiography,* ed. Albert E. Stone (Englewood Cliffs, N.J.: Prentice-Hall, 1981), 48.

15. William C. Spengemann, in one of the most perceptive analyses thus far, comments on this aspect of Knight's *Journal* in *The Adventurous Muse: The Poetics of American Fiction, 1789–1900* (New Haven: Yale University Press, 1977), 39–44.

16. Ibid., 43.

guage itself. Among Madam Knight's writing skills is her ability to employ con-
trasting styles. Much of the time the language in her narrative is earthy, partaking
of the dust of the road itself, humorous for the closeness with which she sticks to
colloquial modes of expression common to the people with whom she interacts.
She is herself a colloquial narrator, as we see on occasions like her visit to the inn at
Dedham, where her efforts to hire a guide are frustrated by the patrons' greater
interest in elbow-bending exercise or, as she puts it, remaining "tyed by the Lipps
to a pewter engine." Likewise, in describing her accommodations in Rye, New
York, after going "up a pair of stairs wch had such a narrow passage that I had
almost stopt [up] by the Bulk of my Body" (probably a clue to her physical shape, a
fact a friendly private audience would know full well), she adds, "Little Miss went
to scratch up my Kennell which Russelled as if shee'd bin in the Barn amongst the
Husks, and supose such was the contents of the tickin." "Little Miss" here is only
one of many menials or country folk described in generic terms, as are the
"Indian-like Animal," "Bumpkin Simpers" and "Jone Tawdry," and even "a
surly old shee Creature, not worthy the name of woman." On other occasions
colloquial expression serves her well to describe more aggressively annoying people, like the boisterous drinker who keeps her awake with his noises at the bar,
bellowing "a thousand Impertinances not worth notice, wch He utter'd with such a
Roreing voice and Thundering blows with the first of wickedness on the Table,
that it peirced my very head." Her own education and reading background sometimes rise to the surface in the middle of humorous passages, as when she tells of
vomiting after supper at an inn, incongruously making a joke of it with a Latin
punch line: "It was down and coming up agen which it did in so plentifull a
manner that my host was soon paid double for his portion, and that in specia."

At other times, though, she varies this bumptious expression with other voices.
For instance, she can become neoclassical in her diction, as when she embellishes a
description of a sunset: "Now was the Glorious Luminary, wth his swift Coursers
arrived at his Stage, leaving poor me wth the rest of this part of the lower world in
darkness, with which *wee* were soon Surrounded." In the very next paragraph,
however, she shifts into a more simply dramatic rendering of her feelings on pursu-
ing an invisible path through the Narragansett country in pitch darkness: "Now
Returned my distressed apprehensions of the place where I was: the dolesome
woods, my Company next to none, Going I knew not whither, and encompased
wth Terrifying darkness; The least of which was enough to startle a more Masculine courage." She shortly lapses back into her neoclassical mode as she regains
confidence with the return of light, this time from the rising of the "Kind Conductress of the night." The sequence culminates in one of the five brief passages of
poetry she inserts in her narrative; here she offers eighteen lines of heroic verse in
imitation of recent Restoration poetry, beginning "Fair Cynthia, all the Homage
that I may / Unto a Creature, unto thee I pay. . . ." Her verse need not be taken

very seriously—indeed, much of it is intentionally comic—but it is better than the "doggerel" label sometimes laid on it.[17]

Increasingly of late, readers have recognized Sarah Kemble Knight's relationship to the major American literary traditions of travel literature and humor. She was not the first to write in either mode, both having existed almost since the first settlement of North America, but she is recognizably part of both traditions, each of which acquired greater strength and identity from the early eighteenth century on. Robert D. Arner observes that Madam Knight's *Journal* "points the way that later American humor would go," representing a summary of many major themes and character types fundamental to the tradition of American humor: "courtship, cultural deprivation, the American Indian, the talkative and taciturn Yankee, the shrewd Yankee trickster, the bumpkin, . . . stylistic techniques [such as] mock epic language, surprising and unusual metaphors—'His shade on his Hors resembled a Globe on a Gate post'—comic colloquialisms, and—an important new dimension—the interplay among sophisticated Bostonian dialect, backwoods speech, and the pidgin English of the Indian." Arner quite correctly concludes that the *Journal* is "a vastly underrated contribution to American comic traditions."[18]

Finally, we need to pay attention to the history of the work's survival. Though written in 1704–1705, it remained in manuscript for several generations until it was finally published in 1825 by Theodore Dwight of New York. Dwight (1796–1866) was a teacher, journalist, and author. His father, Theodore Dwight, Sr., and his uncles, Timothy Dwight and Richard Alsop, had all been poets and members of the group of nationalistic writers known as the Connecticut Wits. Dwight's own writings were in prose and included various travel narratives, biographies, histories, and schoolbooks. The timing of his publication of Knight's *Journal* has not been sufficiently understood. The brief unsigned introduction, written by Dwight, asserts, in the first place, that "the object proposed in printing this little work is not only to please those who have particularly studied the progressive history of our country, but to direct the attention of others to subjects of that descrip-

17. The word *doggerel* is applied by Emily Stipes Watts, *The Poetry of American Women from 1632 to 1945* (Austin: University of Texas Press, 1977), 21. Watts also says, however, that the verse is "honest, funny, and outspoken" (p. 23).

18. "Wit, Humor, and Satire in Seventeenth-Century American Poetry," in *Puritan Poets and Poetics: Seventeenth-Century American Poetry in Theory and Practice,* ed. Peter White (University Park, Penn.: Pennsylvania State University Press, 1985), 283, 284. Others who have recently commented on Knight's place in the tradition of American humor include Thorpe, "Sarah Kemble Knight," 119–21; Kenneth Silverman, Preface to *The Journal of Madam Knight* (New York: Garrett, 1970), v–vii; Jacqueline Hornstein, "Comic Vision in the Literature of New England Women Before 1800," *Regionalism and the Female Imagination* 3 (Fall/Winter 1977): 11–19; Seelye, *Prophetic Waters,* 303–309; Hollis L. Cate, "The Figurative Language of Recall in Sarah Kemble Knight's *Journal,*" *CEA Critic* 43 (1980): 32–35; and Ann Stanford, "Sarah Kemble Knight," *Dictionary of Literary Biography,* vol. 24, ed. Emory Elliott (Detroit: Gale Research, 1984), 187–88.

tion, unfashionable as they still are; and also to remind the public that documents, even as unpretending as the following, may possess a real value, if they contain facts which will be hereafter sought for to illustrate interesting periods in our history." Dwight's statement that subjects of American "history" remain "unfashionable," even half a century after independence, deserves our full attention. Its meaning is clarified in the next paragraph of the introduction, where Dwight observes that "subjects so closely connected with ourselves ought to excite a degree of curiosity and interest, while we are generally so ready to open our minds and our libraries to the most minute details of foreign governments, and the modes and men of distant countries, with which we can have only a collateral connection."

In one sense, such a comment necessarily seems provincial and even potentially isolationist. But in the cultural context of the 1820s it has a rather different value. That decade began with the infamous question by the British reviewer Sydney Smith: "In the four quarters of the globe, who reads an American book?"[19] Ever since the end of the Revolution American writers had addressed the question of what makes for a national culture. A general desire to discover a uniquely American culture was a pressing issue variously dealt with by such writers of the Republican era as the Connecticut Wits, Mercy Otis Warren, Hugh Henry Brackenridge, Royall Tyler, and other early dramatists and novelists—notably, William Dunlap, Charles Brockden Brown, and Susanna Rowson—as well as many journalists in the first three decades of the nineteenth century. James Kirke Paulding published an essay, later titled "National Literature," in *Salmagundi* in 1820, the year not only of Smith's question but of other answers besides Paulding's. Washington Irving issued *The Sketch-Book* with its "Rip Van Winkle" and "The Legend of Sleepy Hollow," and the great mythologizer of the American wilderness, James Fenimore Cooper, published his first novel in 1820. In 1825 the young William Cullen Bryant challenged native authors in his famous *Lectures on Poetry.* Decades of condescension by the British press had finally helped produce a growing confidence that there might yet be something like "American literature," based on American traditions and written from American experience. It would be still longer before the full importance of writing in a distinctly American voice would be entirely realized, though examples had long since been available. Yet Emerson's summary declaration, "We have listened too long to the courtly muses of Europe," was only a dozen years in the future.[20] It was as part of this growing sense of the validity of American expression that Madam Knight's account of her solo journey

19. Review of Adam Seybert, *Statistical Annals of the United States of America* (1818), *Edinburgh Review* 33 (1820): 79. Though Smith was long since identified as the author, his remarks were printed anonymously, in the fashion of the time.

20. *Collected Works of Ralph Waldo Emerson,* vol. 1: *Nature, Addresses, and Lectures,* ed. Robert E. Spiller and Alfred R. Ferguson (Cambridge: Harvard University Press, 1971), 69. Emerson's Phi Beta Kappa address, popularly known as "The American Scholar," was delivered at Harvard on August 31, 1837.

struck her first editor as an eminently suitable text to add to the accumulating body of native materials that would make more appropriate reading matter for Americans than "the modes and men of distant countries." Dwight must have taken wry satisfaction in the fact that excerpts from his edition of Knight's *Journal,* with appreciative editorial comments, quickly appeared in *Blackwood's Edinburgh Magazine,* rival to the *Edinburgh Review,* the journal that had published Smith's condescending query five years before.[21]

Dwight's instincts were sharp. The travel journal of this remarkable colonial American woman surely possesses the flavor of a true native voice, predicting various strands that would grow and flower as the native qualities of America's literature continued to become more pronounced. The voice had spoken a century and more before the generation of Irving and Cooper, but it was presented to the American reader only in the 1820s. In this way Sarah Kemble Knight, all unawares, participated in two key moments in American cultural history—that in which she wrote and that in which her writing received a wider audience through publication. In its vitality and its rich, unaffected humanity, this personal narrative still helps us to know a region, an era, and most of all a delightfully personalized individual.

A   NOTE   ON   THE   TEXT

Theodore Dwight said that his edition of 1825 was printed from a nearly complete manuscript, excepting only where the bottom half of the first sheet was torn away, causing two breaks early in the narrative. Soon afterward most of the manuscript was inadvertently destroyed, and now no portion of it is known to exist. This loss of the manuscript is probably the main cause of occasional rumors that the *Journal* is not authentic. Such claims circulated soon after its first publication; William Deane relates that when he first saw the printed *Journal* (apparently around 1843), "it was stated quite confidently that it was a fiction, written by the late Samuel L. Knapp."[22] Perhaps Dwight unintentionally invited doubts when he began his introduction to the *Journal* by protesting, "This is not a work of fiction," and then even more by his confessed loss of the manuscript soon after publication. Some of the early skepticism about the work's authenticity was also probably based on a condescending opinion by the predominantly male critical establishment that the production of such a work by a woman was unlikely. These doubts, moreover,

21. Alan Margolies, "The Editing and Publication of 'The Journal of Madam Knight,'" *Publications of the Bibliographical Society of America* 58 (1964): 29.

22. Deane, "The Journal of Madam Knight," 963.

would have been fueled by Americans' tendency to an inferiority complex where their native "literature" was concerned. At this late date, however, even the most cautious review of the available facts offers no hard evidence to support a claim that the work is not by Sarah Knight. In the absence of such evidence, and considering not only the first editor's statements about the authenticity of the manuscript but also internal details like the consistency of language usage with early eighteenth-century practice, it seems the earliest editor's account of the matter has a proper claim to our confidence.

Though there have been several editions of the *Journal* since Dwight's, his remains the authoritative text, based as it was on the author's manuscript. The Dwight edition of 1825 (see footnote 13, above) has therefore served as the source text for this edition. The *y* or thorn is converted to *th* and the superscript *e* in the definite article *y^e* is brought down to the line. In all other instances, superscript letters remain as printed in the first edition. Where, very rarely, brackets have been inserted, they enclose a word or punctuation mark added by the present editor for the sake of clarity. Otherwise, Madam Knight's prose is eloquent in its imperfections.

ACKNOWLEDGMENTS

I would like especially to thank John Tedeschi, curator of rare books and special collections at the University of Wisconsin's Memorial Library, for permitting the use of his department's copy of the 1825 edition of the *Journal* in the preparation of the present edition.[23] I am also grateful to my colleague Fred Cassidy, who willingly answered my questions regarding a few of the annotations from his own amazing fund of knowledge and the marvelous resources in the files of his *Dictionary of American Regional English*. Giuseppe Bisaccia, curator of manuscripts at the Boston Public Library; Nathaniel N. Shipton, manuscripts curator of the New England Historic Genealogical Society; Christopher Bickford, director, and Everett C. Wilkie, Jr., Crofut Curator of Rare Books and Manuscripts, both of the Connecticut Historical Society; the late Ross Urquhart, graphics librarian of the Massachusetts Historical Society; Albert T. Klyberg, director of the Rhode Island Historical Society; and Raymond Teichman, supervisory archivist, and Susan Elter, archivist, both of the Franklin D. Roosevelt Library, all deserve thanks as well for their assistance in this project. I have also sought the benefit of advice from scholars who have previously studied Knight's *Journal*, including Alan Margolies, William C. Spengemann, and John Seelye, to all of whom I am grateful for their

23. The University of Wisconsin's copy is in the William B. Cairns Collection of American Women Writers, 1630–1900.

generous sharing of knowledge and ideas. Finally, I would mention the edition of
the *Journal* published by Perry Miller and Thomas H. Johnson in their famous
anthology *The Puritans,*[24] until now the most fully annotated edition. All readers of
the *Journal* in that anthology have benefited from the annotations, including the
present editor.

As any student of Knight's *Journal* quickly discovers, the best single piece of
modern scholarship on the history of the text and the many pertinent biographical
and historical facts is Alan Margolies's essay "The Editing and Publication of 'The
Journal of Madam Knight.' "[25] Not least important in Margolies's discussion is his
identification of certain oft-repeated errors in previous essays. Margolies's work
has been fundamentally important to the preparation of this edition.

BIBLIOGRAPHY

Arner, Robert D. "Sarah Kemble Knight (1666–1727)." In *American Writers before
        1800: A Biographical and Critical Dictionary,* edited by James A. Levernier and
        Douglas R. Wilmes, 857–59. Westport, Conn.: Greenwood Press, 1983.
Arner, Robert D. "Wit, Humor, and Satire in Seventeenth-Century American
        Poetry." In *Puritan Poets and Poetics: Seventeenth-Century American Poetry in The-
        ory and Practice,* edited by Peter White, 283–84. University Park: Pennsyl-
        vania State University Press, 1985.
Cate, Hollis L. "The Figurative Language of Recall in Sarah Kemble Knight's
        Journal." *CEA Critic* 43 (1980), 32–35.
Cate, Hollis L. "Two American Bumpkins." *Research Studies* 41 (1973): 61–63.
Caulkins, Frances Manwaring. *History of New London, Connecticut,* 371–73. New
        London: n.p., 1852.
Deane, William R. Introduction to "Journal of Madam Knight." *The Living Age*
        735 (June 26, 1858): 962–67.
Derounian, Kathryn Zabelle. "Genre, Voice, and Character in the Literature of
        Six Early American Women Writers, 1650–1812." Ph.D. diss., Penn State
        University, 1980.
Freiburg, Malcolm. Introduction to *The Journal of Madam Knight,* [i–v]. Boston:
        Godine, 1972.
Freiburg, Malcolm. "Sarah Kemble Knight." *Notable American Women, 1607–1950: A
        Biographical Dictionary,* edited by Edward T. James, Janet Wilson James,

24. New York: American Book Company, 1938.
25. "Editing and Publication," 25–32.

and Paul S. Boyer, Vol. 2, 340–42. Cambridge: Harvard University Press, 1971.

Hornstein, Jacqueline. "Comic Vision in the Literature of New England Women before 1800." *Regionalism and the Female Imagination* 3 (1977): 11–19.

Learned, William Law, ed. *The Private Journal of a Journey from Boston to New York in the Year 1704 Kept by Madam Knight.* Albany: n.p., 1865.

Margolies, Alan. "The Editing and Publication of 'The Journal of Madam Knight.'" *Publications of the Bibliographical Society of America* 58 (1964): 25–32.

Seelye, John. *Prophetic Waters: The River in Early American Life and Literature,* 292–309. New York: Oxford University Press, 1977.

Silverman, Kenneth. Preface to *The Journal of Madam Knight,* [v]–vii. New York: Garrett, 1970.

Spengemann, William C. *The Adventurous Muse: The Poetics of American Fiction, 1789–1900,* 39–44. New Haven: Yale University Press, 1977.

Stanford, Ann. "Sarah Kemble Knight." In *American Women Writers,* Vol. 2, edited by Lina Mainiero, 476–77. New York: Ungar Publishing, 1980.

Stanford, Ann. "Sarah Kemble Knight." In *Dictionary of Literary Biography,* Vol. 24, edited by Emory Elliott, 187–89. Detroit: Gale Research, 1984.

Stephens, Robert O. "The Odyssey of Sarah Kemble Knight." *CLA Journal* 7 (1964): 247–55.

Thorpe, Peter. "Sarah Kemble Knight and the Picaresque Tradition." *CLA Journal* 10 (1966): 114–21.

Vowell, Faye. "A Commentary on *The Journal of Sarah Kemble Knight.*" *The Emporia Research Studies* 24 (1976): 44–52.

Winship, George Parker. Introductory Note to *The Journal of Madam Knight,* [iii]–viii. Boston: Small, Maynard, 1920; repr. New York: Peter Smith, 1935.

Worthington, Erastus. "Madam Knight's Journal." *Dedham Historical Register* 2 (1891): 36–39.

Ziff, Larzer. *Puritanism in America: New Culture in a New World,* 290–93. New York: The Viking Press, 1973.

Introduction
to the Edition of 1825
[by Theodore Dwight]

This is not a work of fiction, as the scarcity of old American manuscripts may induce some to imagine; but it is a faithful copy from a diary in the author's own hand-writing, compiled soon after her return home, as it appears, from notes recorded daily, while on the road. She was a resident of Boston, and a lady of uncommon literary attainments, as well as of great taste and strength of mind. She was called Madam Knight, out of respect to her character, according to a custom once common in New-England; but what was her family name the publishers have not been able to discover.

The object proposed in printing this little work is not only to please those who have particularly studied the progressive history of our country, but to direct the attention of others to subjects of that description, unfashionable as they still are; and also to remind the public that documents, even as unpretending as the following, may possess a real value, if they contain facts which will be hereafter sought for to illustrate interesting periods in our history.

It is to be regretted that the brevity of the work should have allowed the author so little room for the display of the cultivated mind and the brilliant fancy which frequently betray themselves in the course of the narrative; and no one can rise from the perusal without wishing some happy chance might yet discover more full delineations of life and character from the same practised hand. Subjects so closely connected with ourselves ought to excite a degree of curiosity and interest, while we are generally so ready to open our minds and our libraries to the most minute details of foreign governments, and the modes and men of distant countries, with which we can have only a collateral connection.

In copying the following work for the press, the original orthography has been carefully preserved, in some cases, it may be, so far as to retain the errors of the pen, for fear of introducing any unwarrantable modernism. The punctuation was very hasty, and therefore has not been regarded. Two interruptions occur in the original near the commencement, which could not be supplied; and in a few instances it has been thought proper to make short omissions, but none of them materially affect the narrative.

The reader will find frequent occasion to compare the state of things in the time of our author with that of the present period, particularly with regard to the number of the inhabitants, and the facilities and accommodations prepared for travellers. Over that tract of country where she travelled about a fortnight, on horseback, under the direction of a hired guide, with frequent risks of life and limb, and sometimes without food or shelter for many miles, we proceed at our ease, without exposure and almost without fatigue, in a day and a half, through a well peopled land, supplied with good stage-coaches and public houses, or the still greater luxuries of the elegant steam boats which daily traverse our waters.

The Journal of Madam Knight

Monday, Octb'r. the second, 1704.—About three o'clock afternoon, I begun my Journey from Boston to New-Haven; being about two Hundred Mile. My Kinsman, Capt. Robert Luist, waited on me as farr as Dedham, where I was to meet the Western post.

I vissitted the Reverd. Mr. Belcher,[1] the Minister of the town, and tarried there till evening, in hopes the post would come along. But he not coming, I resolved to go to Billingses where he used to lodg, being 12 miles further. But being ignorant of the way, Mad^m Billings,[2] seing no persuasions of her good spouses or hers could prevail with me to Lodg there that night, Very kindly went wyth me to the Tavern,[3] where I hoped to get my guide, And desired the Hostess to inquire of her guests whether any of them would go with mee. But they being tyed by the Lipps to a pewter engine, scarcely allowed themselves time to say what clownish [Dwight's note: Here half a page of the MS is gone.] . . . Peices of eight, I told her no, I would not be accessary to such extortion.

Then John shan't go, sais shee. No, indeed, shan't hee; And held forth at that rate a long time, that I began to fear I was got among the Quaking tribe,[4] beleeving not a Limbertong'd sister among them could out do Madm. Hostes.

Upon this, to my no small surprise, son John arrose, and gravely demanded what I would give him to go with me? Give you, sais I, are you John? Yes, says he, for want of a Better; And behold! this John look't as old as my Host, and perhaps had bin a man in the last Century. Well, Mr. John, sais I, make your demands. Why, half a pss. of eight and a dram, sais John. I agreed, and gave him a Dram (now) in hand to bind the bargain.

My hostess catechis'd John for going so cheep, saying his poor wife would break her heart [Dwight's note: Here another half page of the MS is gone.] . . . His shade on his Hors resembled a Globe on a Gate post. His habitt, Hors and furniture, its looks and goings Incomparably answered the rest.

---

1. *Reverd. Mr. Belcher:* Joseph Belcher (1669–1723) had been the minister at Dedham since 1693.

2. *Mad^m Billings:* Knight meant to write "Mad^m Belcher"—Abigail Tompson Belcher, a daughter of the poet Benjamin Tompson.

3. *the Tavern:* This would be Fisher's Tavern, which had been licensed "to sell strong waters to relieve the inhabitants" in 1658 and remained a tavern under various names until 1817, when it was torn down (see Erastus Worthington, "Madam Knight's Journal," *Dedham Historical Register* 2 [1891]: 37).

4. *Quaking tribe:* A reproachful reference to Quakers, or Friends.

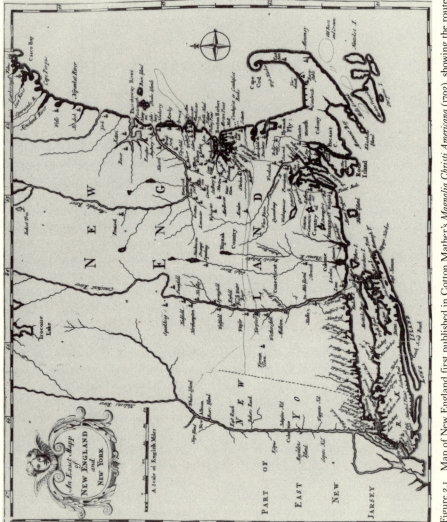

Figure 2.1 Map of New England first published in Cotton Mather's *Magnalia Christi Americana* (1702), showing the route taken by Madam Knight. (Reprinted here from a copy owned by the Massachusetts Historical Society.)

Joseph Belcher.

Figure 2.2   The Reverend Joseph Belcher (1669–1723), minister at Dedham, Massachusetts, from 1693 on. (Anonymous eighteenth-century oil portrait; courtesy of the Dedham Historical Society, Dedham, Massachusetts.)

Figure 2.3   Fisher's Tavern in Dedham (later known as the Woodward-Ames Tavern), where Madam
Knight went with Madam Belcher to find a guide to take her to Billings's Tavern her first night on the road.
(From a sketch by Annie R. Fisher; courtesy of the Dedham Historical Society, Dedham, Massachusetts.)

Thus Jogging on with an easy pace, my Guide telling mee it was dangero's to
Ride hard in the Night, (wh^ch his horse had the sence to avoid,) Hee entertained
me with the Adventurs he had passed by late Rideing, and eminent Dangers he
had escaped, so that, Remembring the Hero's in Parismus and the Knight of the
Oracle,[5] I didn't know but I had mett wth a Prince disguis'd.

When we had Ridd about an how'r, wee come into a thick swamp, wch. by
Reason of a great fogg, very much startled mee, it being now very Dark. But
nothing dismay'd John: Hee had encountered a thousand and a thousand such
Swamps, having a Universall Knowledge in the woods; and readily Answered all
my inquiries wch. were not a few.

In about an how'r, or something more, after we left the Swamp, we come to
Billinges,[6] where I was to Lodg. My Guide dismounted and very Complasantly

5. *Parismus and the Knight of the Oracle:* Elizabethan romances by Emanuel Forde (fl. 1607), *Parismus, the Renouned Prince of Bohemia* (1598) and *The Famous History of Montelion, Knight of the Oracle* (first
published before 1633). Forde's works enjoyed considerable vogue throughout the seventeenth century.

6. *we come to Billinges:* Billings's Inn at old Dorchester, which is now Sharon, Massachusetts, was
well known to Bostonians and is often mentioned in the famous diary of Madam Knight's contemporary, Judge Samuel Sewall of Boston, who nearly always dined at the inn when traveling between
Boston and points south. The location is described in Worthington, "Madam Knight's Journal," 38.

help't me down and shewd the door, signing to me wth his hand to Go in; wch I Gladly did—But had not gone many steps into the Room, ere I was Interogated by a young Lady I understood afterwards was the Eldest daughter of the family, with these, or words to this purpose, (viz.) Law for mee—what in the world brings You here at this time a night?—I never see a woman on the Rode so Dreadfull late, in all the days of my versall[7] life. Who are You? Where are You going? I'me scar'd out of my witts—with much now of the same Kind. I stood aghast, Prepareing to reply, when in comes my Guide—to him Madam turn'd, Roreing out: Lawfull heart, John, is it You?—how de do! Where in the world are you going with this woman? Who is she? John made no Ansr. but sat down in the corner, fumbled out his black Junk,[8] and saluted that instead of Debb; she then turned agen to mee and fell anew into her silly questions, without asking me to sitt down.

I told her shee treated me very Rudely, and I did not think it my duty to answer her unmannerly Questions. But to get ridd of them, I told her I come there to have the post's company with me to-morrow on my Journey, &c. Miss star'd awhile, drew a chair, bid me sitt, And then run up stairs and putts on two or three Rings, (or else I had not seen them before,) and returning, sett herself just before me, showing the way to Reding,[9] that I might see her Ornaments, perhaps to gain the more respect. But her Granam's new Rung sow,[10] had it appeared, would [have] affected me as much. I paid honest John wth money and dram according to contract, and Dismist him, and pray'd Miss to shew me where I must Lodg. Shee conducted me to a parlour in a little back Lento, wch was almost fill'd wth the bedsted, wch was so high that I was forced to climb on a chair to gitt up to the wretched bed that lay on it; on wch having Stretcht my tired Limbs, and lay'd my head on a Sad-coulourd pillow, I began to think on the transactions of the past day.

Tuesday, October the third, about 8 in the morning, I with the Post proceeded forward without observing any thing remarkable; And about two, afternoon, Arrived at the Post's second stage, where the western Post mett him and exchanged Letters. Here, having called for something to eat, the woman bro't in a Twisted thing like a cable, but something whiter; and laying it on the bord, tugg'd for life to bring it into a capacity to spread; wch having wth great pains accomplished, shee serv'd in a dish of Pork and Cabage, I suppose the remains of Dinner. The sause was of a deep Purple, wch I tho't was boil'd in her dye Kettle; the bread was Indian,[11] and every thing on the Table service Agreeable to these. I, being hungry,

7. *versall:* Whole, entire; a colloquial abbreviation of "universal."

8. *Junk:* This word normally meant pieces of old rope; it is thus a denigrating reference to the quality of John's tobacco.

9. *showing the way to Reding:* Gesturing with hands and arms.

10. *Rung sow:* A "rung," or ringed, sow has a ring in its nose to prevent it from rooting.

11. *the bread was Indian:* Indian bread was an unleavened bread made of ground cornmeal (maize) and water, shaped into pones, or rough loaves, and baked; like present-day corn bread.

gott a little down; but my stomach was soon cloy'd, and what cabbage I swallowed serv'd me for a Cudd the whole day after.

Having here discharged the Ordnary for self and Guide, (as I understood was the custom,) About Three afternoon went on with my Third Guide, who Rode very hard; and having crossed Providence Ferry, we come to a River wch they Generally Ride thro'. But I dare not venture; so the Post got a Ladd and Cannoo to carry me to tother side, and hee rid thro' and Led my hors. The Cannoo was very small and shallow, so that when we were in she seem'd redy to take in water, which greatly terrified mee, and caused me to be very circumspect, sitting with my hands fast on each side, my eyes stedy, not daring so much as to lodg my tongue a hair's breadth more on one side of my mouth then tother, nor so much as think on Lott's wife,[12] for a wry thought would have oversett our wherey:[13] But was soon put out of this pain, by feeling the Cannoo on shore, wch I as soon almost saluted with my feet; and Rewarding my sculler,[14] again mounted and made the best of our way forwards. The Rode here was very even and the day pleasant, it being now near Sunsett. But the Post told mee we had neer 14 miles to Ride to the next Stage, (where we were to Lodg.) I askt him of the rest of the Rode, foreseeing wee must travail in the night. Hee told mee there was a bad River we were to Ride thro', wch was so very firce a hors could sometimes hardly stem it: But it was but narrow, and wee should soon be over. I cannot express The concern of mind this relation sett me in: no thoughts but those of the dang'ros River could entertain my Imagination, and they were as formidable as varios, still Tormenting me with blackest Ideas of my Approching fate—Sometimes seing my self drowning, otherwhiles drowned, and at the best like a holy Sister Just come out of a Spiritual Bath in dripping Garments.[15]

Now was the Glorious Luminary, wth his swift Coursers arrived at his Stage, leaving poor me wth the rest of this part of the lower world in darkness, with which *wee* were soon Surrounded. The only Glimering we now had was from the spangled Skies, Whose Imperfect Reflections rendered every Object formidable. Each lifeless Trunk, with its shatter'd Limbs, appear'd an Armed Enymie; and every little stump like a Ravenous devourer. Nor could I so much as discern my Guide, when at any distance, which added to the terror.

Thus, absolutely lost in Thought, and dying with the very thoughts of drowning, I come up wth the post, who I did not see till even with his Hors: he told mee he stopt

12. *Lott's wife:* Lot's wife, while fleeing the destruction of Sodom and Gomorrah, looked behind her and was consequently turned into a pillar of salt (see Genesis 19:1–29). Compare this "wry thought" with Mary Rowlandson's reference to Lot's wife in her description of her Sixth Remove in this volume (p. 41).

13. *wherey:* A wherry is a light riverboat.

14. *sculler:* Oarsman.

15. *Spiritual Bath in dripping Garments:* Possibly a witty allusion to baptism by immersion, as practiced by the Baptists, who had settled in Rhode Island (where Madam Knight then was) in the previous century.

for mee; and wee Rode on Very deliberatly a few paces, when we entred a Thickett of Trees and Shrubs, and I perceived by the Hors's going, we were on the descent of a Hill, w^ch, as wee come neerer the bottom, 'twas totaly dark wth the Trees that surrounded it. But I knew by the Going of the Hors wee had entred the water, wch my Guide told mee was the hazzardos River he had told me off; and hee, Riding up close to my Side, Bid me not fear—we should be over Imediatly. I now ralyed all the Courage I was mistriss of, Knowing that I must either Venture my fate of drowning, or be left like the Children in the wood.[16] So, as the Post bid me, I gave Reins to my Nagg; and sitting as Stedy as Just before in the Cannoo, in a few minutes got safe to the other side, which hee told mee was the Narragansett country.[17]

Here We found great difficulty in Travailing, the way being very narrow, and on each side the Trees and bushes gave us very unpleasent welcomes wth their Branches and bow's, wch wee could not avoid, it being so exceeding dark. My Guide, as before so now, putt on harder than I, wth my weary bones, could follow; so left mee and the way beehind him. Now Returned my distressed aprehensions of the place where I was: the dolesome woods, my Company next to none, Going I knew not whither, and encompased wth Terrifying darkness; The least of which was enough to startle a more Masculine courage. Added to which the Reflections, as in the afternoon of the day that my Call[18] was very Questionable, wch till then I had not so Prudently as I ought considered. Now, coming to the foot of a hill, I found great difficulty in ascending; But being got to the Top, was there amply recompenced with the friendly Appearance of the Kind Conductress of the night, Just then Advancing above the Horisontall Line. The Raptures wch the Sight of that fair Planett produced in mee, caus'd mee, for the Moment, to forgett my present wearyness and past toils; and Inspir'd me for most of the remaining way with very divirting tho'ts, some of which, with the other Occurances of the day, I reserved to note down when I should come to my Stage. My tho'ts on the sight of the moon were to this purpose:

> Fair Cynthia,[19] all the Homage that I may
> Unto a Creature, unto thee I pay;
> In Lonesome woods to meet so kind a guide,
> To Mee's more worth than all the world beside.

16. *Children in the wood:* The title of an English ballad dating from the late sixteenth century which tells of infant orphans, a brother and sister, whose uncle deserts them in the woods, where they die.

17. *Narragansett country:* A large area of southwestern Rhode Island whose exact boundaries were still in doubt in 1704 because of conflicting deeds between the native Narragansett tribe and the white colonists.

18. *my Call:* Her spiritual "vocation," which in the Calvinist understanding of the process of salvation leads the sinner to grace and redemption. She suggests she has treated this matter less seriously than it requires.

19. *Cynthia:* The moon.

Some Joy I felt just now, when safe got or'e
Yon Surly River to this Rugged shore,
Deeming Rough welcomes from these clownish Trees,
Better than Lodgings wth Nereidees.[20]
Yet swelling fears surprise; all dark appears—
Nothing but Light can disipate those fears.
My fainting vitals can't lend strength to say,
But softly whisper, O I wish 'twere day.
The murmer hardly warm'd the Ambient air,
E're thy Bright Aspect rescues from dispair:
Makes the old Hagg her sable mantle loose,
And a Bright Joy do's through my Soul diffuse.
The Boistero's Trees now Lend a Passage Free,
And pleasent prospects thou giv'st light to see.

From hence wee kept on, with more ease th[n] before: the way being smooth and
even, the night warm and serene, and the Tall and thick Trees at a distance, especially w[n] the moon glar'd light through the branches, fill'd my Imagination wth the
pleasent delusion of a Sumpteous citty, fill'd wth famous Buildings and churches, w[th]
their spiring steeples, Balconies, Galleries and I know not what: Granduers w[ch] I
had heard of, and w[ch] the stories of foreign countries had given me the Idea of.

Here stood a Lofty church—there is a steeple,
And there the Grand Parade—O see the people![21]
That Famouse Castle there, were I but nigh,
To see the mote and Bridg and walls so high—
They'r very fine! sais my deluded eye.

Being thus agreably entertain'd without a thou't of any thing but thoughts themselves, I on a suden was Rous'd from these pleasing Imaginations, by the Post's
sounding his horn, which assured mee hee was arrived at the Stage, where we were
to Lodg: and that musick was then most musickall and agreeable to mee.

Being come to mr. Havens',[22] I was very civilly Received, and courteously
entertained, in a clean comfortable House; and the Good woman was very active
in helping off my Riding clothes, and then ask't what I would eat. I told her I had
some Chocolett, if shee would prepare it; which with the help of some Milk, and a

20. *Nereidees:* The Nereids are sea nymphs in classical mythology.
21. *Here . . . steeple / And . . . people:* Here Knight borrows lines from a traditional child's rhyme.
22. *mr. Havens':* Thomas Havens operated Havens' Tavern at Kingstown, Rhode Island, until
his death in 1704, the year of Madam Knight's journey. The Mr. Havens she refers to may have been
one of Thomas's three sons, William, Thomas, or Joseph.

little clean brass Kettle, she soon effected to my satisfaction. I then betook me to my Apartment, wch was a little Room parted from the Kitchen by a single bord partition; where, after I had noted the Occurrances of the past day, I went to bed, which, tho' pretty hard, Yet neet and handsome. But I could get no sleep, because of the Clamor of some of the Town tope-ers in next Room, Who were entred into a strong debate concerning the Signifycation of the name of their Country, (viz.) *Narraganset*. One said it was named so by the Indians, because there grew a Brier there, of a prodigious Highth and bigness, the like hardly ever known, called by the Indians Narragansett; And quotes an Indian of so Barberous a name for his Author, that I could not write it. His Antagonist Replyed no—It was from a Spring it had its name, wch hee well knew where it was, which was extreem cold in summer, and as Hott as could be imagined in the winter, which was much resorted too by the natives, and by them called Narragansett, (Hott and Cold,) and that was the originall of their places name—with a thousand Impertinances not worth notice, wch He utter'd with such a Roreing voice and Thundering blows with the fist of wickedness on the Table, that it peirced my very head. I heartily fretted, and wish't 'um tongue tyed; but wth as little succes as a freind of mine once, who was (as shee said) kept a whole night awake, on a Jorny, by a country Left.[23] and a Sergent, Insigne and a Deacon, contriving how to bring a triangle into a Square. They kept calling for tother Gill,[24] wch while they were swallowing, was some Intermission; But presently, like Oyle to fire, encreased the flame. I set my Candle on a Chest by the bed side, and setting up, fell to my old way of composing my Resentments, in the following manner:

> I ask thy Aid, O Potent Rum!
> To Charm these wrangling Topers Dum.
> Thou hast their Giddy Brains possest—
> The man confounded wth the Beast—
> And I, poor I, can get no rest.
> Intoxicate them with thy fumes:
> O still their Tongues till morning comes!

And I know not but my wishes took effect; for the dispute soon ended w^th 'tother Dram; and so Good night!

Wedensday, Octob^r 4th. About four in the morning, we set out for Kingston (for so was the Town called) with a french Docter[25] in our company. Hee and the Post put

23. *Left.:* Abbreviation for leftenant, now lieutenant.
24. *Gill:* A drinking vessel holding one-fourth of a pint.
25. *a french Docter:* One historian suggests this is Dr. Pierre Ayrault, who fled with other Huguenots from Angers, France, in about 1686 and settled in the "Frenchtown" section of East Greenwich, Rhode Island (see Wilkins Updike, *A History of the Episcopal Church in Narragansett, Rhode Island,* 2nd ed., 3 vols. [Boston: Merrymount, 1907] 1:364).

VII. From Boston Southward to Bristol & Rhode-Island.

PublickHouses		Miles	Towns
Town-Hou			BOSTON
Sheppey's	2	2	Roxbury
Fisher's	9	11	Dedham
Coney's	7	18	Stoughton
Billing's	3	21	Ditto
Hughs's	7	28	Wrentham
Slack's	5	33	Attleborough
French's	5	38	Ditto
Peck's	5	43	Rehoboth
Chapey's	1	44	Ditto
Hunt's	4	48	Ditto
Kelley's	5	53	Swanzey Ferry
Howland's	5	58	BRISTOL Town
Little's	1½	59½	Bristol Ferry
Burden's	1	60½	Portsmouth, on Rhode
Shriev's	4	64½	Ditto (Island
Town House	6½	71	NEWPORT.

From Rhode-Island Eastward to Cape-Cod and Martha's Vineyard.

PublickHouses		Miles	Towns or Places
Town-Hou.			NEWPORT, on Rhode-Island.
Howland's	11	11	Over the Ferry at Ti-
Cecil's	10	21	Dartmouth (verton
Wing's	6	27	Ditto
Pope's	8	35	Ditto
Clap's	5	40	Rochester
Weeks's	10	50	Agawam, an Indian Name.
Newcomb's	10	60	SANDWICH.

From *Sandwich* to *Cape Cod* and the *Vineyard,* as above.

From

From Rhode-Island Southwestward to New-London and New-York.

PublickHouses		Miles	Towns or Places
Town-Hou			Newport
Dodge's			At the Point
Battey's	3	3	Conanicut Island
Sheffield's	1	4	At the other Ferry.
Nichols's	3	7	South Kingston
Case's	3	10	Ditto

N. B. Besides the Ferries.

The Rest as the Road from *Boston* to *New-London,* as follows,

VIII. From Boston to *Providence,* New-London, New-York &c.

PublickHouses		Miles	Towns, or Places
Town-Hou.			BOSTON
French's	38	38	Attleboro', as above
Patuket-Brig	5	43	Parts the Government
The Bridge	4	47	PROVIDENCE Town
Arnold's	5	52	Patuxet
Drake's	10	62	Greenwich
Havens's	6	68	North Kingston
Case's	9	77	South Kingston
Hill's	12	89	Westerly
Tompson's	11	100	Ditto
PaucatukBrig	3	103	Parts the Colonies
Williams's	7	110	Stonington
Seaberry's	8	118	Groton
Shapley's	1	119	Over the Ferry, New-London.

From New-London to New-York, as follows,

To Saybrook	18	To Stradford	4
To Killingsworth	12	To Fairfield	8
To Guilford	10	To Norwalk	12
To Branford	12	To Stanford	10
To New-Haven	10	To Horseneck	7
To Millford	10	To Rye	7
			To

ROADS &c. 203

To New-Rochel	4	To Halfway Houſe	9
To Eaſt Cheſter	4	To New-York	9
To Kings Bridge	6	In all 271 Miles.	

From NEW-YORK to PHILADELPHIA 97 Miles, as follows,

To Flat Buſh	5	To Croſwicks Bridg	4
To the Narrows	5	To Dr. *Brown's*	4
To Amboy	18	To Burlington	9
To Cranbury Brook	20	To Philadelphia	20
To Allens Town	12		

From PHILADELPHIA to JAMES-RIVER in VIRGINIA, 343 Miles, as follows,

To Chriſtiana	38	To *Middleton's*	16
To Elk River	20	To Cedar Neck Poi.	30
To Suſquehanah	20	Over Potowmock Ri.	4
To Gunpowder-Ri.	25	To *Harvey's* Mill	5
To Patapſco	25	To Rapahanock Ri.	12
To Long-Bridge	6	To *Gainſies*	8
To Petuxon Ford	25	To Metapay Ford	30
(Here you may turn off to go to St. *Mary's*)		To Pomonky Ferry	14
		To Madadecum Brid.	5
To *Bell's* Mill	10	To James-Town	50

ADVERTISEMENT.

IF any Gentlemen in the *Southern Provinces* will Pleaſe to ſend to the *Publiſhers* of this *Vade Mecum*, an exact Account of the ſeveral *Counties*, Towns, *Courts*, Fairs, *Roads* &c. in their ſeveral Governments; They ſhall be very gratefully received and added to this Compoſure, to render it more univerſally acceptable and uſeful to the *American Plantations*.

A

Figure 2.4 From *Vade-Mecum for America; Or, a Companion for Traders and Travellers* (Boston: N.p., 1732), giving itineraries between major towns and listing public houses and other landmarks, with mileages between them. Several of the towns and public houses Madam Knight visited are listed, including Fisher's, Billings's, and Havens's inns. These lists show that by 1732 some of the difficult river crossings encountered by Madam Knight had been bridged; note "Patuket-Brig," "The Bridge" at Providence (where she had used a ferry), and "Paucatuk Brig." (Reprinted here from a copy owned by the American Antiquarian Society.)

on very furiously, so that I could not keep up with them, only as now and then they'd stop till they see mee. This Rode was poorly furnished wth accommodations for Travellers, so that we were forced to ride 22 miles by the post's account, but neerer thirty by mine, before wee could bait so much as our Horses, wch I exceedingly complained of. But the post encourag'd mee, by saying wee should be well accommodated anon at mr. Devills,[26] a few miles further. But I questioned whether we ought to go to the Devil to be helpt out of affliction. However, like the rest of Deluded souls that post to the Infernal denn, Wee made all possible speed to this Devil's Habitation; where alliting, in full assurance of good accommodation, wee were going in. But meeting his two daughters, as I suposed twins, they so neerly resembled each other, both in features and habit, and look't as old as the Divel himselfe, and quite as Ugly, We desired entertainm't, but could hardly get a word out of 'um, till with our Importunity, telling them our necesity, &c. they call'd the old Sophister, who was as sparing of his words as his daughters had bin, and no, or none, was the reply's hee made us to our demands. Hee differed only in this from the old fellow[27] in to'ther Country: hee let us depart. However, I thought it proper to warn poor Travailers to endeavour to Avoid falling into circumstances like ours, wch at our next Stage I sat down and did as followeth:

> May all that dread the cruel feind of night
> Keep on, and not at this curs't Mansion light.
> 'Tis Hell; 'tis Hell! and Devills here do dwell:
> Here dwells the Devill—surely this's Hell.
> Nothing but Wants: a drop to cool yo'r Tongue
> Cant be procur'd these cruel Feinds among.
> Plenty of horrid Grins and looks sevear,
> Hunger and thirst, But pitty's bannish'd here—
> The Right hand keep, if Hell on Earth you fear!

Thus leaving this habitation of cruelty, we went forward; and arriving at an Ordinary[28] about two mile further, found tollerable accommodation. But our Hostes, being a pretty full mouth'd old creature, entertain'd our fellow travailer, the french Docter, wth Inumirable complaints of her bodily infirmities; and whisperd to him so lou'd, that all the House had as full a hearing as hee: which was very divirting to the company, (of which there was a great many,) as one might see by their sneering. But poor weary I slipt out to enter my mind in my Jornal, and left my Great Landly with her Talkative Guests to themselves.

26. *mr. Devills:* "The name Davol is very plenty in R.I.—at the time of Madam K. it was Devil on old records" (William R. Deane's note in his edition of the *Journal* published in *The Living Age* [New York], June 26, 1858, 971).
27. *the old fellow:* The devil.
28. *an Ordinary:* An eating place having set prices.

From hence we proceeded (about ten forenoon) through the Narragansett country, pretty Leisurely; and about one afternoon come to Paukataug River, wch was about two hundred paces over, and now very high, and no way over to to'ther side but this. I darid not venture to Ride thro, my courage at best in such cases but small, And now at the Lowest Ebb, by reason of my weary, very weary, hungry and uneasy Circumstances. So takeing leave of my company, tho' wth no little Reluctance, that I could not proceed wth them on my Jorny, Stop at a little cottage Just by the River, to wait the Waters falling, wch the old man that lived there said would be in a little time, and he would conduct me safe over. This little Hutt was one of the wretchedest I ever saw a habitation for human creatures. It was suported with shores[29] enclosed with Clapbords, laid on Lengthways, and so much asunder, that the Light come throu' every where; the doore tyed on wth a cord in the place of hinges; The floor the bear earth; no windows but such as the thin covering afforded, nor any furniture but a Bedd wth a glass Bottle hanging at the head on't; an earthan cupp, a small pewter Bason, A Bord wth sticks to stand on, instead of a table, and a block or two in the corner instead of chairs. The family were the old man, his wife and two Children; all and every part being the picture of poverty. Notwithstanding both the Hutt and its Inhabitance were very clean and tydee: to the crossing the Old Proverb, that bare walls make giddy[30] hows-wifes.

I Blest myselfe that I was not one of this misserable crew; and the Impressions their wretchedness formed in me caused mee on the very Spott to say:

> Tho' Ill at ease, A stranger and alone,
> All my fatigu's shall not extort a grone.
> These Indigents have hunger wth their ease;
> Their best is wors behalfe then my disease.
> Their Misirable hutt wch Heat and Cold
> Alternately without Repulse do hold;
> Their Lodgings thyn and hard, their Indian fare,
> The mean Apparel which the wretches wear,
> And their ten thousand ills wch can't be told,
> Makes nature er'e 'tis midle age'd look old.
> When I reflect, my late fatigues do seem
> Only a notion or forgotten Dreem.

I had scarce done thinking, when an Indian-like Animal come to the door, on a creature very much like himselfe, in mien and feature, as well as Ragged cloathing; and having 'litt,[31] makes an Awkerd Scratch wth his Indian shoo, and a Nodd,

---

29. *shores:* Props or buttresses to support a building; here, upright posts.
30. *giddy:* Frivolous, inattentive.
31. *'litt:* Alit, that is, alighted.

sitts on the block, fumbles out his black Junk, dipps it in the Ashes, and presents it piping hott to his muscheeto's,[32] and fell to sucking like a calf, without speaking, for near a quarter of an hower. At length the old man said how do's Sarah do? who I understood was the wretches wife, and Daughter to the old man: he Replyed—as well as can be expected, &c. So I remembred the old say, and suposed I knew Sarah's case. Butt hee being, as I understood, going over the River, as ugly as hee was, I was glad to ask him to show me the way to Saxtons, at Stoningtown; wch he promising, I ventur'd over wth the old mans assistance; who having rewarded to content, with my Tattertailed guide, I Ridd on very slowly thro' Stoningtown, where the Rode was very Stony and uneven. I asked the fellow, as we went, divers questions of the place and way, &c. I being arrived at my country Saxtons, at Stonington, was very well accommodated both as to victuals and Lodging, the only Good of both I had found since my setting out. Here I heard there was an old man and his Daughter to come that way, bound to N. London; and being now destitute of a Guide, gladly waited for them, being in so good a harbour, and accordingly, Thirsday, Octob^r the 5th, about 3 in the afternoon, I sat forward with neighbor Polly and Jemima, a Girl about 18 Years old, who hee said he had been to fetch out of the Narragansetts, and said they had Rode thirty miles that day, on a sory lean Jade, wth only a Bagg under her for a pillion, which the poor Girl often complain'd was very uneasy.

Wee made Good speed along, wch made poor Jemima make many a sow'r face, the mare being a very hard trotter; and after many a hearty and bitter Oh, she at length Low'd out: Lawful Heart father! this bare mare hurts mee Dingeely,[33] I'me direfull sore I vow; with many words to that purpose: poor Child sais Gaffer—she us't to serve your mother so. I don't care how mother us't to do, quoth Jemima, in a pasionate tone. At which the old man Laught, and kik't his Jade o' the side, which made her Jolt ten times harder.

About seven that Evening, we come to New London Ferry: here, by reason of a very high wind, we mett with great difficulty in getting over—the Boat tos't exceedingly, and our Horses capper'd at a very surprizing Rate, and set us all in a fright; especially poor Jemima, who desired her father to say so jack to the Jade, to make her stand. But the careless parent, taking no notice of her repeated desires, She Rored out in a Passionate manner: Pray suth father, Are you deaf? Say so Jack to the Jade, I tell you. The Dutiful Parent obey's; saying so Jack, so Jack, as gravely as if hee'd bin to saying Catechise after Young Miss, who with her fright look't of all coullers in the Rain Bow.

Being safely arrived at the house of Mrs. Prentices in N. London, I treated neighbour Polly and daughter for their divirting company, and bid them farewell; and between nine and ten at night waited on the Rev^d Mr. Gurdon Saltonstall,[34]

32. *muscheeto's:* Mustache whiskers.

33. *Dingeely:* To ding is defined in Samuel Johnson's *Dictionary of the English Language* (1755) as meaning "to bounce or to dash with violence."

34. *The Rev^d Mr. Gurdon Saltonstall:* Gurdon Saltonstall (1666-1724) was the minister at New London, Connecticut, from 1691 to 1707; in 1707 he was elected governor of Connecticut, a post to which he was annually reelected until his death.

Figure 2.5 Anonymous 18th-century American oil portrait of Governor Gurdon Saltonstall of Connecticut. In 1704–1705 this "affable, courteous, Genero's" host of Madam Knight on both the westbound and homeward-bound legs of her journey was still the minister at New London. (Courtesy of the Yale University Art Gallery, gift of Roswell Saltonstall.)

minister of the town, who kindly Invited me to Stay that night at his house, where I was very handsomely and plentifully treated and Lodg'd; and made good the Great Character I had before heard concerning him: viz. that hee was the most affable, courteous, Genero's and best of men.

Friday, Octo^r 6th. I got up very early, in Order to hire somebody to go with mee to New Haven, being in Great parplexity at the thoughts of proceeding alone; which my most hospitable entertainer observing, himselfe went, and soon return'd wth a young Gentleman of the town, who he could confide in to Go with mee; and about eight this morning, wth Mr. Joshua Wheeler my new Guide,[35] takeing leave of this worthy Gentleman, Wee advanced on towards Seabrook. The Rodes all along this way are very bad, Incumbred wth Rocks and mountainos passages, wch were very disagreeable to my tired carcass; but we went on with a moderate pace wch made the Journy more pleasent. But after about eight miles Rideing, in going over a Bridge under wch the River Run very swift, my hors stumbled, and very narrowly 'scaped falling over into the water; wch extreemly frightened mee. But through God's Goodness I met with no harm, and mounting agen, in about half a miles Rideing, come to an ordinary, were well entertained by a woman of about seventy and vantage,[36] but of as Sound Intellectuals as one of seventeen. Shee entertain'd Mr. Wheeler wth some passages of a Wedding awhile ago at a place hard by, the Brides-Groom being about her Age or something above, Saying his Children was dredfully against their fathers marrying, wch shee condemned them extreemly for.

From hence wee went pretty briskly forward, and arriv'd at Saybrook ferry about two of the Clock afternoon; and crossing it, wee call'd at an Inn to Bait, (foreseeing we should not have such another Opportunity till we come to Killingsworth.) Landlady come in, with her hair about her ears, and hands at full pay scratching. Shee told us shee had some mutton wch shee would broil, wch I was glad to hear; But I supose forgot to wash her scratchers; in a little time shee brot it in; but it being pickled, and my Guide said it smelt strong of head sause,[37] we left it, and p^d sixpence a piece for our Dinners, wch was only smell.

So wee putt forward with all speed, and about seven at night come to Kill-

---

35. *Mr. Joshua Wheeler my new Guide:* "Below the houses of Mr. Saltonstall and Mrs. Prentis and on the opposite side of the way stood the Wheeler house. . . . John Wheeler was one of the early shipping merchants of New London. His son Joshua, born in 1681, was undoubtedly Madam Knight's guide" (William Law Learned's note in his edition of *The Private Journal of a Journey from Boston to New York in the Year 1704,* published in 1865, as quoted in Alan Margolies, "The Editing and Publication of 'The Journal of Madam Knight,'" *Publications of the Bibliographical Society of America* 58 [1964]: 28).

36. *seventy and vantage:* Over seventy.

37. *Head sause:* Pickled pig's head (or sometimes calf's head), including ears, jowls, and other parts. Also called head souse or, in a jelled form, head cheese.

ingsworth, and were tollerably well with Travillers fare, and Lodgd there that night.

Saturday, Oct. 7th, we sett out early in the Morning, and being something una-quainted wth the way, having ask't it of some wee mett, they told us wee must Ride a mile or two and turne down a Lane on the Right hand; and by their Direction wee Rode on but not Yet comeing to the turning, we mett a Young fellow and ask't him how farr it was to the Lane which turn'd down towards Guilford. Hee said wee must Ride a little further, and turn down by the Corner of uncle Sams Lott. My Guide vented his Spleen at the Lubber; and we soon after came into the Rhode, and keeping still on, without any thing further Remarkabell, about two a clock afternoon we arrived at New Haven, where I was received with all Posible Respects and civility. Here I discharged Mr. Wheeler with a reward to his satisfaction, and took some time to rest after so long and toilsome a Journey; and Inform'd myselfe of the manners and customs of the place, and at the same time employed myselfe in the afair I went there upon.

They are Govern'd by the same Laws as wee in Boston, (or little differing,) thr'out this whole Colony of Connecticot, And much the same way of Church Government, and many of them good, Sociable people, and I hope Religious too: but a little too much Independant in their principalls, and, as I have been told, were formerly in their Zeal very Riggid in their Administrations towards such as their Lawes made Offenders, even to a harmless Kiss or Innocent merriment among Young people. Whipping being a frequent and counted an easy Punishment, about w[ch] as other Crimes, the Judges were absolute in their Sentences. They told mee a pleasant story about a pair of Justices in those parts, w[ch] I may not omit the relation of.

A negro Slave belonging to a man in the Town, stole a hogs head from his master, and gave or sold it to an Indian, native of the place. The Indian sold it in the neighbourhood, and so the theft was found out. Thereupon the Heathen was Seized, and carried to the Justices House to be Examined. But his worship (it seems) was gone into the feild, with a Brother in office, to gather in his Pompions.[38] Whither the malefactor is hurried, And Complaint made, and satisfaction in the name of Justice demanded. Their Worships cann't proceed in form without a Bench: whereupon they Order one to be Imediately erected, which, for want of fitter materials, they made with pompions—which being finished, down setts their Worships, and the Malefactor call'd, and by the Senior Justice Interrogated after the following manner. You Indian why did You steal from this man? You sho'dn't do so—it's a Grandy wicked thing to steal. Hol't Hol't cryes Justice Jun[r.] Brother, You speak negro to him. I'le ask him. You sirrah, why did You steal this man's

38. *Pompions:* Pumpkins.

Hoggshead? Hoggshead? (replys the Indian,) me no stomany.[39] No? says his Worship; and pulling off his hatt, Patted his own head with his hand, sais, Tatapa[40]—You, Tatapa—you; all one this. Hoggshead all one this.[41] Hah! says Netop,[42] now me stomany that. Whereupon the Company fell into a great fitt of Laughter, even to Roreing. Silence is comanded, but to no effect: for they continued perfectly Shouting. Nay, sais his worship, in an angry tone, if it be so, *take mee off the Bench.*

Their Diversions in this part of the Country are on Lecture days and Training days mostly: on the former there is Riding from town to town.

And on training dayes The Youth divert themselves by Shooting at the Target, as they call it, (but it very much resembles a pillory,) where hee that hitts neerest the white has some yards of Red Ribbin presented him, wch being tied to his hattband, the two ends streeming down his back, he is Led away in Triumph, wth great applause, as the winners of the Olympiack Games. They generally marry very young: the males oftener as I am told under twentie than above; they generally make public wedings, and have a way something singular (as they say) in some of them, viz. Just before Joyning hands the Bridegroom quitts the place, who is soon followed by the Bridesmen, and as it were, dragg'd back to duty—being the reverse to the former practice among us, to steal m^s Pride.[43]

There are great plenty of Oysters all along by the sea side, as farr as I Rode in the Collony, and those very good. And they Generally lived very well and comfortably in their famelies. But too Indulgent (especially the farmers) to their slaves:

39. *stomany:* Understand(?).

40. *Tatapa:* The same as, equal to (one definition of the verb *tatuppe* in James Hammond Trumbull, *Natick Dictionary,* Bureau of American Ethnology, bulletin 25 [1903]: 159–60).

41. *all one this:* "All one" is a translation of *Tatapa;* "this" refers to the speaker's head. The judge is therefore saying to the Indian, A hogshead is like—all one with—this head. In pointing to the Indian and saying *you* he means to suggest the similarity between the Indian's head and the hogshead, but he seems to his listeners to be likening his own head to a hog's head, thus the uproarious laughter. The context leaves in doubt whether the object stolen was the large barrel or cask known as a hogshead or the actual head of a slaughtered hog. The latter would have been easier to carry off than the former.

42. *Netop:* A word meaning "adult male" or sometimes, when used by white colonists, simply "Indian man." J. Hammond Trumbull cites several variations in Massachusetts, Narragansett, and Powhatan dialects of Algonquian, observing that "the familiar *'netop'* of the early colonists, sometimes translated 'brother,' but by Roger Williams, more accurately 'friend,'—denotes a brother by *adoption* or *affinity,* one who is regarded *as* a brother" ("On Algonkin Names for *Man,*" *Transactions of the American Philological Association* [1871]: 11).

43. *steal m^s Pride:* Steal Mistress Pride, a familiar expression for the popular wedding ritual in early rural America called "stealing" the bride, the reverse of the related custom of the groom's running away from the bride. The custom involved taking the bride (or groom) away to a local tavern where she (or he) was redeemed with the purchase of dinner for the captors (see David Watters, "'I here, thou there, yet both but one': Popular and Elite Literature in Early New England" [paper presented at "Prospects: A Conference on Early American Literature," Chapel Hill, North Carolina, March-April, 1989] 19). Alice Morse Earle says this sport "lingered long in the Connecticut valley" (*Customs and Fashions in Old New England* [1893; rpt. Williamstown, Mass.: Corner House Publishers, 1983], 77).

sufering too great familiarity from them, permitting th^m to sit at Table and eat with them, (as they say to save time,) and into the dish goes the black hoof as freely as the white hand. They told me that there was a farmer lived nere the Town where I lodgd who had some difference wth his slave, concerning something the master had promised him and did not punctualy perform; wch caused some hard words between them; But at length they put the matter to Arbitration and Bound themselves to stand to the award of such as they named—wch done, the Arbitrators Having heard the Allegations of both parties, Order the master to pay 40^s to black face, and acknowledge his fault. And so the matter ended: the poor master very honestly standing to the award.

There are every where in the Towns as I passed, a Number of Indians the Natives of the Country, and are the most salvage of all the salvages of that kind that I had ever Seen: little or no care taken (as I heard upon enquiry) to make them otherwise. They have in some places Landes of their owne, and Govern'd by Law's of their own making;—they marry many wives and at pleasure put them away, and on the least dislike or fickle humour, on either side, saying *stand away* to one another is a sufficient Divorce. And indeed those uncomely *Stand aways* are too much in Vougue among the English in this (Indulgent Colony) as their Records plentifully prove; and that on very trivial matters, of which some have been told me, but are not proper to be Related by a Female pen, tho some of that foolish sex have had too large a share in the story.

If the natives committ any crime on their own precincts among themselves, the English takes no Cognezens of. But if on the English ground, they are punishable by our Laws. They mourn for their Dead by blacking their faces, and cutting their hair, after an Awkerd and frightfull manner; But can't bear You should mention the names of their dead Relations to them: they trade most for Rum, for wch they^d hazzard their very lives; and the English fit them Generally as well, by seasoning it plentifully with water.

They give the title of merchant to every trader; who Rate their Goods according to the time and spetia they pay in: viz. Pay, mony, Pay as mony, and trusting. *Pay* is Grain, Pork, Beef, &c. at the prices sett by the General Court that Year; *mony* is pieces of Eight, Ryalls, or Boston or Bay shillings (as they call them,) or Good hard money, as sometimes silver coin is termed by them; also Wampom, vizt. Indian beads wch serves for change. *Pay as mony* is provisions, as afores^d one Third cheaper then as the Assembly or Gene^l Court sets it; and *Trust* as they and the merch^t agree for time.

Now, when the buyer comes to ask for a comodity, sometimes before the merchant answers that he has it, he sais, *is Your pay redy?* Perhaps the Chap Reply's Yes: what do You pay in? say's the merchant. The buyer having answered, then the price is set; as suppose he wants a sixpenny knife, in pay it is 12d[44]—in pay as

44. *12d:* Twelve pence. The abbreviation comes from the name of the Roman coin *denarius* and the later French coin *denier*. The denier, like the English penny, was a copper coin.

money eight pence, and hard money its own price, viz. 6d. It seems a very Intricate way of trade and what Lex Mercatoria[45] had not thought of.

Being at a merchants house, in comes a tall country fellow, wth his alfogeos[46] full of Tobacco; for they seldom Loose their Cudd, but keep Chewing and Spitting as long as they'r eyes are open,—he advanc't to the middle of the Room, makes an Awkward Nodd, and spitting a Large deal of Aromatick Tincture, he gave a scrape with his shovel like shoo, leaving a small shovel full of dirt on the floor, made a full stop, Hugging his own pretty Body with his hands under his arms, Stood staring rown'd him, like a Catt let out of a Baskett. At last, like the creature Balaam Rode on,[47] he opened his mouth and said: have You any Ribinen for Hatbands to sell I pray? The Questions and Answers about the pay being past, the Ribin is bro't and opened. Bumpkin Simpers, cryes its confounded Gay I vow; and beckning to the door, in comes Jone Tawdry, dropping about 50 curtsees, and stands by him: hee shows her the Ribin. *Law, You,* sais shee, *its right Gent,* do You, take it, *tis dreadfull pretty.* Then she enquires, *have You any hood silk I pray?* w[ch] being brought and bought, Have You any *thred silk to sew it w[th]* says shee, w[ch] being accomodated wth they Departed. They Generaly stand after they come in a great while speachless, and sometimes dont say a word till they are askt what they want, which I Impute to the Awe they stand in of the merchants, who they are constantly almost Indebted too; and must take what they bring without Liberty to choose for themselves; but they serve them as well, making the merchants stay long enough for their pay.

We may Observe here the great necessity and bennifitt both of Education and Conversation; for these people have as Large a portion of mother witt, and sometimes a Larger, than those who have bin brought up in Cities; But for want of emprovements, Render themselves almost Ridiculos, as above. I should be glad if they would leave such follies, and am sure all that Love Clean Houses (at least) would be glad on't too.

They are generaly very plain in their dress, throuout all the Colony, as I saw, and follow one another in their modes; that You may know where they belong, especially the women, meet them where you will.

Their Cheif Red Letter day is St. Election, w[ch] is annualy Observed according to Charter, to choose their Goven[r]: a blessing they can never be thankfull enough for, as they will find, if ever it be their hard fortune to loose it. The present Govenor in Conecticott is the Hon[ble] John Winthrop Esq.[48] A Gentleman of an Ancient and Honourable Family, whose Father was Govenor here sometime before, and his

45. *Lex Mercatoria:* Mercantile law.

46. *alfogeos:* Probably an approximate spelling of *alforjas,* the Spanish word for "saddlebags," here used colloquially for cheeks.

47. *the creature Balaam rode on:* An ass (see Numbers 22:20–35).

48. *the Hon[ble] John Winthrop Esq.:* Fitz-John Winthrop (1639–1707) was the governor of Connecticut from 1698 to 1707.

Grand father had bin Gov[r] of the Massachusetts. This gentleman is a very curteous and afable person, much Given to Hospitality, and has by his Good services Gain'd the affections of the people as much as any who had bin before him in that post.

Dec[r] 6th. Being by this time well Recruited and rested after my Journy, my business lying unfinished by some concerns at New York depending thereupon, my Kinsman, Mr. Thomas Trowbridge[49] of New Haven, must needs take a Journy there before it could be accomplished, I resolved to go there in company wth him, and a man of the town w[ch] I engaged to wait on me there. Accordingly, Dec. 6th we set out from New Haven, and about 11 same morning came to Stratford ferry; w[ch] crossing, about two miles on the other side Baited our horses and would have eat a morsell ourselves, But the Pumpkin and Indian mixt Bred had such an Aspect, and the Bare-legg'd Punch so awkerd or rather Awfull a sound, that we left both, and proceeded forward, and about seven at night come to Fairfield, where we met with good entertainment and Lodg'd; and early next morning set forward to Norowalk, from its halfe Indian name *North-walk,* when about 12 at noon we arrived, and Had a Dinner of Fryed Venison, very savoury. Landlady wanting some pepper in the seasoning, bid the Girl hand her the spice in the little *Gay* cupp on the shelfe. From hence we Hasted towards Rye, walking and Leading our Horses neer a mile together, up a prodigios high Hill; and so Riding till about nine at night, and there arrived and took up our Lodgings at an ordinary, w[ch] a French family kept. Here being very hungry, I desired a fricasee, w[ch] the Frenchman undertakeing, mannaged so contrary to my notion of Cookery, that I hastned to Bed superless; And being shewd the way up a pair of stairs w[ch] had such a narrow passage that I had almost stopt by the Bulk of my Body; But arriving at my apartment found it to be a little Lento Chamber furnisht amongst other Rubbish with a High Bedd and a Low one, a Long Table, a Bench and a Bottomless chair,—Little Miss went to scratch up my Kennell w[ch] Russelled as if shee'd bin in the Barn amongst the Husks, and supose such was the contents of the tickin—nevertheless being exceeding weary, down I laid my poor Carkes (never more tired) and found my Covering as scanty as my Bed was hard. Annon I heard another Russelling noise in The Room—called to know the matter—Little miss said shee was making a bed for the men; who, when they were in Bed, complained their leggs lay out of it by reason of its shortness—my poor bones complained bitterly not being used to such Lodgings, and so did the man who was with us; and poor I made but one Grone, which was from the time I went to bed to the time I Riss, which was about three in the morning, Setting up by the Fire till Light, and having discharged our ordinary w[ch] was as dear as if we had had far Better fare—wee took our leave of Monsier and about seven in the morn come to New Rochell a french town, where we had a good

---

49. *Mr. Thomas Trowbridge:* Identified by William Deane as the brother of Caleb Trowbridge, whose will Sarah Knight was helping to settle (see Deane, "The Journal of Madam Knight," 966).

Breakfast. And in the strength of that about an how'r before sunsett got to York. Here I applyd myself to Mr. Burroughs, a merchant to whom I was recommended by my Kinsman Capt. Prout, and received great Civilities from him and his spouse, who were now both Deaf but very agreeable in their Conversation, Diverting me with pleasant stories of their knowledge in Brittan from whence they both come, one of which was above the rest very pleasant to me viz. my Lord Darcy had a very extravagant Brother who had mortgaged what Estate hee could not sell, and in good time dyed leaving only one son. Him his Lordship (having none of his own) took and made him Heir of his whole Estate, which he was to receive at the death of his Aunt. He and his Aunt in her widowhood held a right understanding and lived as become such Relations, shee being a discreat Gentlewoman and he an Ingenios Young man. One day Hee fell into some Company though far his inferiors, very freely told him of the Ill circumstances his fathers Estate lay under, and the many Debts he left unpaid to the wrong of poor people with whom he had dealt. The Young gentleman was put out of countenance—no way hee could think of to Redress himself—his whole dependance being on the Lady his Aunt, and how to speak to her he knew not—Hee went home, sat down to dinner and as usual sometimes with her when the Chaplain was absent, she desired him to say Grace, wch he did after this manner:

> Pray God in Mercy take my Lady Darcy
> Unto his Heavenly Throne,
> That Little John may live like a man,
> And pay every man his own.

The prudent Lady took no present notice, But finishd dinner, after wch having sat and talk't awhile (as Customary) He Riss, took his Hatt and Going out she desired him to give her leave to speak to him in her Clossett, Where being come she desired to know why hee prayed for her Death in the manner aforesaid, and what part of her deportment towards him merritted such desires. Hee Reply'd, none at all, But he was under such disadvantages that nothing but that could do him service, and told her how he had been affronted as above, and what Impressions it had made upon him. The Lady made him a gentle reprimand that he had not informed her after another manner, Bid him see what his father owed and he should have money to pay it to a penny, And always to lett her know his wants and he should have a redy supply. The Young Gentleman charm'd with his Aunts Discrete management, Beggd her pardon and accepted her kind offer and retrieved his fathers Estate, &c. and said Hee hoped his Aunt would never dye, for shee had done better by him than hee could have done for himself.—Mr. Burroughs went with me to Vendue[50] where I bought about 100 Rheem of paper wch was retaken in a fly-boat from Holland and sold very Reasonably here—some ten, some Eight shillings per

---

50. *Vendue:* A market where goods were sold by auction.

Rheem by the Lott wch was ten Rheem in a Lott. And at the Vendue I made a great many acquaintances amongst the good women of the town, who curteosly invited me to their houses and generously entertained me.

The Cittie of New York is a pleasant, well compacted place, situated on a Commodius River wch is a fine harbour for shipping. The Buildings Brick Generaly, very stately and high, though not altogether like ours in Boston. The Bricks in some of the Houses are of divers Coullers and laid in Checkers, being glazed look very agreeable. The inside of them are neat to admiration, the wooden work, for only the walls are plasterd, and the Sumers and Gist[51] are plained and kept very white scowr'd as so is all the partitions if made of Bords. The fire places have no Jambs (as ours have) But the Backs run flush with the walls, and the Hearth is of Tyles and is as farr out into the Room at the Ends as before the fire, wch is Generally Five foot in the Low'r rooms, and the peice over where the mantle tree should be is made as ours with Joyners work, and as I supose is fasten'd to iron rodds inside. The House where the Vendue was, had Chimney Corners like ours, and they and the hearths were laid wth the finest tile that I ever see, and the stair cases laid all with white tile which is ever clean, and so are the walls of the Kitchen wch had a Brick floor. They were making Great preparations to Receive their Govenor, Lord Cornbury[52] from the Jerseys, and for that End raised the militia to Gard him on shore to the fort.

They are Generaly of the Church of England and have a New England Gentleman for their minister,[53] and a very fine church[54] set out with all Customary requsites. There are also a Dutch and Divers Conventicles as they call them, viz. Baptist, Quakers, &c. They are not strict in keeping the Sabbath as in Boston and other places where I had bin, But seem to deal with great exactness as farr as I see or Deall with. They are sociable to one another and Curteos and Civill to strangers and fare well in their houses. The English go very fasheonable in their dress. But the Dutch, especially the middling sort, differ from our women, in their habitt go

51. *Sumers and Gist:* Summers and joists. The summer beam was a central floor timber holding the crossbeams, or joists, which were set into it. In early colonial homes the absence of plaster ceilings made these beams supporting the floor of the second story visible from the ground floor.

52. *Lord Cornbury:* Edward Hyde, Viscount Cornbury (1661–1724), a first cousin of Queen Anne, was captain-general and governor of New York and New Jersey from 1702 to 1708. His administration was a failure, characterized by graft, bigotry, and numerous other corruptions. On at least one public occasion, Cornbury appeared dressed in women's clothing, purportedly in imitation of his cousin, the queen. He had his portrait painted in such attire. His political enemies, in fact, referred to him as a transvestite.

53. *a New England Gentleman for their minister:* William Vesey (1674–1746), a native of Braintree, Massachusetts, and a Harvard graduate, was ordained in England and installed as minister in New York in 1697 (see his biography in Clifford K. Shipton, *Biographical Sketches of Those Who Attended Harvard College in the Classes 1690–1700,* vol. 4 of *Sibley's Harvard Graduates* [Cambridge: Harvard University Press, 1933], 173–79).

54. *a very fine church:* Trinity Church, still standing on Broadway at the head of Wall Street, was completed in 1698.

loose, were French muches wch are like a Capp and a head band in one, leaving their ears bare, which are sett out wth Jewells of a large size and many in number. And their fingers hoop't with Rings, some with large stones in them of many Coullers as were their pendants in their ears, which You should see very old women wear as well as Young.

They have Vendues very frequently and make their Earnings very well by them, for they treat with good Liquor Liberally, and the Customers Drink as Liberally and Generally pay for't as well, by paying for that which they Bidd up Briskly for, after the sack[55] has gone plentifully about, tho' sometimes good penny worths are got there. Their Diversions in the Winter is Riding Sleys about three or four Miles out of Town, where they have Houses of entertainment at a place called the Bowery, and some go to friends Houses who handsomely treat them. Mr. Burroughs cary'd his spouse and Daughter and myself out to one Madame Dowes, a Gentlewoman that lived at a farm House, who gave us a handsome Entertainment of five or six Dishes and choice Beer and metheglin,[56] Cyder, &c. all which she said was the produce of her farm. I believe we mett 50 or 60 slays that day—they fly with great swiftness and some are so furious that they'le turn out of the path for none except a Loaden Cart. Nor do they spare for any diversion the place affords, and sociable to a degree, they'r Tables being as free to their Naybours as to themselves.

Having here transacted the affair I went upon and some other that fell in the way, after about a fortnight's stay there I left New-York with no Little regrett, and Thursday, Dec. 21, set out for New Haven wth my Kinsman Trowbridge, and the man that waited on me about one afternoon, and about three come to half-way house about ten miles out of town, where we Baited and went forward, and about 5 come to Spiting Devil,[57] Else Kings bridge, where they pay three pence for passing over with a horse, which the man that keeps the Gate set up at the end of the Bridge receives.

We hoped to reach the french town and Lodg there that night, but unhapily lost our way about four miles short, and being overtaken by a great storm of wind and snow which set full in our faces about dark, we were very uneasy. But meeting one Gardner who lived in a Cottage thereabout, offered us his fire to set by, having but one poor Bedd, and his wife not well, &c. or he would go to a House with us, where he thought we might be better accommodated—thither we went, But a surly old shee Creature, not worthy the name of woman, who would hardly let us go into her Door, though the weather was so stormy none but shee would have turnd out a Dogg. But her son whose name was gallop, who lived Just by Invited us to his house and shewed me two pair of stairs, viz. one up the loft and tother up the Bedd, w^{ch}

55. *sack:* A variety of sweet wine imported chiefly from the Canary Islands.

56. *metheglin:* A liquor made of honey and water, boiled and fermented, and often flavored with spices.

57. *Spiting Devil:* Spuyten Duyvil, a Dutch name still used for the place where the Hudson and Harlem rivers join at the northernmost tip of Manhattan Island.

was as hard as it was high, and warmed it with a hott stone at the feet. I lay very uncomfortably, insomuch that I was so very cold and sick I was forced to call them up to give me something to warm me. They had nothing but milk in the house, wch they Boild, and to make it better sweetened wth molasses, which I not knowing or thinking oft till it was down and coming up agen wch it did in so plentifull a manner that my host was soon paid double for his portion, and that in specia.[58] But I believe it did me service in Cleering my stomach. So after this sick and weary night at East Chester, (a very miserable poor place,) the weather being now fair, Friday the 22^d Dec. we set out for New Rochell, where being come we had good Entertainment and Recruited ourselves very well. This is a very pretty place well compact, and good handsome houses, Clean, good and passable Rodes, and situated on a Navigable River, abundance of land well fined and Cleerd all along as wee passed, which caused in me a Love to the place, wch I could have been content to live in it. Here wee Ridd over a Bridge made of one entire stone of such a Breadth that a cart might pass with safety, and to spare—it lay over a passage cutt through a Rock to convey water to a mill not farr off. Here are three fine Taverns within call of each other, very good provision for Travailers.

Thence we travailed through Merrinak,[59] a neet, though little place, wth a navigable River before it, one of the pleasantest I ever see—Here were good Buildings, Especialy one, a very fine seat, wch they told me was Col. Hethcoats, who I had heard was a very fine Gentleman. From hence we come to Hors Neck, where wee Baited, and they told me that one Church of England parson officiated in all these three towns once every Sunday in turns throughout the Year; and that they all could but poorly maintaine him, which they grudg'd to do, being a poor and quarelsome crew as I understand by our Host; their Quarelling about their choice of Minister, they chose to have none—But caused the Government to send this Gentleman to them. Here wee took leave of York Government, and Descending the Mountainos passage that almost broke my heart in ascending before, we come to Stamford, a well compact Town, but miserable meeting house,[60] wch we passed, and thro' many and great difficulties, as Bridges which were exceeding high and very tottering and of vast Length, steep and Rocky Hills and precipices, (Buggbears to a fearful female travailer)[.] About nine at night we come to Norrwalk, having crept over a timber of a Broken Bridge about thirty foot long, and perhaps fifty to the water.[61] I was exceeding tired and cold when wc come to our Inn, and

---

58. *in specia:* In kind.

59. *Merrinak:* Mamaroneck, New York.

60. *miserable meeting house:* The Stamford church's congregation voted in 1702 to build a new, larger meeting house, but in late 1704 "Madam Knight was too early by some eighteen months" to see the completed new building (E. B. Huntington to William R. Deane, August 22, 1865, William R. Deane Collection, New England Historic Genealogical Society; see also Huntington's *History of Stamford, Connecticut* [Stamford: N.p., 1868], 134–35).

61. *a Broken Bridge . . . fifty to the water:* Probably at the Norwalk River. E. B. Huntington sug-

could get nothing there but poor entertainment, and the Impertinant Bable of one of the worst of men, among many others of which our Host made one, who, had he bin one degree Impudenter, would have outdone his Grandfather. And this I think is the most perplexed night I have yet had. From hence, Saturday, Dec. 23, a very cold and windy day, after an Intolerable night's Lodging, wee hasted forward only observing in our way the Town to be situated on a Navigable river wth indiferent Buildings and people more refind than in some of the Country towns wee had passed, tho' vicious enough, the Church and Tavern being next neighbours. Having Ridd thro a difficult River wee come to Fairfield where wee Baited and were much refreshed as well with the Good things wch gratified our appetites as the time took to rest our wearied Limbs, wch Latter I employed in enquiring concerning the Town and manners of the people, &c. This is a considerable town, and filld as they say with wealthy people—have a spacious meeting house and good Buildings. But the Inhabitants are Litigious, nor do they well agree with their minister, who (they say) is a very worthy Gentleman.

They have aboundance of sheep, whose very Dung brings them great gain, with part of which they pay their Parsons sallery, And they Grudg that, prefering their Dung before their minister. They Lett[62] out their sheep at so much as they agree upon for a night; the highest Bidder always caries them, And they will sufficiently Dung a Large quantity of Land before morning. But were once Bitt by a sharper who had them a night and sheared them all before morning—From hence we went to Stratford, the next Town, in which I observed but few houses, and those not very good ones. But the people that I conversed with were civill and good natured. Here we staid till late at night, being to cross a Dangerous River ferry, the River at that time full of Ice; but after about four hours waiting with great difficulty wee got over. My fears and fatigues prevented my here taking any particular observation. Being got to Milford, it being late in the night, I could go no further; my fellow travailer going forward, I was invited to Lodg at Mrs. ———, a very kind and civill Gentlewoman, by whom I was handsomely and kindly entertained till the next night. The people here go very plain in their apparel (more plain than I had observed in the towns I had passed) and seem to be very grave and serious. They told me there was a singing Quaker lived there, or at least had a strong inclination to be so, His Spouse not at all affected that way. Some of the singing Crew come there one day to visit him, who being then abroad, they sat down (to the woman's no small vexation) Humming and singing and groneing after their conjuring way—Says the woman are you singing quakers? Yea says They—Then take my squalling Brat of a child here and sing to it says she for I have almost split

---

gested this location in a letter of August 22, 1865, to William R. Deane, and was further "inclined to think, that [Knight] must have exaggerated the hight [*sic*] of the bridge some fifteen or twenty feet" (Deane Collection).

62. *Lett:* Rent.

my throat wth singing to him and cant get the Rogue to sleep. They took this as a great Indignity, and mediately departed. Shaking the dust from their Heels left the good woman and her Child among the number of the wicked.

This is a Seaport place and accomodated with a Good Harbour, But I had not opportunity to make particular observations because it was Sabbath day—This Evening.

December 24. I set out with the Gentlewomans son who she very civilly offered to go with me when she see no parswasions would cause me to stay which she pressingly desired, and crossing a ferry having but nine miles to New Haven, in a short time arrived there and was Kindly received and well accommodated amongst my Friends and Relations.

The Government of Connecticut Collony begins westward towards York at Stanford[63] (as I am told) and so runs Eastward towards Boston (I mean in my range, because I dont intend to extend my description beyond my own travails) and ends that way at Stonington—And has a great many Large towns lying more northerly. It is a plentiful Country for provisions of all sorts and its Generally Healthy. No one that can and will be dilligent in this place need fear poverty nor the want of food and Rayment.

January 6th. Being now well Recruited and fitt for business I discoursed the persons I was concerned with, that we might finnish in order to my return to Boston. They delay^d as they had hitherto done hoping to tire my Patience. But I was resolute to stay and see an End of the matter let it be never so much to my disadvantage—So January 9th they come again and promise the Wednesday following to go through with the distribution of the Estate which they delayed till Thursday and then come with new amusements. But at length by the mediation of that holy good Gentleman, the Rev. Mr. James Pierpont,[64] the minister of New Haven, and with the advice and assistance of other our Good friends we come to an accommodation and distribution, which having finished though not till February, the man that waited on me to York taking the charge of me I sit out for Boston. We went from New Haven upon the ice (the ferry being not passable thereby) and the Rev. Mr. Pierpont wth Madam Prout Cuzin Trowbridge and divers others were taking leave wee went onward without any thing Remarkabl till wee come to New London and Lodged again at Mr. Saltonstalls—and here I dismist my Guide, and my Generos entertainer provided me Mr. Samuel Rogers of that place to go home with me—I stayed a day here Longer than I intended by the Commands of the Honble Govenor Winthrop to stay and take a supper with him whose wonderful civility I may not

63. *Stanford:* That is, Stamford, Connecticut.

64. *the Rev. Mr. James Pierpont:* Pierpont (1660–1714) was minister at New Haven from 1685 until his death. His daughter, Sarah, later married Jonathan Edwards (1703–1758), the great Calvinist minister, theologian, and philosopher.

Figure 2.6 Portrait of the minister at New Haven, the Reverend James Pierpont, artist unknown, painted in 1711, six years after Pierpont was instrumental in helping to achieve "accommodation and distribution" of the Trowbridge estate in January, 1705. (Courtesy of the Yale University Art Gallery, bequest of Allen Evarts Foster, B.A. 1906.)

Figure 2.7   Mary Winthrop Livingston, (ca. 1676–1713), daughter of Governor Fitz-John Winthrop, one of the ladies who accompanied Madam Knight to the ferryboat at New London on her return trip. (18th-century American painting, New York, artist unidentified, ca. 1705, oil on canvas, oval 29¾ × 25″. Courtesy of The Harvard University Portrait Collection, gift of Robert Winthrop, 1964.)

omitt. The next morning I Crossed the Ferry to Groton, having had the Honor of the Company, of Madam Livingston[65] (who is the Govenors Daughter) and Mary Christophers[66] and divers others to the boat—And that night Lodg^d at Stonington and had Rost Beef and pumpkin sause for supper. The next night at Haven's and had Rost fowle, and the next day wee come to a river which by Reason of The Freshetts coming down was swell'd so high wee fear^d it impassable and the rapid stream was very terryfying—However we must over and that in a small Cannoo. Mr. Rogers assuring me of his good Conduct, I after a stay of near an how'r on the shore for consultation went into the Cannoo, and Mr. Rogers paddled about 100 yards up the Creek by the shore side, turned into the swift stream and dexterously steering her in a moment wee come to the other side as swiftly passing as an arrow shott out of the Bow by a strong arm. I staid on the shore till Hee returned to fetch our horses, which he caused to swim over himself bringing the furniture[67] in the Cannoo. But it is past my skill to express the Exceeding fright all their transactions formed in me. Wee were now in the colony of the Massachusetts and taking Lodgings at the first Inn we come too had a pretty difficult passage the next day which was the second of March by reason of the sloughy ways then thawed by the Sunn. Here I mett Capt. John Richards of Boston who was going home, So being very glad of his Company we Rode something harder than hitherto, and missing my way going up a very steep Hill, my horse dropt down under me as Dead; this new surprize no little hurt me meeting it Just at the Entrance into Dedham from whence we intended to reach home that night. But was now obliged to gett another Hors there and leave my own, resolving for Boston that night if possible. But in going over the Causeway at Dedham the Bridge being overflowed by the high waters comming down I very narrowly escaped falling over into the river Hors and all wch twas almost a miracle I did not—now it grew late in the afternoon and the people having very much discouraged us about the sloughy way wch they said wee should find very difficult and hazardous it so wrought on mee being tired and dispirited and disapointed of my desires of going home that I agreed to Lodg there that night wch wee did at the house of one Draper,[68] and the next day being March 3d wee got safe home to Boston, where I found my aged and tender mother and my Dear and only Child in good health with open arms redy to receive me, and my Kind relations and friends flocking in to welcome mee and hear the story of my transactions and travails I having this day bin five months from home and now I cannot fully express my Joy and Satisfaction. But desire sincearly to adore my Great Benefactor for thus graciously carying forth and returning in safety his unworthy handmaid.

65. *Madam Livingston:* Mary Winthrop Livingston, who had married John Livingston in the spring of 1701 (see Lawrence H. Leder, *Robert Livingston, 1654–1728, and the Politics of Colonial New York* [Chapel Hill: University of North Carolina Press, 1961], 159).

66. *Mary Christophers:* It was the Christophers family that preserved the manuscript of Knight's *Journal* after Elizabeth Knight Livingston's death on March 17, 1736 (see Frances Manwaring Caulkins, *History of New London, Connecticut* [New London, Conn.: N.p., 1852], 373, 365).

67. *furniture:* Movable goods, baggage.

68. *one Draper:* Mrs. Abigail Whiting Draper, widow of James Draper, Jr. She is identified in a letter from Abijah Draper of West Roxbury, Massachusetts, to William R. Deane, August 22, 1865, Deane Collection.

Some Account of the Fore Part
of the Life of Elizabeth Ashbridge

Edited, with an Introduction, by
DANIEL B. SHEA

Elizabeth Ashbridge and the Voice Within

I

Though never entirely unknown to the relatively small audience who have read Quaker autobiography, Elizabeth Ashbridge now makes her appearance to a generation of readers prepared as never before to respond to the significance of her plainspoken yet astutely imagined narrative for the history of women's autobiography.[1] That significance may not emerge at first glance, despite or even because of the melodramatic adventures that give the narrative immediate interest: adolescent marriage, followed in quick order by widowhood and parental banishment to Ireland; virtual enslavement as an indentured servant, in America; a more prolonged but no less painful trial as the wife of an alcoholic and abusive husband; cycles of religious seeking and despair punctuated by voices, visions, and temptations to suicide; and finally deliverance, when Elizabeth Ashbridge arrives at a secure faith among the Society of Friends and shortly afterward is informed that she is once again a widow.

Abstracted from the narrative interest of such trials, the achievement of Elizabeth Ashbridge as autobiographer may remain indistinct. Since we do not have the original manuscript of her *Account,* we have access only through the hands of copyists to what she may actually have written, revised, reinstated. The autobiographical persona, although admirable in her endurance, may strike some readers as depending too much for her heroism on a long-suffering passivity. The textual Elizabeth Ashbridge might also appear a creature of male-dominated autobiographical discourse defined, albeit in opposition, by her relation to a series of masters, so that even her final triumph contains an irony: in the end she is delivered into the hands of a master both paternal and divine, a sublimation that only emphasizes patriarchy's dominance over woman's autobiographical act.

Perhaps so, by a strict accounting. But Elizabeth Ashbridge is an autobiographer who defeats expectation and overwhelms first surmise. Referentially, her narrative may be "about" a number of things, including, as she herself would

---

1. In a recent doctoral dissertation, Cristine Levenduski has set Elizabeth Ashbridge fully in context. describing the ways in which contemporary "cultural mythologies" about Quakers assured her marginalization and deriving from her autobiography the personal patterns that meshed with the Quakers' sense of themselves as "a peculiar people" ("Elizabeth Ashbridge's 'Remarkable Experiences': Creating the Self in a Quaker Personal Narrative" [Ph.D. diss., University of Minnesota, 1989], 6–7 passim).

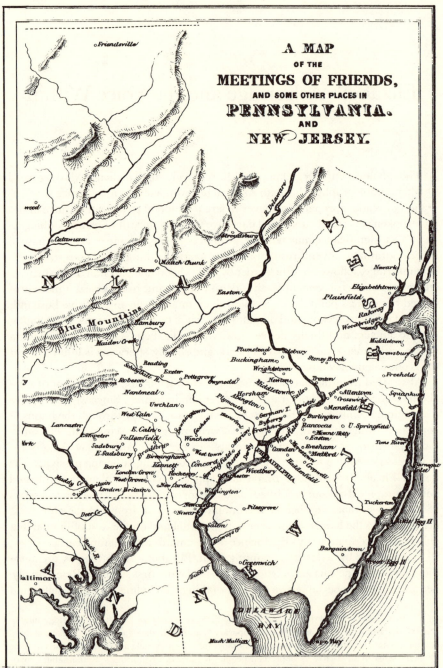

Figure 3.1   Much of the itinerary Elizabeth Ashbridge was compelled to follow by her husband Sullivan may be traced on this map, which shows Philadelphia at the center of a network of Quaker meetings. Goshen, Pennsylvania, west and north of Philadelphia, became her home after her marriage to Aaron Ashbridge. (From James Bowden, *The History of the Society of Friends in America,* vol. 1 [London: N.p., 1850].)

have insisted, the discovery of religious truth. What the narrative enacts, however, is the writer's committed refusal to accept any voice as her own which she has not encountered as central to her own interiority. Her autobiography is at once the product of her status as an American immigrant-vagabond, a Quaker, and a woman. If it is true that the autobiographical product, first given to the world in 1774 at Nantwich, Cheshire, not far from her birthplace, makes a small circle of her life, and in language submissive to convention, it is also true that the auto-biographical dynamic in which Elizabeth Ashbridge involved herself contained a potential for self-definition which she sought, found, and realized. The terms on which the Quaker autobiographer accepted her task may seem, like Quaker customs and testimonies in general, extraordinarily limiting. What Elizabeth Ashbridge suggests is that boundedness is not bondage, that all writing defines itself against limits, and that the inward space of autobiography could be a place of discovery for the self-writer who was both a woman and a Quaker.

I I

Almost everything we know about Elizabeth Ashbridge is derived from her autobiography, although the period from the death of her second husband, whom we know only as Sullivan, through her marriage to Aaron Ashbridge and her departure for a missionary journey to England and Ireland, where she died in 1755, holds promise for further investigation. Given the scarcity of biographical infor-mation, it is useful to grasp at least the general outlines of the historical moment of which she was a part, a moment at which the doctrines of the Society of Friends were being spread throughout the transatlantic community and had found a par-ticularly hospitable region for growth in the New World colonies of Pennsylvania and East and West Jersey.[2] When Elizabeth Ashbridge was born in Middlewich, Cheshire, in 1713, the colonial settlements along the Delaware River, many of them predominantly Quaker, were already flourishing. What one scholar has called the golden age of Quakerism in America had begun: the struggle for survival in the wilderness had been won while the more subtle struggle between spiritual values and material success remained to be decided.[3] Antipathy against the Quakers and their characteristic doctrines and practices had scarcely disappeared, however, as

2. See Frederick B. Tolles, *Quakers and the Atlantic Culture* (New York: Macmillan, 1960).

3. Howard H. Brinton, *Friends for 300 Years: The History and Beliefs of the Society of Friends Since George Fox Started the Quaker Movement* (New York: Harper and Brothers, 1952), 183. See also Frederick B. Tolles, *Meeting House and Counting House: The Quaker Merchants of Colonial Philadelphia, 1682–1763* (Chapel Hill: University of North Carolina Press, 1948).

the experience of Elizabeth Ashbridge makes clear. From their beginning the Quakers had been identified as a radical Protestant sect, inveterate travelers who were also fearlessly evangelical. George Fox had begun to gather followers in the 1640s, but the sacred history of his Society dates its founding from 1652 and the vision he reports in his *Journal* from the top of a mount called Pendle Hill in Lancashire. By 1660 his followers had carried his mystical, egalitarian, prophetic version of Christianity beyond England, Scotland, and Ireland into every part of the New World.[4]

The Massachusetts Puritans reacted more violently against Quaker missionaries than had any government in England, and more often than not the Quakers who came to preach and prophesy in New England were women. When Mary Fisher and Ann Austin arrived in Boston in 1656, Deputy Governor Bellingham and a specially convened council of magistrates, citing the Quakers' intention to propagate "corrupt, heretical, and blasphemous doctrines," ordered one hundred of their books confiscated and burned and the two women confined to the Boston jail, where they were physically examined as possible witches. Citizens who sought to speak with them through the window of the prison were threatened with a fine of £5. Fisher and Austin were then transported to Barbados, but by the end of 1661 four Quakers had been executed in Massachusetts. Longest remembered among these had been Mary Dyer, who was hanged in 1660 and who is memorialized by a statue on the grounds of the Boston State House. Mary Dyer's offenses were double. She not only challenged repeatedly the laws against Quaker proselytizing; she was also a reminder of the Antinomian heresies of Anne Hutchinson, whose ardent follower she had been more than twenty years before, when Mrs. Hutchinson was tried for heresy and banished from Massachusetts.[5]

Doctrinally linked, Quaker and Antinomian theologies posed a serious challenge to male institutional authority, a challenge that constitutes an essential theme in the autobiography of Elizabeth Ashbridge. It is not surprising that Mary Dyer should eventually have sought doctrinal sanction in Quakerism for the impulse toward inward, immediate, and individual revelation which was at the heart of the Antinomian heresy.[6] Nor is it merely coincidental that Katherine Marbury Scott, a sister of Anne Hutchinson's, should also have become a Quaker, returning to Massachusetts twenty years after her sister's banishment to undertake her own

4. Wesley Frank Craven, *The Colonies in Transition, 1660–1713* (New York: Harper and Row, 1968), 183.

5. See Margaret Hope Bacon, *The Quiet Rebels: The Story of the Quakers in America* (New York: Basic Books, 1969), 25–33; James Bowden, *The History of the Society of Friends in America* (vol. 1, 1850; vol. 2, 1854; rpt. in 1 vol., New York: Arno, 1972). 42–205.

6. See Mary Maples Dunn, "Women of Light," in *Women of America: A History,* ed. Carol Berkin and Mary Norton (Boston: Houghton Mifflin, 1979), 120; Amy Schrager Lang, *Prophetic Woman: Anne Hutchinson and the Problem of Dissent in the Literature of New England* (Berkeley and Los Angeles: University of California Press, 1987), 155–60.

encounter with the magistracy, as a result of which she was whipped and imprisoned.[7] The doctrines articulated by George Fox and his followers carried the Reformation idea of a priesthood of all believers to its furthest extent: that priesthood would include women.

George Fox's missionary trip to America in 1671 did not take him to New England, but by that time the characteristic ideas of the Quakers did not require his personal sponsorship. Chief among those ideas was the doctrine of an inward Christ or Spirit of God, epitomized in Paul's proclamation to the Thessalonians, "Ye are all the children of light" (1 Thess. 5:5). The Inner Light, the Quakers believed, was promised universally, whereas for the Calvinist Puritans the divine life of grace was awarded only to those few whom God had chosen from all eternity. Moreover, the process of seeking, by which the Inner Light was realized, did not depend on the ministrations of a hierarchical church or its patristic genealogy of trained, ordained priests. William Penn, founder and proprietor of the colony of Pennsylvania, had said, "Sexes made no Difference; since in Souls there is none: and they are the subjects of Friendship."[8] Crucial to the empowering of a female ministry were the arguments advanced by Fox that inequality between the sexes was a condition of the Fall which was repealed in all those who came to dwell in the Light, and that for those new-made persons in whom the Spirit dwelled there was the possibility of continuing revelation beyond that already contained in Scripture.[9] At a stroke, then, the rationale for male proprietorship over revelation was undone. The closed book, its doctrines articulated and elaborated by the male exegete only, was closed no more. The Spirit was as likely to speak in a female as in a male voice. George Fox was unequivocal about the Spirit's androgynous vocality:

So be ashamed for ever and let all your mouths be stopped for ever, that despise the spirit of prophesy in the daughters, and do cast them into prison, and do hinder the women labourers in the gospel. . . . For the light is the same in the male, and in the female, which cometh from Christ, . . . and who is it that dare stop Christ's mouth?[10]

7. Emery Battis, *Saints and Sectaries: Anne Hutchinson and the Antinomian Controversy in the Massachusetts Bay Colony.* (Chapel Hill: University of North Carolina Press, 1962), 10[1]n.

8. Quoted in Margaret Hope Bacon, *Mothers of Feminism: The Story of Quaker Women in America* (New York: Harper and Row, 1986), 25[1]n.

9. See Mary Maples Dunn, "Saints and Sisters: Congregational and Quaker Women in the Early Colonial Period," in *Women in American Religion,* ed. Janet Wilson James (Philadelphia: University of Pennsylvania Press, 1980), 41; idem, "Women of Light," 118.

10. George Fox, "The Woman Learning in Silence," in *The Works of George Fox,* 8 vols. (Philadelphia: Gould, 1831), 4:109.

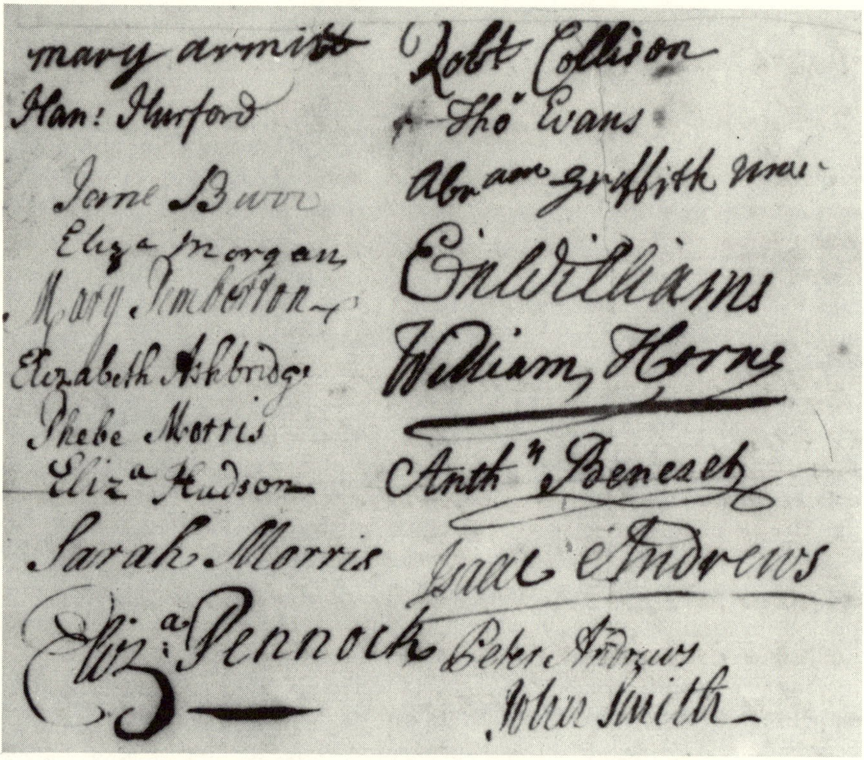

Figure 3.2   The only known sample of Elizabeth Ashbridge's handwriting appears with the signatures of Quaker ministers and elders, twenty-three women and thirty-four men from Pennsylvania and New Jersey, at the end of an epistle dated "the 16th day of the 3 month 1752." (Used with the permission of the Library of the Religious Society of Friends, Friends House, London.)

III

The achieved public role from which Elizabeth Ashbridge finally spoke was that of a traveling Friend, authorized by her local Quaker meeting to preach the Light in distant places. Although the evidence is scant, it is clear that in the period of her expanded participation in the life of Pennsylvania Quakers, working out of her local meeting at Goshen, she was recognized as speaking with increasing authority. In 1752 her signature appears, together with those of such prominent and influential Quakers as Anthony Benezet, Jane Hoskens, Israel Pemberton, and John Woolman on an epistle from the General Spring Meeting of ministers and elders held in Philadelphia to a meeting of ministers and elders in London.[11] Almost two years after the death of Elizabeth, Aaron Ashbridge, writing from Goshen, forwarded a copy of his wife's "journal" (the usual term for a Quaker autobiography) to Israel Pemberton, a wealthy trading and landholding member of the Society and clerk of the Yearly Meeting in Philadelphia (see Figure 3.3 for a facsimile of the letter). Furthermore, and most significantly, Aaron asked that the manuscript "be sent to John Woolman at Mount Holly who hath requested the perusal thereof." Woolman's own *Journal,* which he began to write in 1756, would become the classic and prototypical Quaker autobiography, claiming readers far beyond its own sect and century after its posthumous publication in 1774, the year in which Elizabeth Ashbridge's *Account* also appeared. From Aaron Ashbridge's letter we may infer that Elizabeth Ashbridge was known to Woolman from her activity in the area about Philadelphia and perhaps from her brief residence in Woolman's Mount Holly, New Jersey. It seems likely as well that he had the opportunity to read her journal while he was still in the process of writing his own.

Elizabeth Ashbridge, public Friend, is the product of the process described in her autobiography. That process is composed of a number of elements involving the narrator's geographical wanderings, her confrontation with both a male priesthood and an oppressive marriage, and the inward journey, sometimes symbolically rendered, toward a self whose hiding place is silence but which eventually proclaims itself in a new voice, the achieved voice of the autobiographer.

The geography of Elizabeth Ashbridge's quest claims attention early. As the narrative progresses, unchosen itinerancy gradually yields to increasingly willed and purposive seeking, the metaphor of the journey changing value as its literal vehicle gives way to spiritual tenor. The narrator's first departure from home is a kind of original sin, an end to innocence, when she disobeys her parents and elopes to marry, at age fourteen, an impoverished stocking weaver, "the darling of my heart," she says, still wistfully, of the young man who died five months after their marriage. Exile follows when her mother arranges a visit to a Quaker relative in Ireland, and a definitive pattern is initiated. The narrator's recoil from her first acquaintance with Quakers establishes the irony of her final arrival in their center

---

11. The epistle simply advises the Second Day Morning Meeting of ministers and elders in London that the visit of Mary Weston, a Friend who had arrived in Philadelphia bearing a London certificate, had been "very acceptable." But the signatories suggest the total network of Philadelphia-area Quakers who helped shape Elizabeth Ashbridge's mature thinking about her faith and experience. Women and men signed in separate columns, and the family names are those encountered repeatedly in studies of eighteenth-century Pennsylvania–New Jersey Quakerism. Thomas Carleton, who sent greetings to Elizabeth Ashbridge on her missionary trip, is one of the signers, as is William Hammans, whose preaching Elizabeth Ashbridge says played an important part in her conversion. The epistle is part of the holdings of the Friends Library, London, filed as Gibson 3/75.

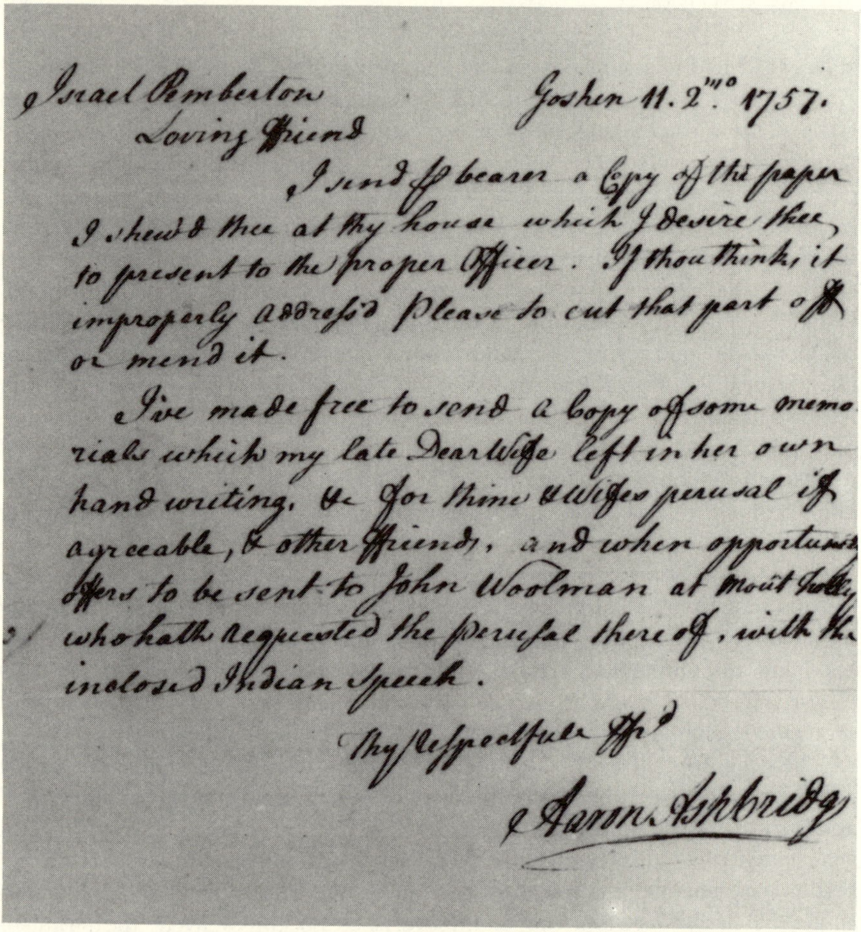

Israel Pemberton Goshen 11. 2d mo 1757.

Loving Friend

I send pr bearer a Copy of the paper I shew'd thee at thy house which I desire thee to present to the proper Officer. If thou thinks it improperly address'd Please to cut that part off or mend it.

I've made free to send a Copy of some memorials which my late Dear Wife left in her own hand writing. &c for thine & Wifes perusal if agreeable, & other friends, and when opportunity offers to be sent to John Woolman at Mount Holly who hath requested the perusal thereof, with the inclosed Indian Speech.

Thy Respectfull Frd

Aaron Ashbridge

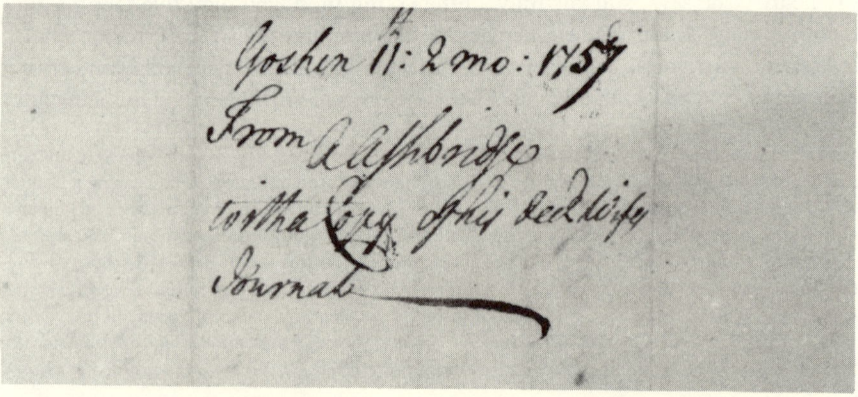

Goshen 11: 2 mo: 1757

From A Ashbridge

with a Copy of his dead Wifes

Journal

Figure 3.3 Letter from Aaron Ashbridge to the prominent Philadelphia Friend Israel Pemberton, accompanying "a Copy of some memorials which my late Dear Wife left in her own handwriting" and suggesting that the copy be forwarded to John Woolman, who had requested it. On the reverse side, another hand refers to the manuscript as "a Copy of his dead Wifes Journal." (Used with the permission of the Haverford College Library, Quaker Collection.)

in Pennsylvania and foreshadows the indirection of all the Spirit's leadings. Both her banishment to Ireland and her willful escape from it have much to do with her relation to paternal authority. Her mother, though a member of the Church of England, is represented as the source of spiritual principle, her father as the predominance of a severe kind of justice over mercy. His continued rejection of his daughter in refusing to recall her to England inspires counter-rejection. Finding herself "quite shut out of his affections," Elizabeth concludes that "since my absence was so Agreeable he should have it," and she therefore propels herself into the arrangement that results in her going to America as an indentured servant. Loving her unloving father, she punishes both him and herself. Fleeing and seeking him at once, she goes to sea, just as he had done "in many long voyages" until she was twelve.

The passages in which Elizabeth Ashbridge unwittingly binds herself as an indentured servant, then escapes that Old World arrangement only to fall into another and worse one in her transport to the New World, might have been taken from any of several important eighteenth-century novels titled after their heroines. Daniel Defoe's resilient anti-heroine, Moll Flanders, "in the despicable Quality of Transported Convicts destin'd to be sold for Slaves," eventually recovers her fortunes in Maryland and relates the account of her life, she says, for "Instruction, Caution, Warning and Improvement to every Reader." Samuel Richardson's fallen Clarissa Harlowe is advised by her sister to remove to Pennsylvania until her parents can be satisfied "that you behave like a true and uniform penitent." Susanna Rowson's heroine, Charlotte Temple, is duped into eloping unmarried to America and is abandoned in New York by her lover, there to sink into an early grave.

Whatever its fictional analogues, the autobiography of Elizabeth Ashbridge is firmly grounded in history. Many indentured servants were in fact vagrants and criminals, under sentence or escaping from one. Not all were "filled with the thought of coming to America," as Elizabeth Ashbridge describes herself, but many saw themselves delineated in advertisements directed at persons "disgusted with the frowns of fortune of their native land."[12] This inherently exploitative trade flourished through the agency of just such opportunists as the gentlewoman and her brother-in-law depicted by Elizabeth Ashbridge. The unsavory dealings of these "crimps," "spirits," and "men stealers" ranged from simple fraud to kidnapping. The essential contract of the indentured servant involved the obligation of servitude for a stated period of time in exchange for payment of the servant's fare to America. When, however, the contract was passed forward into other hands, the servant lost all control over his or her fate.[13] This is in effect what happens to

12. Cheesman A. Herrick, *White Servitude in Pennsylvania: Indentured and Redemption Labor in Colony and Commonwealth* (Philadelphia: McVey, 1926), 144.

13. Ibid., 144–47.

Elizabeth Ashbridge after she frees herself from the Irish gentlewoman. Just arrived in New York, "a Stranger in a Strange Land," she is forced by the ship's captain into signing a second indenture, which is promptly sold to a New York master. For such reasons, emigrants contemplating indentured servitude were advised to make their contracts before leaving England and to guard the indenture in case of later disputes.[14]

Elizabeth Ashbridge's new master is one in a series of superficially righteous members of the traditional churches, a series that bridges her experiences in England, Ireland, and America. The standpoint from which she characterizes churchmen—clergy or laity, Roman Catholic, Anglican, or Presbyterian—is established at the outset. From her youth, she tells the reader, she was always in awe of religious ministers "and sometimes wept with Sorrow, that I was not a boy that I might have been one." The religious quest that follows and that results in her own ordination by the Spirit proceeds in large part by an interrogation of the churches' patriarchy. Although characters are individualized, they share the same general profile. Like her father, whose power and whose absence from his family are equally unquestioned, these are figures whose authority derives from the institutions they control, whether family or church. Their credentials and their articles of belief do not bear close examination. When Elizabeth, even after conceding to an Irish Catholic priest the authority to confess her, examines his principles for herself, she discovers them to be "ridiculous stuff," ultimately political in their concern to return the Roman Catholic Pretender to the English throne while disenfranchising those beyond the pale, like her Anglican mother. In a much later scene, Elizabeth Ashbridge is at great pains to describe the trial of a Presbyterian minister, sketching context and reporting heated conversations as they converge finally on the question of the minister's salary. The scene is an important one because it is a figure for the sustained narrative trial of the patriarchal priesthood, and it provokes from the narrator an explicit judgment: "for I now saw beyond the Men made Ministers, and what they preached for."

Like the churchman to whom she is indentured, most of these male clerics are characterized by outward righteousness and inward dissoluteness, by easy, nominal belief and a reliance on rote prayer and sacramental form. At worst, they are raging hypocrites. In one episode her master intends to have Elizabeth whipped because she has revealed to a confidante the "difference" they have had, most likely his attempt to take sexual advantage of his young servant, a not uncommon result of the servant's status as property.[15] But a more complex case is that of the husband Sullivan, whom Elizabeth Ashbridge reveals as alternately brutal and pitiable. His abuses of domestic power, his moral weakness, and his superficial

14. See Sharon V. Salinger, *"To Serve Well and Faithfully": Labor and Indentured Servants in Pennsylvania, 1682–1800* (Cambridge: Cambridge University Press, 1987), 11.

15. Ibid., 111.

adherence to his status as a church member—he fears that Elizabeth will stop singing and dancing if she leaves the Church of England—link him to his fellows among the ordained patriarchy. Yet as autobiographer, Elizabeth Ashbridge twines the thread of his salvation with her own, exempting him by a kind of narrative grace from the condemnation he would otherwise have shared with his drinking and preaching companions. Reclaimed from outward power, he lives to assert the Quaker testimony for peace against the British army, which he has joined in a drunken and perhaps fatalistic attempt to preserve his wife by ending their marriage. His "sufferings for Truth," as the Quakers expressed that experience among their members, are a mirror image in the great world of those his wife endured domestically at his hands, and Elizabeth Ashbridge portrays his testimony and principled death as the final, indeed the only, fruit of their marriage.

To speculate on the husband's motivations as he departs from the narrative is to be reminded of his fictionality; not that Elizabeth Ashbridge intended a fiction—quite the opposite—but because autobiography necessarily invents all its characters in relation to its central character, the autobiographical persona. The reader has no access to fact, only to the narrative process that creates the husband's deliverance and integrates it with that of the autobiographer, a process that relates her struggle to his as substance to shadow. Indeed, the power relationship between character and autobiographer is precisely opposite that of the husband and wife depicted in the narrative. As "my husband," the historical Sullivan depends entirely for his textual being on Elizabeth Ashbridge as autobiographer. His purging from the narrative is necessary to her final identification, even at a cost, since the autobiographer must surrender a dimension of her autobiographical self along with him.. The woman he marries for her singing and dancing, whom the narrator describes as "airy and wild," and whom we see in an instant's image contemplating a career as actress, turning the pages of playbooks and missing her sleep in colonial New York: that Elizabeth Ashbridge too is a necessary sacrifice to the autobiographical process.

In the same way, Elizabeth Ashbridge as narrator endows her husband with a capacity for deliverance which, as creator, she denies to the other churchmen and assorted lounge-abouts who come to life under her hand. The autobiographical Elizabeth Ashbridge must listen to a great many other voices before she can discern, within, the sound of her own. Yet her narrative grants a comparable discovery as gift, or grace, to her husband. In one scene he lies alone and is spoken to, hearing the words, "Lord where shall I fly to shun thee?" His fragment of autobiographical act—the scene unfolds "as he afterwards told me"—would have no life without the enabling life of hers. And the creation for the husband of an interiority that is continuous with her own creates a further possibility: as a fictional character, he becomes more real by virtue of participating in the autobiographer's realization. He is granted a brief sight of the autobiography's central process of becoming when, propelled by the voice he has heard, he rides to join his wife at meeting and grudgingly, brokenly acknowledges: "Well I'll E'en give you up, for I see it don't avail to Strive; if it be of God I can't over throw it, & if it be of your self it will soon fall."

I V

Integral as the figure of the husband may be, Elizabeth Ashbridge's account of her early life cannot finally be read as the autobiography of a marriage. It is not only that she writes as a widow, before her marriage to Aaron Ashbridge. Her journey into the inmost spaces of identity is one she undertakes alone, its conflicting impulses and contending voices notwithstanding, for these are the imagery of her single-minded will to create her identity, set against all temptations to surrender the idea of a separate self. The journey is not without its element of mystery. Over the journey's route the autobiographer has arched what she will call Providence, a term by which she concedes that there is more to soul-making than earnest, purposive striving. The persona, Elizabeth, intends from the beginning of her travels to get to Pennsylvania, an autobiographical trope for her buried intention to join the Quakers. Yet it may seem almost fortuitous that she should arrive there, after an early plan to return to England is deflected into a pattern of wanderings over which she has little control. Her husband, she says, was much "given to ramble, which was very Disagreeable to me, but I must submit." He "had led me," she says later, "thro' the Country like a Vagabond." America, like the question of identity for the eighteenth-century female autobiographer, must have seemed mapless, a succession of names without pattern or history, like a deceptively bountiful offering of external roles without a self to inhabit them. Walt Whitman's poetry of the open road and the "extra-vagant" language of Thoreau would later suffuse American geography with spiritual meaning, but Elizabeth Ashbridge attempted a like project in a period when the itinerant female ministry and its aspiring voices earned only terms of contempt: "she preacher," "audacious virago," "vagabond Quakers."[16]

Still, the idea of a Pennsylvania of the soul abides in the autobiography of Elizabeth Ashbridge. Its most telling symbolic expression is the woman carrying a lamp who in a dream reports an offer of mercy to Elizabeth from the very source of her creation, a source seemingly outside yet also deeply within herself. Her own lamp, Elizabeth learns, will not be put out, though she cannot at first obey her

16. Robert J. Leach, *Women Ministers: A Quaker Contribution* (Wallingford, Pa.: Pendle Hill, 1979), 6, 10.

visionary instruction. The lamp is in a sense the light by which the autobiographer illuminates the idea of an achieved identity even before the persona can give it a name. Doctrinally, it is the Quaker Inner Light. Within the narrative, it is light cast by a powerfully expressed intention of identity.

Appearing early as a resolve "never to leave Searching till I had found the Truth," the intention is periodically renewed. "Come Life or Death," Elizabeth says later, "I'll fight through, for my Salvation is at Stake." Toward the end of the narrative the autobiographical persona feels the light to be nearly extinguished— her husband tells her that as a seamstress she does not earn her candle—yet she asserts that light against his authority. His commands, she tells him, would no longer be obeyed; "where they imposed upon my Conscience, I no longer Durst: For I had already done it too Long, & wronged my Self by it. . . ."

The light, salvation, conscience, the self: these terms all tend to converge on a single, central point, the finally unnameable subject, end, origin, and sanctum sanctorum of this and all autobiography, the place, everywhere and nowhere in the text, where the "I" is focused. The reader who finds that, after all, Elizabeth Ashbridge only attempted to fill that unfillable space with a conventional identity (the conscientious Friend) habited in conventional form (the Quaker journal) needs to shift attention from categories to processes.

The categories available for a woman's self-definition were particularly rigid as Elizabeth Ashbridge wrote, probably sometime in the late 1740s, even though her reading experience would have extended beyond spiritual autobiography to include perhaps, during her play-reading phase, heroic drama with its conflict between love and honor as well as comedies of sexual wit and sentiment. An entire category of women's self-writing, the so-called scandalous memoirs, depended, according to one scholar, on the public construction of a character whose virtue has been questioned, to stand in the stead of a private self.[17] Identity imagined as character posed equally frustrating literary alternatives: either gender differences were stereotypical or they enforced the idea that character, properly, belonged to only one gender, as when Samuel Johnson quoted with approval the verses, "Nothing so true as what you once let fall / Most women have no *characters at all.*[18] Attempting to "imagine a self," women writers were able to enter the large new field of the novel but for the most part were constrained to "affirm the social order that limit[ed] them" and to achieve articulation at the price of apology; at best in eighteenth-century fiction, woman makes "a mythology of her victimization, verbally converting it into the badge of her freedom."[19]

17. Felicity Nussbaum, "Heteroclites: The Gender of Character in the Scandalous Memoirs," in *The New Eighteenth Century: Theory, Politics, English Literature,* ed. Felicity Nussbaum and Laura Brown (New York: Methuen, 1987), 160.

18. Quoted in ibid., 147.

19. Patricia Meyer Spacks, *Imagining a Self: Autobiography and Novel in Eighteenth-Century England* (Cambridge: Harvard University Press, 1976), 58, 73.

Elizabeth Ashbridge writes herself into autobiographical being on ground other than that of character. The reader sees very little of the character of Elizabeth Ashbridge as public Friend. For that moral distillation of externally observed word and act and gesture we depend on the testimonies of those who wrote about her after her death and who saw her character in the light of her exemplary service. The narrative provides at most a few shadowy types of the Quaker to come, when, for example, Elizabeth unknowingly encounters her future self in her aunt, a Quaker preacher, or when she responds with unvoiced irony to a Quaker woman she hears preaching in Boston, "I am sure you are a fool, for if ever I should turn Quaker, which will never be, I would not be a preacher." To endow herself with a "character" from whatever stock of religious, social, or literary models would have presumed to answer the question she asks rhetorically in concluding the narrative, "Lord, what was I; that thou should have revealed to me the knowledge of thy Truth?" In the case of Elizabeth Ashbridge, autobiography's interrogation— "What was I?"—proceeds not for the sake of an answer but in order to re-create the very process of coming to identity and to dis-cover the voice that speaks it. The autobiography is the phenomenon of a woman speaking of her coming to speak.

For such an event to unfold there need to be both space and silence. Elizabeth's essential seeking takes place away from others: in a garden, where she first hears the voice of Truth, in a garret, in the woods, in a stable, most often lying awake beside yet a world away from her husband. In this pattern of searching in secret, remote, and estranged places it is as if, in order to go about her work, the auto-biographer has to clear spaces entirely free from enforced role and sanctioned stereotype.

These are not, however, places of certain peace, but rather of potential conflict. Elizabeth enters them at the risk of self-destruction. Voices exhort her to suicide. The ascent to identity must overcome the downward pull of a negative self whose voice is that of the devil, for whom Elizabeth Ashbridge has a large fund of names: the "crooked serpent," of course, crooked as Truth is not; but other terms too, more appropriate for dramatizing the inner dialectic of autobiography: "the old enemy," "the restless adversary," "the old accuser." As shadow, that devil attempts to negate the light of her woman's identity, and it is a compound of many negations: the denial of the right to exist other than as a dependent; the denial of an original voice, for which echo and all the contortions of mimicry must be sub-stituted; the denial implicit in normative patriarchal history, summed up in the specter of the father's approval, therefore the denial of becoming.

The introjected accusatory power of these voices is enormous. To escape their will to her nonbeing, Elizabeth must deprive herself of the instruments of self-destruction—the apron and garters of her given female identity, the knife she will eventually, as autobiographer, exchange for a pen. She will not be safe from the wounding power of negative identity until she is healed by "the true balm of Gilead." As a reader of Scripture, Elizabeth Ashbridge would have understood these words of Jeremiah (8:22; 46:11) to mean, by a New Testament extension, the solace of grace, the healing power of the Spirit. We are free as well to imagine these words reading Elizabeth Ashbridge, translating her autobiographical vision of a heart at rest in a centered self. Within the narrative spaces she has cleared, Elizabeth Ashbridge discovers—that is, she simultaneously finds and reveals—a secret self and secret tongue.

For the persona, these are necessarily dangerous secrets, as their narrative imagery consistently announces. On board the ship that takes her to America, Elizabeth harbors the secret of her Irish tongue, but her possession of it carries her into the power struggle between indentured servants and the ship's masters and endangers her life. The persona is bilingual both in fact and figure, speaking English and hiding her Irish, fluent among her masters in the language of duty and deference while making, as she says, her private remarks, remarks that will eventually flower into autobiography. Throughout the period in which she comes to accept Quaker faith and practice she must hide her emergent self from her husband and others, even at one point denying and distorting it by affecting an un-Quakerlike flamboyance in dress. Her denials, which say in effect, "Do not think me anything so threatening as a creature of Inner Light," are virtually a metaphor for woman's protective adaptations. Elizabeth Ashbridge compares them to Peter's denial of Christ. Sitting in company with others, who hear only thunder, Elizabeth hears a voice indicting her and leaving her "speechless." The silence is broken when self and tongue connect vitally and disturbingly. After a separation from her husband of four months, she proclaims her new identity to him through the familiar Quaker usage of "thee": "My dear, I am glad to see thee," she tells him. The secret is out, and it is a threatening one. In response, he invokes her adversary and in alarm speaks as if her new tongue had power to transform him, as indeed it does. "The Divel *thee thee*; don't *thee* me."

In Quaker autobiography, the new-made Friend's rising out of communal silence to speak in meeting is always climactic, an uncovering of the Light within and a validation of the Spirit's presence. For Elizabeth Ashbridge's persona, that moment is particularly daunting because it is an approach to the threshold of autobiography, where inner becomes outer, and because the power associated with an essential rather than a borrowed voice is the fearsome power to make and unmake selves, both first- and third-persons. And so, Elizabeth Ashbridge says, "it was required of me in a more Publick manner to Confess to the world what I was and to give up in Prayer in a Meeting, the sight of which and the power attending made me Tremble, & I could not hold my Self still." With respect to her husband, her fear proves justified. Though she has remained largely silent under his abuse, her voice breaks that silence when she calls him a "Vile Man" and prays to be delivered from him. His death, the unexpected granting of her request, seems so stunningly to demonstrate the power of her voice that she fears divine displeasure. With the same voice, however, Elizabeth Ashbridge as autobiographer creates her

Figure 3.4   Painting of a Quaker meeting attributed to Egbert van Heemskerk the younger (1645–1704). The painting violates the Quaker prohibition against images and memorials and has a satiric rather than a reverential purpose, as suggested in the figure of the woman preaching while standing on a tub. However, the illumination of the speaker, the pathos of eloquence in her pose, and the rapt attention of her hearers create a sympathetic effect. Numerous copies and engravings exist, several of them at Friends House, London. (Used with the permission of the Haverford College Library, Quaker Collection.)

husband's final scene and finest hour, when he tells his military commanders, in language that recalls his wife's speeches to him, "I have but one Life, & you may take that if you Please, but I'll never take up Arms." At the close of the narrative, the autobiographer has accepted the burden of the power of such a voice, its divine prerogative for damning and blessing, creating and uncreating. Having arisen out of silence, her voice now silences all its old adversarial opposites.

V

No reader will approach the *Account* of Elizabeth Ashbridge anticipating formal complexities such as those we find in Gertrude Stein's *Autobiography of Alice B. Toklas* or Maxine Hong Kingston's *Woman Warrior.* Her relevance for the present critical moment may be a little difficult to make out. That moment has been described by some feminist critics as one of opportunity but also as one that is problematic for the reading of women's autobiography. The difficulty is that just as the terms *self* and *identity*, entering a newly chromatic range of gendered meanings, have begun to acquire special valence for writing by women, readers of autobiography are now told that such terms signify no substantive reality.[20] There are no selves in auto- biographies, say some theorists, only words, and the autobiographer has not made those words, only borrowed them from the verbal culture. In a vast system of signifiers interacting with one another, heated and cooled, privileged and dis- privileged by a culture, the autobiographical self becomes a kind of mirror trick, no more "there" than the elephant once the mirrors have been taken away. As Katherine Goodman has pointed out, the casualty in this theoretical description is the sense of choice that accompanies a concept of self, precisely at a time when women's sense of choice has begun to define their reading of history and their enactment of a present identity.[21] By contrast, the universe of signifiers gathers the autobiographer into its own impersonal system and expels the naively alien idea of autobiography as willed self-creation.

The text of Elizabeth Ashbridge's autobiography is not innocent of some of these implications, but it knows better—and what her text knows, it knows because of the narrator's Quakerism. In her account, patriarchal history and the patri- archal priesthood are put on trial, and we arrive narratively at a time in which a woman's voice is delivered up out of silence. No Quaker, though, would enter-

20. See Sidonie Smith, *A Poetics of Women's Autobiography: Marginality and the Fictions of Self-Repre- sentation* (Bloomington: Indiana University Press, 1987), 3–19; Katherine Goodman, *Dis/Closures: Women's Autobiography in Germany Between 1790 and 1914* (New York: Lang, 1986), ii–iii.
21. *Dis/Closures,* xvi.

tain a pride of representation. The text nowhere assumes that either the Inner Light or the self irradiated by the Light can be adequately mirrored or contained by any of its verbal signs. If anything, the autobiographical self represents less at the end than at the beginning of the narrative, having shed its stereotypical roles and their readily identifiable behavior in favor of pure potential, a principle of becoming whose content has yet to be filled in. Most important, the text knows that to arrive at an awareness of a self that refuses characterization is deliverance into a new kind of freedom of choice. The representable selves of romantic adolescent, oppressed servant, aspiring actress, and long-suffering spouse promise narrative predictability rather than choice. The idea of an unrepresentable spirit within, which is always yet to be spoken, gives admission to a new world of seeking words.

The voice discovered through the process of Elizabeth Ashbridge's autobiography says all these things, however time- and culture-bound we may find the Quaker minister who wrote it. Her language, historically described, will appear no different from that of her contemporaries, male or female. In its time it necessarily derived from what feminist critics call a "phallologocentric" lexicon, but precisely because Elizabeth Ashbridge, in her innocence, was free to locate the source of language elsewhere than in gender, we are free to find the voice that underlies her language prophetic. The prophecy does not concern an alternative lexicon, one for women only. The voice makes no attempt to pronounce "gynologocentric" and probably would not care to. But it is centered in an essential paradigm for the development of women's autobiography. Speaking of what happened under the dispensation of the father, that voice grows increasingly less accented by the past until finally it arrives at a present it can celebrate, and in a new act of verbal self-consciousness, speaks itself, not only as a woman who has become a Quaker but as woman becoming.

A NOTE ON BIOGRAPHY

The principal published source of information on Elizabeth Ashbridge and her last husband, Aaron Ashbridge, has been *The Ashbridge Book*, a family genealogy in which Elizabeth plays only a small part. A "Biographical Sketch" of Elizabeth Ashbridge appeared in the Philadelphia Quaker journal *The Friend* in 1857, but the sketch is drawn almost entirely from her autobiography and from testimonials issued after her death, including the memorial issued by the Goshen, Pennsylvania Monthly Meeting of which she was a member. Additionally, the sketch includes an anecdote from the journal of Sarah Stephenson giving the author's recollection of the visit of Elizabeth Ashbridge and Sarah Worrell to the Stephenson home in

Worcester early in the missionary journey through England and Ireland that claimed both their lives. The story provides a brief glimpse of Elizabeth Ashbridge in the period after she had given up what she called her airy ways. Sarah Stephenson recalls:

> One evening, during this time, Elizabeth, in a very weighty manner, addressed me, in the language of unspeakable love; remarking also, "What a pity that child should have a ribbon on her head." Her words were piercing and deeply affected my mind. I do not know that I closed my eyes to sleep that night; and in the morning, not daring to put on my ribbon, I came down without it.[22]

Sources for further biographical study are the records of the various Quaker meetings with which Elizabeth Ashbridge associated. Chief among these, and the basis for information contained in *The Ashbridge Book*, is the Goshen Monthly Meeting, whose minutes are collected at the Friends Historical Library of Swarthmore College, with copies in the Quaker Collection, Haverford College Library. It is possible that the records of the meetings at Bordentown, Mount Holly, and Burlington between the time of Elizabeth Ashbridge's reception into the ministry in 1738 and her marriage in 1746 to Aaron Ashbridge would yield a fuller picture of her life as a public Friend. A historical novel by Shirley A. Weitzel, *Land O' Goshen,* provides a portrait of George Ashbridge, brother of Aaron, and of the activity around the mill on the Ashbridge property in the period of the Revolution.[23]

An important discovery is the inclusion of Elizabeth's Ashbridge's signature on an epistle from the General Spring Meeting of ministers and elders held in Philadelphia on March 16, 1752. The twenty-three women and thirty-four men who signed the letter were among the most prominent and influential of contemporary Quakers, including the autobiographers Jane Hoskens and John Woolman as well as Anthony Benezet, who like Woolman was a leader in the Society's antislavery movement. It is significant too that Elizabeth Ashbridge's voice had already become a distinctive one to leading Quakers quite apart from any influence her journal might have had later through the distribution of manuscript copies after her death. Such is the evidence of the letter of 1757, reprinted in Figure 3.3, from Aaron Ashbridge to Israel Pemberton, another signatory to the epistle of 1752, who

22. "Biographical Sketches of Ministers and Elders and Other Concerned Members of the Yearly Meeting of Philadelphia," *The Friend* 31 (September 1857): 254.

23. George Ashbridge was sponsored, unsuccessfully, by Benjamin Franklin for Speaker of the Pennsylvania House in 1764 (see Jack D. Marietta, *The Reformation of American Quakerism, 1748–1783* [Philadelphia: University of Pennsylvania Press, 1984], 329). An appendix to Weitzel's novel gives current locations of such relevant sites as the Ashbridge mill and Goshen meetinghouse (*Land O' Goshen: A Tale of Chester County, 1776–1778* [Philadelphia: Rochambeau, 1979], 262).

was the eldest of three successful and philanthropic Philadelphia Quakers and a member of the original editorial committee that oversaw publication of John Woolman's *Journal*.

We are accustomed to thinking of Woolman's spiritual autobiography, long established as a Quaker classic, as the summit of Friends writing in this genre, a work more influential than influenced. Aaron Ashbridge's letter, alluding to Woolman's request to peruse a copy of his late wife's journal, suggests instead the textual network of the Quaker autobiographers, who wrote as individual men and women but also as interdependent members of a group literary culture. It is possible that Elizabeth Ashbridge met Woolman during the time she spent in Mount Holly, since Woolman moved there in 1741 and Elizabeth may well have remained there for the two years after her husband's enlistment in 1740 until she received, as Aaron tells us, certain news of Sullivan's death. Woolman's *Journal* states only that in November 1758 he attended "a family meeting at our friend's Aaron Ashbridge's, where the channel of gospel love was opened and my mind was comforted after a hard day's labour."[24] The next day, Woolman says, he attended the Goshen Monthly Meeting. Whether Ashbridge's late wife was at that point, three years after her death, a matter for comment and testimony, we can only speculate.

From *The Ashbridge Book* we learn that Aaron Ashbridge was married both before and after his marriage to Elizabeth Sampson Sullivan. Born in 1712, Aaron became a farmer and eventually lived on a plot of 331 acres deeded to him by his father, George Ashbridge, in 1737, following his marriage to Sarah Davies. The land lay along the Goshentown and Chester roads northwest of Philadelphia, just south of the Friends' Goshen meetinghouse and immediately to the west of the father's farm. In 1746, by this time a widower, Aaron Ashbridge requested a certificate from the Goshen to the Burlington meeting "in order to marry Elizabeth Sullivan." In October he issued the following wedding invitation: "My sweetheart as well as myself desire (if it may suit thy convenience and freedom), that thou wilt favor us with thy company at our marriage, which is intended to be at Burlington the 4th of next month."[25] Within a few months, Elizabeth Ashbridge had become a member of the Goshen Meeting, and presumably she and her husband lived on the nearby Ashbridge farm from 1746 until she left for England and Ireland in 1753.

Elizabeth and Aaron Ashbridge appear to have enjoyed both content and respect during the brief period of their marriage. Aaron was appointed an overseer of the Goshen Meeting in 1748 and became a justice of the peace in 1749. The Goshen records note that Elizabeth, with other Friends, was appointed to visit families in 1748. Her standing in the Society appears to have been secure. A 1751 entry in the Goshen records notes that one Hannah Eachus was complained of "for

24. *The Journal and Major Essays of John Woolman,* ed. Phillips P. Moulton (New York: Oxford University Press, 1971), 94.

25. Wellington T. Ashbridge, *The Ashbridge Book* (Toronto: Copp Clark, 1912), 47.

aspersing the character of Elizabeth Ashbridge" and was herself disowned by the meeting two months later.[26]

When Elizabeth Ashbridge informed the Goshen Meeting in February 1753 that she felt "drawings" to visit Friends abroad, she was required to pass a kind of character test in order to obtain a certificate from her local meeting to those in England and Ireland, satisfying a committee of three who had been appointed to "inquire concerning her conversation and ministry." A month later the certificate was signed for her. Two letters written by Thomas Carleton of Kennett, Pennsylvania, available in the Quaker Collection of Haverford College, inquire after Elizabeth Ashbridge during her missionary trip and mention Margaret Ellis as a member of her company. The letters, dated December 17, 1753, and November 18, 1754, and sent to a British cousin, convey the writer's respects and news of Aaron Ashbridge's good health. The details of Elizabeth Ashbridge's itinerary are unclear. Like other Friends, she may well have begun her journey in London. The Goshen Meeting at any rate received a certificate from London testifying that her conduct and ministry there were "very acceptable." We know of her visit to the Stephenson home in Worcester. We do not know whether she visited her family at Middlewich, only sixty miles away. But in a "Memorandum relating to Travelling Publick Friends at Darlington [Durham]," an anonymous Quaker historian suggests that Elizabeth Ashbridge's itinerary was both ambitious and laborious:

Some time this Spring (as I understand) Two women friends from America, their names (I think) Sarah Worral & Elizabeth Ashbridge both died in Ireland, after having visited part of that nation & some part of this. One of them [Elizabeth Ashbridge] before She died left it as a caution to such as might be under a like concern, not to travel too hard, intimating it had been fatal to herself & Companion who dyed but a very little before her.[27]

The area in County Carlow, Ireland, reached by Elizabeth Ashbridge in the final stage of her illness had been settled by members of the Lecky and Watson families, immigrants from Cumbria, England, since the early seventeenth century. The meetinghouse at Kilconner was founded by Samuel Watson in 1670, and the burying ground at nearby Ballybromhill was part of the Watson lands. Leckys and Watsons intermarried from the seventeenth century on, so it was natural that Elizabeth Ashbridge, having died in the Lecky house at Kilnock, should be buried at Ballybromhill. That the Kilnock-Kilconner settlement was a usual stop on the missionary trail of visiting Friends can be gathered from the journal of John

26. Ibid., 50.

27. Memorandum relating to Travelling publick Friends at Darlington 1754-5-6 with other occurrences, MS Box Q1/5, Library of the Society of Friends, Friends House, London.

Figure 3.5   The ruins of the seventeenth-century Quaker meetinghouse built by the Watson family and used as well by the Leckys, the family in whose house Elizabeth Ashbridge died. If Elizabeth Ashbridge attended a meeting or preached during the period of her final illness it would have been here. The ruins lie near Fennagh, County Carlow, Ireland, on private property, formerly the township of Kilconner.

Churchman, who traveled at about the same time as Elizabeth Ashbridge: "After a meeting at Newton, we went to Samuel Watson's, at Kilconner, whose wife (late Abigail Bowles) had been on a religious visit in America several years past."[28]

The burying ground and meetinghouse may still be seen. Because the early Quakers rejected any memorial but their testimonies to the Truth, no gravestones remain at Ballybromhill, save a tablet to a nineteenth-century descendant of the Lecky-Watson family which also memorializes the other members of the Quaker family buried there. An early twentieth-century entrance gate now names the plot "God's Acre." Only a place in the road, the burying ground is nevertheless conspicuous for the enormous beech trees that cover it and that are home to a cacophony of rooks, evidently appointed to call attention by contrast to the permanent peaceableness of the Friends below. The small stone meetinghouse at Kilconner is fallen in and much overgrown after years of disuse. In its latter days it reverted to the Church of Ireland and was used as a dance hall for parish youth, an irony students of Elizabeth Ashbridge can best appreciate. Kilnock is marked only by the remains of

28. *An Account of the Gospel Labours and Christian Experiences of a Faithful Minister of Christ, John Churchman* (London: N.p., 1780), 167.

Figure 3.6   Entrance to the Friends burying ground at Ballybromhill, County Carlow, Ireland. The entrance gate is of modern construction and gives the name "God's Acre" to the property, approximately two miles from both the meetinghouse at Kilconner and from Kilnock, where Elizabeth Ashbridge died.

Kilnock House, also a ruin but possibly, considering its age and its history of Lecky-Watson ownership, the house in which Elizabeth Ashbridge died on May 16, 1755.

The career of Aaron Ashbridge, after the death of his wife in 1755, bears an ironic resemblance to the life of Elizabeth's second husband, Sullivan, who progressed from dissolute drunkenness to the virtual Quakerism of his pacifist refusal to bear arms. The irony lies in the fact that Aaron's life reversed the pattern. As a justice of the peace in 1757 he was charged by Captain Moore of the Royal American Regiment with refusing to swear in recruits and with discouraging them from entering the king's service, though he denied these apparent demonstrations of Quaker conscience after receiving an inquiry from Lt. Gov. William Denny. Toward the end of his life, however, he was twice complained of in the Goshen Meeting for drinking to excess, the second time, in January 1775, "so as to be disguised therewith on a public road." Two months later he was disowned by the meeting with the observation that he had been "a serviseable member for many years past."[29] He died in 1776, and his will, probated on May 31, left £300 for the education of poor children, primarily those of Friends.

29. Ashbridge, *The Ashbridge Book*, 49.

A NOTE ON THE TEXT

Unless the original manuscript of the autobiography of Elizabeth Ashbridge should someday be found, any edition must be based on a manuscript copy or collation of copies or on the first edition of 1774. Although the 1774 edition has now been reprinted in full in the third edition of *The Norton Anthology of American Literature,* comparison of that text with early manuscript copies indicates typesetter's errors, deletions, and rewordings for fluency which may reflect the work's original publication under the auspices of the author's family. The autobiography was first published in Nantwich, Cheshire. Elizabeth Sampson, as she tells us, was born in Middlewich, ten miles away.

The basis for later copies of the autobiography outside this country is most likely a copy made by Aaron Ashbridge shortly after he received news of his wife's death in Ireland, which he would have sent to Friends there, together with his "Lamentation" and his continuation of her life's story to the point of her departure from Pennsylvania in 1753. He may also have made a copy for his wife's survivors among the Sampson family, and we know from his letter to Israel Pemberton in 1757 that he made at least one copy for circulation in this country. However, none of the numerous copies available in historical collections appears to be in Aaron's handwriting when it is compared with the handwriting in the Pemberton letter. Hence none can claim the authority, such as it might be, of having been copied by Aaron directly from his wife's manuscript. It is possible, of course, that Elizabeth carried abroad either her original manuscript or a copy she had made of it, even possible that she left a copy with her family in Middlewich, and that copies available in England derive from a manuscript of hers rather than of Aaron's.

In these circumstances, and given the unauthorized variants and erratic typesetting of the 1774 edition, the choice of the text that most likely represents the words of Elizabeth Ashbridge has inherent limitations, but these limitations can at least be minimized by choosing a very early manuscript copy to which a minimum of "improvements" or miscopyings would have accrued in successive stages through the late eighteenth and early nineteenth centuries. There are a number of candidates. The Boston Public Library and the Quaker Collection of the Haverford College Library each has a copy. The Friends Historical Library at Swarthmore College has three: one dated 1781; another dated 1784 in the hand of, and probably copied by, Abigail Mott; and a third, possibly of earlier origin, that is incomplete, beginning about a third of the way through the narrative and ending with the conclusion of the narrative proper. A manuscript book in the hand of Anne Emlen, dated 1784, was the basis for an edition of Elizabeth Ashbridge's narrative by Charles Caleb Cresson (Philadelphia, 1886), but the book, then owned by Mary Leggett Williams, can no longer be located. The Library of the Society of Friends in London has two copies, both by Quaker ministers. One is primarily in the hand of Solomon Chapman (1750–1838) of Sunderland; the other appears to be in several hands, but is ascribed to John Gripper (1755–1826) of Layer Breton (Essex) on the basis of the cover inscription.

Possibly the most eligible candidates for copy text are part of the collection of the Friends Library at Swanbrook House, Dublin. Because Elizabeth Ashbridge died in Ireland and because the Dublin Yearly Meeting noted her death by means of a testimonial, which is sometimes published at the conclusion of the autobiography, any eighteenth-century copy preserved by the Society of Friends in Dublin has great interest. Three copies are available at the Friends Library. One copy, running to forty-five pages, was probably made by Samuel Russel, whose name appears on the inside cover with the date "16th 3rd mo. 1759," although the date on the title page reads Dublin 1757. A second, undated copy, with an elaborately decorated title page, runs to sixty-one pages and is followed by Aaron Ashbridge's sequel, as is the forty-five page copy by Russel. A third, probably later, copy has the date "22. 1. 72" and has been copied into a small notebook, probably by its owner Thomas Pim. None of these copies is the missing holograph, then, and because the undated copy contains the Irish account of Elizabeth Ashbridge's last illness and the Russel copy contains an index, both in the same hand as the autobiography proper, neither of these can be Aaron's copy. The first two of these Dublin manuscripts have been photographed and consulted for this edition—the Russel manuscript because of its early date, and the second manuscript, whose readings sometimes vary from Russel's, because it alone provides a calendar of dates for the narrative of Elizabeth Ashbridge's final illness.

The manuscript copies used as the basis for the present edition belong to the Woodbrooke Quaker Study Centre, Birmingham, England, and are part of the Bevan-Naish Library. Of the two manuscripts, BN 2432 and BN 1172, the first is in a clearer but later hand. The second is earlier, cruder both in script and orthography, and is missing the first four pages. Excepting these pages, where this edition follows BN 2432, the basis for the present edition has been BN 1172 because it appears to be a very early copy and because the copyist appears free of editorial sophistication or bias, copying dutifully and artlessly. One may speculate, but not assert, that this early manuscript of Midlands derivation was copied locally from a manuscript in the possession of the Sampson family.

The textual variants given following the narrative suggest but do not exhaust patterns of difference among the manuscripts consulted. No choice of readings can be authoritative, and even the selected variants illustrate the difficulties of editorial choice. Egregious misreadings in the 1774 edition—*Babylon* for *Baptism, amuser* for *accuser*—can be readily corrected by consulting the manuscript copies, but choices among copies are more difficult, particularly when a reading from BN 1172 stands alone against readings in the other manuscripts. Does this mean, for example, that an interpolation has been copied and recopied through a succession of manuscripts, or is the explanation that the BN 1172 copyist failed to represent the original text accurately? For the most part, original spelling and capitalization have been retained, but an exact reproduction of these features of BN 1172 would only have reproduced the copyist, not necessarily Elizabeth Ashbridge, whose spelling, punctuation, habits of capitalization, and paragraphing have been reproduced variously in other copies. Quotation marks, for instance, appear in other copies but not in BN 1172. They have been adopted here. Paragraphing has been introduced and punctuation added only when it seemed necessary to clarify meaning. Where idiosyncratic spellings seemed likely to confuse the reader (e.g., *their* for *there*, *two* for *too*), they have been silently altered.

This edition also assembles materials traditionally associated with Elizabeth Ashbridge's own narrative. Aaron's postscript continuation of his wife's story and his elegiac "Lamentation" are also based on BN 1172, but other manuscripts have been consulted to supply the information that, for instance, Elizabeth Ashbridge was left not simply "several score" but £80 in debt following the death of Sullivan. A manuscript of the "Lamentation" held in the Friends Library, London, contains readings unavailable elsewhere, but they appear to be highly poetic elaborations peculiar to this copyist and have not been adopted. The testimonies from Irish Friends regarding Elizabeth Ashbridge's ministry among them and her death in County Carlow were transmitted by and are possibly the work of John Gough (1720–91) and have been transcribed from copies available in the Friends Library, London. Gough was a prominent Irish Friend, an educator, and a historian of the Society, and his name appears at the end of the 1755 memorial testimony to Elizabeth Asbridge from the National Meeting of Ireland. Gough is probably also the "J.G." whose initials follow the Waterford testimony to Elizabeth Ashbridge, which is also available in the London Friends Library collection.

There were numerous nineteenth-century editions of Elizabeth Ashbridge's autobiography, both in Britain and America, including the first American edition by Benjamin and Thomas Kite (Philadelphia, 1807). Two previous editions of the autobiography have appeared in this century. *Quaker Grey*, with an introduction by A. C. Curtis, presents the narrative (based on BN 2432) in a modernized format and divided into chapters.[30] *Remarkable Experiences in the Life of Elizabeth Ashbridge*, edited by Edmund Hatcher, was based on the 1847 edition but also profited from consulting BN 2432, mistakenly assuming it to be "her husband's original copy of her accounts."[31]

30. Guildford, Eng.: Astolat, 1904.
31. Birmingham, Eng.: N.p., 1927.

BIBLIOGRAPHY

Ashbridge, Wellington T. *The Ashbridge Book.* Toronto: Copp Clark, 1912.

Bacon, Margaret Hope. *Mothers of Feminism: The Story of Quaker Women in America.* New York: Harper and Row, 1986.

Bacon, Margaret Hope. *The Quiet Rebels: The Story of the Quakers in America.* New York: Basic Books, 1969.

Battis, Emery. *Saints and Sectaries: Anne Hutchinson and the Antinomian Controversy in the Massachusetts Bay Colony.* Chapel Hill: University of North Carolina Press, 1962.

"Biographical Sketches of Ministers and Elders and Other Concerned Members of the Yearly Meeting of Philadelphia." *The Friend* 31 (September 1857): 220–54.

Bowden, James. *The History of the Society of Friends in America.* Vol. 1, 1850; vol. 2, 1854. Rpt. in 1 vol., New York: Arno, 1972.

Brinton, Howard H. *Friends for 300 Years: The History and Beliefs of the Society of Friends Since George Fox Started the Quaker Movement.* New York: Harper and Brothers, 1952.

Brinton, Howard H. *Quaker Journals: Varieties of Religious Experience Among Friends.* Wallingford, Pa.: Pendleton Hill, 1972.

Dunn, Mary Maples. "Saints and Sisters: Congregational and Quaker Women in the Early Colonial Period." In *Women in American Religion,* edited by Janet Wilson James, 21–46. Philadelphia: University of Pennsylvania Press, 1980.

Dunn, Mary Maples. "Women of Light." In *Women of America: A History,* edited by Carol Berkin and Mary Norton, 114–36. Boston: Houghton Mifflin, 1979.

Edkins, Carol. "Quest for Community: Spiritual Autobiographies of Eighteenth-Century Quaker and Puritan Women in America." *Women's Autobiography: Essays in Criticism,* edited by Estelle C. Jelinek, 39–52. Bloomington: Indiana University Press, 1980.

Fox, George. *The Journal of George Fox.* Edited by John L. Nickalls. London: Religious Society of Friends, 1975.

Fox, George. "The Woman Learning in Silence." In *The Works of George Fox,* 4: 104–10. 8 vols. Philadelphia: Gould, 1831.

Grimes, Mary Cochran. "Saving Grace Among Puritans and Quakers: A Study of 17th and 18th Century Conversion Experiences." *Quaker History* 72 (1983): 3–26.

Hoskens, Jane. *The Life and Spiritual Sufferings of That Faithful Servant of Christ, Jane Hoskens, a Public Preacher Among the People Called Quakers.* Philadelphia: Evitt, 1771.

Lang, Amy Schrager. *Prophetic Woman: Anne Hutchinson and the Problem of Dissent in the*

Literature of New England. Berkeley and Los Angeles: University of California Press, 1987.

Leach, Robert J. *Women Ministers: A Quaker Contribution.* Wallingford, Pa.: Pendle Hill, 1979.

Levenduski, Cristine. "Elizabeth Ashbridge's 'Remarkable Experiences': Creating the Self in a Quaker Personal Narrative." Ph.D. diss., University of Minnesota, 1989.

Marietta, Jack D. *The Reformation of American Quakerism, 1748–1783.* Philadelphia: University of Pennsylvania Press, 1984.

Nussbaum, Felicity. "Eighteenth Century Women's Autobiographical Commonplaces." In *The Private Self: Theory and Practice of Women's Autobiographical Writings,* edited by Shari Benstock, 147–71. Chapel Hill: University of North Carolina Press, 1988.

Nussbaum, Felicity. "Heteroclites: The Gender of Character in the Scandalous Memoirs." In *The New Eighteenth Century: Theory, Politics, English Literature,* edited by Felicity Nussbaum and Laura Brown, 144–67. New York: Methuen, 1987.

Ross, Isabel. *Margaret Fell: Mother of Quakerism.* London: Longman's, 1949.

Salinger, Sharon V. *"To Serve Well and Faithfully": Labor and Indentured Servants in Pennsylvania, 1682–1800.* Cambridge: Cambridge University Press, 1987.

Shea, Daniel B. *Spiritual Autobiography in Early America.* 1968. Rpt. Madison: University of Wisconsin Press, 1988.

Tolles, Frederick B. *Meeting House and Counting House: The Quaker Merchants of Colonial Philadelphia, 1682–1763.* Chapel Hill: University of North Carolina Press, 1948.

Tolles, Frederick B. *Quakers and the Atlantic Culture.* New York: Macmillan, 1960.

Weitzel, Shirley A. *Land O' Goshen: A Tale of Chester County, 1776–1778.* Philadelphia: Rochambeau, 1979.

Woolman, John. *The Journal and Major Essays of John Woolman.* Edited by Phillips P. Moulton. New York: Oxford University Press, 1971.

Wright, Luella M. *The Literary Life of the Early Friends, 1650–1725.* New York: Columbia University Press, 1932.

Some Account of the
Fore Part of the Life of
Elizabeth Ashbridge,

who died in Truth's service at the house of Robert Lecky at
Kilnock in the County of Carlow Ireland; the 16th of 5th mo.
1755. Written by her own Hand many years ago.

My Life being attended with many uncommon Occurences, some of which I
through disobedience brought upon myself, and others I believe were for my
Good, I therefore thought proper to make some remarks on the Dealings of Divine
Goodness to me, and have often had cause with David to say, it was good for me
that I have been afflicted &c.[1] and most earnestly I desire that whosoever reads the
following lines, may take warning and shun the Evils that I have thro' the Deceit-
fulness of Satan been drawn into.

To begin with my beginning. I was born in Middlewich in Cheshire in the year
1713 of Honest Parents, my Father a Doctor of Physick or Surgeon; his name was
Thomas Sampson, my Mother's name was Mary. My Father was a Man that bore
a good Character, but not so Strictly religious as my Mother, who was a pattern of
Virtue to me. I was the only Child of my Father but not of my Mother, she being a
Widow when my Father married her, and had two Children by her former Husband, a Son & a daughter. Soon after my birth, my Father took to the sea &
followed his Profession on board a ship, in many long voyages, till I arrived to the
Age of twelve years, & then left off; so that my Education lay mostly on my
Mother, in which She discharged her duty by endeavoring to instill in me, in my
tender Age, the principles of virtue; for which I have since had Cause to be
thankful to the Lord, & that he blessed me with such a parent, whose good Advice
and Counsel to me has been as Bread cast on the Waters, & may all Parents have
the same Testimony in their Children's breasts; in a word She was a good Example
to all about her, and Beloved by most that Knew her, Tho' not of the same religious
perswasion I am now of. But Alas for me, as soon as the time came that she might

---

1. *it was good . . . afflicted:* "It is good for me that I have been afflicted, that I may learn your
statutes" (Psalm 119:71).

reasonably have expected the benefit of her Labours, & have had Comfort in me, I left her—of which I shall speak in its place.

In my very Infancy, I had an awful regard for religion & a great love for religious people, particularly the Ministers, and sometimes wept with Sorrow, that I was not a boy that I might have been one; believing them all Good Men & so beloved of God. Also I had a great Love for the Poor, remembering I had read that they were blessed of the Lord; this I took to mean such as were poor in this World. I often went to their poor Cottages to see them, and used to think they were better off than me, and if I had any money or any thing else I would give it to them, remembering that those that gave to such, lent to the Lord; for I had when very young earnest desires to be beloved by him, and used to make remarks on those that pretended to religion; and when I heard the Gentlemen swear it made me sorry, for my Mother told me, if I used any Naughty words God would not love me.

As I grew up, I took notice there were several different religious societies, wherefore I often went alone and wept; with desires that I might be directed to the right. Thus my young years were attended with these & such like tender desires tho' I was sometimes guilty of faults incident to Children; and then I always found something in me that made me sorry. From my Infancy till fourteen years of age I was as innocent as most Children, about which time my Sorrows began, and have continued for the most part of my life ever since; by giving way to a foolish passion, in Setting my affections on a young man who Courted me without my Parents' consent; till I consented, and with sorrow of Heart may say, I suffered myself to be carried off in the night, and before my Parents found me, was married, tho' as soon as they missed me, all possible search was made, but all in vain till too late to recover me.

This precipitate action plunged me into a deal of Sorrow. I was soon smote with remorse, for thus leaving my parents, whose right it was to have disposed of me to their contents, or at least to have been consulted in the Affair. I was soon Chastised for my disobedience—Divine Providence let me see my error. In five months I was stripped of the Darling of my Soul, and left a young & disconsolate Widow. I had then no home to fly to. My Husband was poor, had nothing but his Trade, which was a Stocking Weaver, & my Father was so displeased, he would do nothing for me. My Dear Mother had some Compassion & used to keep me Amongst the Neighbours. At last by her Advice I went over to Dublin, to a relation of hers in hopes that Absence would regain my Father's Affection. But he continued Inflexible, & would not send for me again & I durst not return without it.

This relation was one of the People called Quakers; his Conduct was so different from the Manner of my Education (which was in the way of the Church of England) that it proved very disagreeable to me for tho' (as I have said) I had a Religious Education, yet I was allowed to sing & dance, which my Cousin disallow'd of, & I having great Vivacity in my Natural Disposition, could not bear to give way to the Gloomy Sense of Sorrow & Convictions; therefore let it have the wrong effect, so gave up to be more Wild & Airy than ever, for which he often reproved me. But I then thought (as many do now of this Society), 'Twas the Effect of Singularity, & therefore would not bear it, nor be controuled, & having a distant relation in the West of Ireland, left Dublin and went thither; And here I might take my Swing, for what rendered me disagreeable to the former, was quite pleasing to the latter.

Between these two relations I spent Three Years and three Months. While I was in Ireland, I contracted an intimate Acquaintance with a Widow & her Daughter that were Papists, with whom I used to have a deal of discourse about religion, they in defence of their Faith & I of mine. And tho' I was then wild, yet it often made me very thoughtful. The Old Woman would tell me of such mighty miracles done by their Priests, that I began to be shaken, & thought if these things were so they must of a Truth be the Apostles' Successors.

The Old woman perceived it & one day in a rapture said "Oh! if I can under God, be the happy Instrument to convert you to the Holy Catholick Faith, all the sins that ever I committed will be forgiven." In a while it got so far that the priest came to converse with me, & I being young & my Judgment weak, was ready to believe what they said, and wild as I was, it cost me many Tears, with desires that I might be rightly directed; for some time I frequented their place of Worship, but none of my Relations knew what was my motive. At length I concluded never to be led darkly into their Belief, & if their Articles of Faith are good, they'll not be against my Knowing them, so the next time I had an Opportunity with the priest I told him I had some thoughts of becoming one of his flock but did not care to join till I knew all I must agree to; I therefore desired him to let me see their principles. He answered I must first confess my Sins to him: & gave me till the next day to consider them.

I was not much against it, for thought I, "I have done nothing if all the World Knew that any can hurt me for: And if what this Man says be true, it will be for my Good," & when he came again I told him all that I could remember, which for my part I thought bad enough, but he thought me (as he said) the most Innocent Creature that ever made Confession to him. When I had done, He took a book out & read it; all which I was to swear to, if I joined with them; and tho' young made my remarks[2] as he went on, but I shall neither give myself the Trouble of Writing, nor any of reading a deal of the ridiculous stuff it contained; But what made me sick of my new intention (I believe I should have swallowed the rest) was to swear that I believed the Pretender[3] to be the true heir to the Crown of England; & that he was King James' Son and also that whosoever died out of the Pale of that Church was damned.

2. *made my remarks:* Noticed, remarked privately.

3. *the Pretender:* James Edward Stuart, declared rightful successor to the throne of England by his father, the Catholic James II, who was exiled to Ireland and France following the Glorious Revolution of 1689 and replaced by the Protestant monarchs William and Mary of Orange; also known as the Old Pretender.

As to the first, I did not believe it essential to Salvation, whether I believed it or not, and to take an Oath to any such thing would be very unsafe; And the Second struck directly against Charity, which The Apostle preferred before all other Graces,[4] & Besides I had a religious Mother who was not of that opinion. I thought it therefore barbarous in me, to believe she would be damned, Yet concluded to take it into Consideration.—But before I saw him again a Sudden Turn Took hold, which put a final end to it.

My Father still keeping me at such a distance that I thought myself quite shut out of his Affections, I therefore Concluded since my Absence was so Agreeable, he should have it; and getting acquainted with a Gentlewoman that then lately came from Pensilvania (& was going back again) where I had an Uncle, my Mother's Brother, I soon agreed with her for my passage & being ignorant of the Nature of an Indenture[5] soon became bound, tho' in a private manner, (for fear I should be found out) tho' this was repugnant to law.—As soon as this was over, She invited me to go & see the Vessel I was to go in, to which I readily consented, not Knowing what would follow, & when I came on board, I found a Young Woman I afterward understood was of a very good Family and had been deluded away by this creature. I was extremely pleased to think I should have such an agreeable Companion & while we were in discourse, our Kidnapper left us & went on shore, & when I wanted to go, was not permitted.

Here I was kept near three weeks; at the end thereof the Friends of the other young Woman found her out & fetched her on shore; by which means mine found me, & sent the Water Bailif, who took me also on shore. Our Gentlewoman was forced to keep Incog[nito] or she would have been laid fast.[6]

I was Kept close for two weeks, but at last found means to get away, for I was so filled with the thought of coming to America, that I could not give it up, & meeting with the Captain I enquired when they sailed. He told me, I got on board & came in the same ship, & have cause to believe there was a Providential hand in it.

There was Sixty Irish Servants on board (I came now unindentured) & several English Passengers, but not one of them understood the Irish language but myself: I had taken no small pains to learn it. I could understand so much as to discover any thing they discoursed upon, which was of great service to us all. There was also on board the Gentlewoman beforementioned & a Young Man her Husband's

---

4. *Charity, . . . before all other Graces:* "So there abide faith, hope, and charity, these three; but the greatest of these is charity" (1 Corinthians 13:13).

5. *Indenture:* An agreement that, when legally executed, bound an emigrant to a period of service under a master who paid the servant's passage to America. William Penn hoped to foster settlement in Pennsylvania by allowing fifty acres of land for each servant brought to the colony (see Cheesman A. Herrick, *White Servitude in Pennsylvania* [Philadelphia: McVey, 1926], 32–34.) The "gentlewoman" of whom Elizabeth Ashbridge speaks may well have had prostitution rather than settlement in mind for her.

6. *laid fast:* That is, imprisoned.

Brother (Twenty of those Servants belonged to her). While we were on the Coast of Ireland (For the Wind kept us there some weeks) I overheard those Creatures contriving how they should be free when they came to America; to accomplish their design they concluded to rise & kill the Ship's crew & all the English on board, & the abovementioned Young Man was to navigate the Vessel. The same night I discovered their barbarous design privately to the Captain, who let the English know it. The next day they bore for the shore & some small distance off the Cove of Cork lowered sail & dropped Anchor under pretence that the Wind was not fair to stand their Course; so hoisted out the Boat, and invited the Passengers to go on shore to divert themselves, & among the rest the Rebels' Captain; he did, which was all they wanted. As soon as he was on shore the rest left him and came on board. Our Captain immediately ordered to weigh Anchor and hoist Sail, but there were great Outcries for the Young Man on Shore. The Captain told them the Wind freshened up, & that he would not stay for his own Son. So[7] their Treachery was betrayed in good time; & in such a manner that they did not mistrust it, for it was thought most advisable to keep it private, least any of them should do me a mischief; but at Length they found out that I understood Irish, by my Smiling at an Irish Story they were telling, and from that time they Devised many ways to hurt me, & several of them were corrected and Put in Irons for it.

In Nine Weeks from the time I left Ireland we arrived at New York, (viz)[8] on the 15th of the 7 mo 1732 & then those to whom I had been Instrumental under Providence to save Life, proved Treacherous to me: I was a Stranger in a Strange Land.[9] The Captain got an Indenture wrote & Demanded of me to Sign it, withal Threatning a Gaol[10] if I refused; I told him I could find means to Satisfy him for my Passage without becoming bound: they then told me I might take my Choice Either to Sign that, or have that I had signed in Ireland in force against me (by this time I had learned the Character of the afforesaid Woman, that she was a Vile Creature, & feared that if ever I was in her Power she would use me Ill on her Brother's Account). I therefore in a fright Signed that, & tho' there was no Magistrate present, I being Ignorant In such Cases, it Did well enough to Make me a Servant four Years.

In Two Weeks time I was Sold, & Were it Possible to Convey in Characters a sense of the Sufferings of my Servitude, it would make the most strong heart pity the Misfortunes of a young creature as I was, who had a Tender Education; for tho' my Father had no great Estate, yet he Lived well. I had been used to Little but my School, but now it had been better for me if I had been brought up to more hard-

7. The Bevan Naish (Birmingham, England) Library's manuscript BN 1172 begins at this point.

8. *(viz):* Abbreviation for Latin *videlicet,* used as we now use "i.e." or "e.g."

9. *a Stranger in a Strange Land:* Moses so describes himself living among the Egyptians (see Exodus 2:22).

10. *Gaol:* Archaic and British for "jail"; spelled *goal,* however, in several of the manuscript copies.

ship. For a While at first I was Pretty well used, but in a Little time the Scale turned, Occasioned by a Difference that happened between my Master & me, wherein I was Innocent: from that time he set himself against me and was Inhuman. He would not suffer me to have Clothes to be Decent in, having to go barefoot in his Service in the Snowey Weather & the Meanest drudgery, wherein I Suffered the Utmost Hardship that my Body was able to Bear, which, with the afforesaid Troubles, had like to have been my Ruin to all Eternity had not Almighty God in Mercy Interposed.

My Master would seem to be a Very Religious Man, taking the Sacrament (so called),[11] & used to Pray every Night in his family, except when his Prayer Book was Lost, for he never Pray'd without it that I knew of. The Afforesaid Difference was of Such a kind that it made me Sick of his Religion; for tho' I had but little my Self yet I had an Idea what sort of People they should be that were so.—At Length the old Enemy by insinuations made me believe there was no such thing as Religion, & that the Convictions I had felt from my Infancy was no other than the prejudice of Education, which Convictions were at times so Strong that I have gone alone & fallen with my face to the Ground crying for mercy: but now I began to be hardened, and for Some months I do not Remember that I felt any such thing, so was Ready to Conclude that there was no God; that such thoughts were foolish & all but Priest Craft: and though I had a Great Veneration for that set of men in my youth, I now looked on them in another Manner: & what corroborated me in my Atheistical opinion was, my Master's house used to be a place of Great resort of the Clergy, which gave me much opportunity to make my Remarks. Sometimes those that Came out of the Country lodged there & their Evening Diversion used to be Cards & Singing, & a few minutes after, Prayers and Singing Psalms to Almighty God. I used to think, if there be a God he is a pure being, & will not hear the Prayers of Polluted Lips: But he that hath in an abundant manner shewn mercy to me (as will be seen in the sequel) did not Long Suffer me to Doubt in this Matter, but in a moment, when my feet were near the Bottomless Pit, Pluckt me Back.

To one Woman (& no other) I had Discovered the Nature of the Difference which Two years before had happened between my Master & Me; by her means he heard of it, & tho' he knew it was True yet he sent for the Town Whipper to Correct me. I was Called In; he never asked me Whether I had told any such thing but ordered me to strip; at which my heart was ready to burst; for I could as freely have given up my Life as Suffer such Ignominy. I then said if there be a God, be graciously Pleased to Look down on one of the most unhappy Creatures & plead my Cause for thou knows what I have said is the truth; and were it not for a principle

---

11. *the Sacrament (so called):* The sacrament of the Lord's Supper, or Communion. Quakers rejected the sacraments of the Church of England as empty outward forms, as when Elizabeth Ashbridge refers disparagingly to baptism as sprinkling, or to confirmation as merely passing under a bishop's hands. She mistrusts the set prayer of the Church of England's Book of Common Prayer for the same reason.

more noble than he was Capable of I would have told it before his wife. I then fixed my Eyes on the Barbarous man, & in a flood of Tears said: "Sir, if you have no Pity on me, yet for my Father's Sake spare me from this Shame (for before this time he had heard of my Father &C. several ways) & if you think I deserve such punishment, do it your Self." He then took a turn over the Room & bid the Whipper go about his business, and I came off without a blow, which I thought something Remarkable, but now I began to think my Credit was gone (for they said many things of me which I blessed God were not True) & here I suffer so much Cruelty I cannot bear it.

The Enemy Immediately Came in & put me in a way how to be rid of it all & tempted me to End my Miserable Life: I joyn'd with it & for that Purpose went into the garret to hang my Self. Now it was I was convinced there was a God, for as my feet Entered the Place Horrour seized to that degree, I trembled much, and as I stood like one in Amaze, it seemed as tho' I heard a Voice say, "there is a Hell beyond the grave;" at which I was greatly astonished, & now Convinced that there was an almighty Power, to whom I then Prayed, saying, "God be merciful & Enable me to bear what thou in thy Providence shall bring or Suffer to Come upon me for my Disobedience." I then went Down again but Let none know what I had been about. Soon after this I had a Dream, & tho' some make a ridicule of Dreams, yet this seemed a significant one to me & therefore shall mention it. I thought somebody knocked at the Door, by which when I had opened it there stood a Grave woman, holding in her right hand an oil lamp burning, who with a Solid Countenance fixed her Eyes upon me & said—"I am sent to tell thee that If thou'l return to the Lord thy God, who hath Created thee, he will have mercy on thee, & thy Lamp shall not be put out in obscure darkness;" upon which the Light flamed from the Lamp in an extraordinary Manner, & She left me and I awoke.

But alas! I did not give up nor Comply with the heavenly Vision, as I think I may Call it, for after this I had like to have been caught in another Snare, which if I had would Probably have been my Ruin, from which I was also preserved. I was Counted a fine Singer & Dancer, in which I took great Delight, and once falling in with some of the Play house company then at New York, they took a Great fancy to me, as they said, & Perswaded me to become an Actress amongst them, & they would find means to get me from my cruel Servitude, & I should Live Like a Lady—The Proposal took with me & I used no small Pains to Qualify my Self for it in Reading their Play Books, even when I should have Slept, yet was put to the Demur when I came to Consider what my Father would say who had forgiven my Disobedience in marrying and earnestly desiring to see me again had sent for me home, but my proud heart would not Consent to return in so mean a Condition; therefore I chose Bondage rather.

So when I had Served near three years, I bought off the remainder of my Time & then took to my Needle, by which I could maintain my Self handsomely: but, alas, I was not Sufficiently Punished; I had got released from one cruel Servitude

& then not Contented got into another, and this for Life. A few months after, I married a young man that fell in Love with me for my Dancing, a Poor Motive for a man to Choose a Wife, or a Woman a Husband. But for my Part I fell in Love with nothing I saw in him and it seems unaccountable that I who had refused several, both in this Country & Ireland, at Last married a man I had no Value for.

In a few Days after we were Married he took me from [New] York. Being a Schoolmaster he had hired in the Country to keep school; he led me to New England and there settled in a place called Westerly in Rhode Island Government. With regard to Religion he was much like my Self, without any, and when in Drink would use the worst of Oaths. I do not mention this to Expose my husband; but to Shew the Effect it had on me, for I now saw my Self ruined as I thought, being joyned to a man I had no Love for & that was a Pattern of no good to me; then I began to think what a Couple we were, like two joyning hands and going to destruction, & there upon Concluded if I was not forsaken of heaven to alter my Course of Life. But to Set my Affections upon the Divine being & not Love my husband seemed Impossible: therefore I Daily Desired with Tears that my Affections might be in a right manner set upon my husband, and can say in a little time my Love was Sincere to him.

I now resolved to do my Duty to God; & Expecting I must come to the knowledge of it by the Scriptures I took to reading them with a Resolution to follow their Directions, but the more I read the more uneasy I grew, especially about Baptism; for altho' I had reason to believe I had been Sprinkled in my Infancy, because at the age of Thirteen I Passed under the Bishop's hands for Confirmation (as twas Called) yet I could not find any Precedent for that Practice & lighting on that place where it is said, "he that believes & is Baptized" &C.,[12] here I observed Belief went before Baptism, which I was not Capable of when Sprinkled: hence grew much Dissatisfied, & Living in a Neighbourhood that were mostly Seventh day Baptists, I Conversed much with them. At Length thinking it my Real Duty, I was In the Winter time Baptised by one of their Teachers, but Did not joyn Strictly with them, tho' I began to think the Seventh Day was the true Sabbath, & for some time kept it. My husband Did not Oppose me, for he saw I grew more Affectionate to him. I did not Leave off Singing & Dancing so, but that I could divert him when he'd ask me. But I did not find that Satisfaction in what I had done as I Expected.

Soon after this my husband & I concluded to go for England & for that End went to Boston & there found a Ship bound for Liverpool. We agreed for our Passage & Expected to Sail in two Weeks:—but my time was not to go yet, for there Came a Gentleman who hired the Ship to Carry him & his Attendance to Philadelphia & to take no other Passengers; & there being no other Ship near Sailing we for that time gave it out. We stayed Several weeks in Boston, & I still continued Dissat-

---

12. *"he . . . is Baptized":* "He who believes and is baptized shall be saved, but he who does not believe shall be condemned" (Mark 16:16).

isfy'd as to Religion; tho' I had reformed my Conduct so as to be accounted by those that knew me a sober Woman yet was not Content, for Even then I expected to find the Sweets of Such a Change, & though several thought me Religious, I durst not think so my Self, but what to Do to be so was an utter Stranger. I used to Converse with People of all societies as Opportunity offer'd & like many others had got a Pretty Deal of Head Knowledge, & Several Societies thought me of their Opinions severally; But I joyned Strictly with none, resolving never to leave Searching till I had found the truth: this was in the Twenty Second year of my age.

While we were in Boston I one Day went into the Quaker Meeting not Expecting to find what I wanted, but out of Curiosity. At this Meeting there was a Woman friend spoke, at which I was a Little surprised, for tho' I had heard of Women's preaching I had never heard one before. I looked on her with Pity for her Ignorance (as I thought) & Contempt of her Practise, saying to my self, "I am sure you are a fool, for if ever I should turn Quaker, which will never be, I would not be a preacher."—In these and such like thoughts, I sat while She was Speaking; after she had done there Stood up a man, which I could better Bear. He spoke well & I thought raised sound Doctrine from good Joshua's resolution (Viz) "as for me and my house we will serve the Lord,"[13] & C. After he had sat silent a while he went to prayer, which was something so awful & Affecting as drew tears from my Eyes yet a Stranger to the Cause.

Soon after this we Left Boston, & my husband being Given to ramble, which was very Disagreeable to me, but I must submit, we Came to Rhode Island by Water, from thence to the East End of Long Island, where we hired to keep School. This Place was mostly Settled with Presbyterians. I soon got Acquainted with some of the most Religious of them, for tho' I was poor yet was favoured with Reception amongst People of the Best Credit, & had frequent Discourses with them, but the more I was acquainted, the worse I liked their Opinions, so Remained Dissatisfy'd; & the old Enemy of my Happiness knowing that I was Resolved to Abandon him and Seek peace for my Soul, he fresh Assaults me & laid a bait, with which I had like to have been caught. One Day having been Abroad, at my return home I found the People at whose house we had taken a room had left some flax in an apartment thro' which I Passed to my own, at sight of which I was Immediately tempted to steal some to make me some thread. I went to it & took a small Bunch in my hand, at which I was smote with remorse. Being of such a kind that my Very Nature abhored it, I laid it Down, saying, "Lord keep me from such a Vile Action as this"; but the twisting serpent did not Leave me yet, but Assaulted again so strong & prevalent that I took it into my own Room; but when I came there Horror Seized me, & bursting into Tears Cryed, "Oh thou God of Mercy, enable me to resist this Temptation," which he in his Mercy did, and gave me power to say, "get thee behind me Satan, I'll resist till I'll die before I'll yield"; &

13. *"as for me . . . serve the Lord"*: Joshua 24:15.

then I Carryed it back, and returning to my Room was fill'd with thanksgiving to God, and wrapt in such a frame, as I have not words to Express, neither can any guess but those who have resisted Temptations; these have it in their own Experience to taste the sweet Peace that flows to the Soul.

My Husband soon hired further up the Island where we were nearer a Church of England to which I used to go, for tho' I Disliked some of their ways, yet I liked them best; but now a fresh Exercise fell upon me, and of such a Sort as I had never heard of any being in the like, & while under it I thought my self alone.—I was in the Second month sitting by a fire in Company with Several, my Husband also present; there arose a Thunder Gust, & with the Noise that struck my Ear, a voice attended, even as the Sound of a mighty Trumpet, piercing thro' me with these words, "O! Eternity, Eternity, the Endless term of Long Eternity:" at which I was Exceedingly Surprized, sitting speechless as in a trance, and in a moment saw my Self in such a state as made me Despair of ever being in a happy one. I seemed to see a Long Roll wrote in Black Characters, at sight whereof I heard a Voice say to me, "this is thy Sins;" I then saw Sin to be Exceeding Sinful, but this was not all, for Immediately followed another Saying, "and the Blood of Christ is not Sufficient to wash them out; this is shewn thee that thou mays't Confess thy Damnation is just & not in order that they should be forgiven."

All this while I sat Speechless; at Last I got up trembling, & threw my self on a Bed: the Company thought my Indisposition proceeded only from a fright at the Thunder, but Alas, it was of another kind, and from that time for several months I was in the utmost Despair, and if any time I would endeavour to hope or lay hold of any Gracious promise, the old Accuser would Come in, telling me, it was now too Late, I had withstood the day of Mercy till it was over, & that I should add to my Sins by praying for Pardon & provoke Divine Vengeance to make a Monument of Wrath of me. I was like one already in torment; my Sleep Departed from me, I Eat little, I became extremely melancholy, and took no delight in any thing. Had all the world been mine & the Glory of it, I would now have Gladly a given it for one glimpse of hope; My husband was Shock'd, to See me so changed, I that once Could divert him with a Song (in which he greatly delighted), nay after I grew Religious as to the outward, could now Do it no longer. My Singing now was turned into mourning & my Dancing into Lamentations: my Nights and Days were one Continual Scene of Sorrows: I let none know my Desperate Condition— My husband used all means in his power to divert my Melancholy, but in vain, the wound was too Deep to be healed with any thing short of the true Balm of Gilead.[14] I Durst not go much alone for fear of Evil Spirits, but when I did my husband

14. *Balm of Gilead:* Literally, an ointment, as in the rhetorical question of Jeremiah 8:22, "Is there no balm in Gilead?" But by extension the phrase suggests a spiritual annointing, as in Jeremiah 46:11: "Go up to Gilead and take balm, O virgin daughter of Egypt! In vain you have used many medicines; there is no healing for you." In the Christian typological tradition the balm of Gilead suggests the grace of conversion.

would not Suffer it, & if I took the Bible, he would take it from me saying, "how you are altered, you used to be agreeable Company but now I have no Comfort of you." I endeavoured to bear all with Patience, expecting soon to bear more than man could inflict upon me.

At Length I went to the Priest to see if he Could relieve me, but he was a Stranger to my Case: he advised me to take the Sacrament & use some innocent diversions, & lent me a Book of prayers, which he said was fit for my Condition, but all was in Vain. As to the Sacrament, I thought my Self in a State very unfit to receive it worthily, and could not use the Prayers, for I then thought if Ever my Prayers would be acceptable, I should be enabled to pray without form. Diversions were burdensome, for as I said above, my husband used all means tending that way to no Purpose, yet he with some others once perswaded me to go to the Raising of a building (where such Company were Collected) in Expectation of Aleviating my grief, but contrarywise it proved a means of adding to my Sorrow: for in the mean time there came an officer to summon a jury to Enquire concerning the Body of a man that had hanged himself, which as soon as I understood seemed to be attended with a Voice saying, "thou shall be the next Monument of such Wrath, for thou art not worthy to Die a natural Death," and for Two Months was Daily tempted to destroy myself, and some times so strong that I could hardly resist, thro' fear of that sort when I went alone, I used to throw off my apron & garters, & if I had a knife cast it from me Crying, "Lord keep me from taking that Life thou gave, & which thou Would have made happy if I had on my Part joyned with the Offers of Thy Grace, and had regarded the Convictions attending me from my youth: the fault is my own, thou O Lord art clear;" & yet so great was my Agony that I desired Death that I might know the worst of my Torments, of which I had so sharp a foretaste. All this while I Could not shed a Tear; my heart was as hard as a Stone & my Life Miserable, but God that's full of Mercy and Long forbearance, in his own good time delivered my Soul out of this Thraldom.

For one night as I Lay in Bed (my husband by me a Sleep) bemoaning my Miserable Condition, I had strength to Cry, "O, my God, hast thou no mercy left, Look Down, I beseech thee, for Christ's Sake, who has promised that all manner of Sins & blasphemies Shall be forgiven; Lord, if thou will graciously please to Extend this Promise to me an unWorthy Creature trembling before thee; there is nothing thou shalt Command but I will obey."—In an Instant my heart was tendered, & I dissolved in a flow of tears, abhoring my Past Offentes, & admiring the mercy of God, for I now was made to hope in Christ my Redeemer, & Enabled to Look upon him with an Eye of Faith, & saw fulfilled what I believed when the Priest lent me his Book, (Viz.) that if ever my Prayers would be Acceptable I should be Enabled to pray without form & so used form no more.

Nevertheless I thought I ought to join with Some religious Society but met with none I liked in everything; yet the Church of England seeming nearest, I joined with them & took the Sacrament (So called) & can say in truth, I did it with reverence & fear. Being now released from Deep Distress I seemed Like another Creature, and often went alone without fear, & tears abundantly flowed from my Eyes & once as I was abhorring my Self in great Humility of mind, I heard a gracious Voice full of Love, saying, "I will never Leave thee, nor forsake thee, only obey what I shall make known to thee." I then entered into Covenant saying: "My soul Doth Magnify thee the God of mercy, if thou'l Vouchsafe thy Grace the rest of my Days shall be Devoted to thee, & if it be thy Will that I beg my Bread, I'll be content and Submit to thy Providence."

I now began to think of my Relations in Pennsylvania whom I had not yet seen; and having a great Desire that way, Got Leave of my Husband to go & also a Certificate from the Priest on Long Island in order that if I made any stay, I might be receiv'd as a Member wherever I came; Then Setting out, my husband bore me Company to the Blazing Star Ferry, saw me Safe over & then returned. On the way near a place called Maidenhead [New Jersey] I fell from my horse & I was Disabled from Traveling for some time: In the interval I abode at the house of an Honest Like Dutchman, who with his wife were very kind to me, & tho' they had much trouble going to the Doctor and waiting upon me, (for I was Several Days unable to help my self) yet would have nothing for it (which I thought Exceeding kind) but Charged me if ever I came that way again to call and Lodge there.—I mention this because by and by I shall have occasion to remark this Place again.

Hence I came to Trenton [New Jersey] Ferry, where I met with no small Mortification upon hearing that my Relations were Quakers, & what was the worst of all my Aunt a Preacher. I was Sorry to hear it, for I was Exceedingly prejudiced against these People & have often wondered with what face they Could Call them Selves Christians. I Repented my Coming and had a mind to have turned back. At Last I Concluded to go & see them since I was so far on my journey, but Expected little Comfort from my Visit. But see how God brings unforeseen things to Pass, for by my going there I was brought to my Knowledge of his Truth.—I went from Trenton to Philadelphia by Water, thence to my Uncle's on Horseback, where I met with very kind reception; for tho' my Uncle was dead and my Aunt married again, yet both her husband and She received me in a very kind manner.

I had not been there three Hours before I met with a Shock, & my opinion began to alter with respect to these People.—For seeing a Book lying on the Table (& being much for reading) I took it up: My Aunt Observing said, "Cousin that is a Quakers' Book," for Perceiving I was not a Quaker, I suppose she thought I would not like it: I made her no answer but revolving in my mind, "what can these People write about, for I have heard that they Deny the Scriptures & have no other bible but George Fox's Journal, & Deny all the holy Ordinances?" So resolved to read, but had not read two Pages before my very heart burned within me and Tears Issued from my Eyes, which I was Afraid would be seen; therefore with the Book (Saml. Crisp's Two Letters)[15] I walked into the garden, sat Down, and the

15. *Saml. Crisp's Two Letters:* Edmund Hatcher's edition, *Remarkable Experiences in the Life of*

piece being Small, read it through before I went in; but Some Times was forced to Stop to Vent my Tears, my heart as it were uttering these involuntary Expressions; "my God must I (if ever I come to the true knowledge of thy Truth) be of this man's Opinion, who has sought thee as I have done & join with these People that a few hours ago I preferred the Papists before? O thou, the God of my Salvation & of my Life, who hast in an abundant manner manifested thy Long Suffering & tender Mercy, Redeeming me as from the Lowest Hell, a Monument of thy grace: Lord, my soul beseecheth thee to Direct me in the right way & keep me from Error, & then According to thy Covenant, I'll think nothing too near to Part with for thy name's Sake. If these things be so, Oh! happy People thus beloved of God."

After I came a little to my Self again I washed my face least any in the House should perceive I had been weeping. But this night got but Little Sleep, for the old Enemy began to Suggest that I was one of those that wavered & was not Steadfast in the faith, advancing several Texts of Scripture against me & them, as, in the Latter Days there should be those that would deceive the very Elect:[16] & these were they, & that I was in danger of being deluded. Here the Subtile Serpent transformed himself so hiddenly that I verily believed this to be a timely Caution from a good Angel—so resolved to beware of the Deceiver, & for Some weeks Did not touch any of their Books.

The next Day being the first of the week I wanted to have gone to Church, which was Distant about four Miles, but being a Stranger and having nobody to go along with me, was forced to Give it out, & as most of the Family was going to Meeting, I went with them, but with a resolution not to like them, & so it was fully Suffered: for as they sat in silence I looked over the Meeting, thinking with my self, "how like fools these People sit, how much better would it be to stay at home & read the Bible or some good Book, than to come here and go to Sleep." For my Part I was very Sleepy & thought they were no better than my Self. Indeed at Length I fell a sleep, and had like to fallen Down, but this was the last time I ever fell asleep in a Meeting, Tho' often Assaulted with it.[17]

Now I began to be lifted up with Spiritual Pride & thought my Self better than they, but thro' Mercy this did not Last Long, for in a Little time I was brought Low & saw that these were the People to whom I must join.—It may seem strange that I who had Lived so long with one of this Society in Dublin, should yet be so great a Stranger to them. In answer let it be Considered that During the time I was there I never read one of their Books nor went to one Meeting, & besides I had heard such

---

Elizabeth Ashbridge (Birmingham, Eng.: n.p., 1927), reprints these two letters.

16. *those that would deceive the very Elect:* "For false Christs and false prophets will arise, and will show great signs and wonders, so as to lead astray if possible, even the elect" (Matthew 24:24).

17. Compare the experience of Benjamin Franklin on his first entry into Philadelphia: "I sat down among them, and after looking round a while and hearing nothing said, being very drowsy thro' Labour and want of Rest the preceding Night, I fell fast asleep and continu'd so till the Meeting broke up, when one was kind enough to rouse me" (*Autobiography,* ed. J. A. Leo Lemay and P. M. Zall [New York: Norton, 1986], 20–21).

ridiculous stories of them as made me Esteem them the worst of any Society of People; but God that knew the Sincerity of my heart looked with Pity on my Weakness & soon Let me see my Error.

In a few weeks there was an afternoon's Meeting held at my Uncle's to which came that Servant of the Lord Wm. Hammans who was made then Instrumental to the Convincing me of the truth more Perfectly, & helping me over Some great Doubts: tho' I believe no one did ever sit in Greater opposition than I did when he first stood up; but I was soon brought Down for he preached the Gospel with such Power I was forced to give up & Confess it was the truth. As soon as meeting Ended I Endeavoured to get alone, for I was not fit to be seen, I being So broken; yet afterward the Restless adversary assaulted me again, on this wise. In the morning before this meeting, I had been Disputing with my Uncle about Baptism, which was the subject this good Man Dwelt upon, which was handled so Clearly as to answer all my Scruples beyond all objection: yet the Crooked Serpent alleged that the Sermon that I had heard did not proceed from divine Revelation but that my Uncle and Aunt had acquainted the Friend of me; which being Strongly Suggested, I fell to Accusing them with it, of which they both cleared themselves, saying they had not seen him Since my Coming into these Parts until he came into the meeting. I then Concluded he was a messenger sent of God to me, & with fervent Cryes Desired I might be Directed a right and now Laid aside all Prejudice & set my heart open to receive the truth in the Love of it. And the Lord in his own good time revealed to my Soul not only the Beauty there is in truth, & how those should shine that continue faithful to it, but also the Emptiness of all shadows, which in the day were Gloryous, but now he the Son of Glory was come to put an end to them all, & to Establish Everlasting Righteousness in the room thereof, which is a work in the Soul. He likewise let me see that all I had gone through was to prepare me for this Day & that the time was near that he would require me to go forth & declare to others what he the God of Mercy had done for my Soul; at which I was Surprized & begged to be Excused for fear I should bring dishonour to the truth, and cause his Holy name to be Evil spoken of.

All the while, I never Let any know the Condition I was in, nor did I appear like a Friend, & fear'd a Discovery. I now began to think of returning to my husband but found a restraint to stay where I was. I then Hired to keep School & hearing of a place for him, wrote desiring him to come to me, but Let him know nothing how it was with me. I loved to go to meetings, but did not like to be seen to go on week days, & therefore to Shun it used to go from my school through the Woods, but notwithstanding all my care the Neighbours that were not friends began to revile me, calling me Quaker, saying they supposed I intended to be a fool and turn Preacher; I then receiv'd the same censure that I (a little above a year before) had Passed on one of the handmaids of the Lord at Boston, & so weak was I, alas! I could not bear the reproach, & in order to Change their Opinions got into greater Excess in Apparel than I had freedom to Wear for some time before I came Acquainted with Friends.

In this Condition I continued till my Husband came, & then began the Tryal of
my Faith. Before he reached me he heard I was turned Quaker, at which he stampt,
saying, "I'd rather heard She had been dead as well as I Love her, for if so, all my
comfort is gone." He then came to me & had not seen me before for four Months. I
got up & met him saying, "My Dear, I am glad to see thee," at which he flew in a
Passion of anger & said, "the Divel thee thee, don't thee me."[18] I used all the mild
means I could to pacify him, & at Length got him fit to go & Speak to my Relations, but he was Alarmed, and as soon as we got alone said, "so I see your Quaker
relations have made you one." I told him they had not, which was true, nor had I
ever told him how it was with me: But he would have it that I was one, & therefore
would not let me stay among them; & having found a place to his mind, hired and
came Directly back to fetch me hence, & in one afternoon walked near thirty Miles
to keep me from Meeting, the next Day being first Day; & on the Morrow took me
to the Afforesaid Place & hired Lodgings at a churchman's house; who was one of
the Wardens, & a bitter Enemy to Friends & used to Do all he could to irritate my
Husband against them, & would tell me abundance of Ridiculous Stuff; but my
Judgement was too Clearly convinced to believe it.

I still did not appear like a Friend, but they all believed I was one. When my
Husband and he Used to be making their Diversion & reviling, I used to sit in
Silence, but now and then an involuntary Sigh would break from me: at which he
would tell my husband: "there, did not I tell you that your wife was a Quaker; &
She will be a preacher." Upon which My Husband once in a Great rage came up to
me, & Shaking his hand over me, said, "you had better be hanged in that Day." I
then, Peter like, in a panick denied my being a Quaker, at which great horror
seized upon me, which Continued near three Months: so that I again feared that
by Denying the Lord that Bought me, the heavens were Shut against me; for great
Darkness Surrounded, & I was again plunged into Despair. I used to Walk much
alone in the Wood, where no Eye saw nor Ear heard, & there Lament my miserable
Condition, & have often gone from Morning till Night and have not broke my
Fast.

Thus I was brought so Low that my Life was a burden to me; the Devil seem'd
to Vaunt that tho' the Sins of my youth were forgiven, yet now he was sure of Me,
for that I had Committed the unpardonable Sin & Hell inevitable would be my
portion, & my Torment would be greater than if I had hanged my Self at first. In
this Doleful State I had none to bewail my Doleful Condition; & Even in the Night
when I Could not Sleep under the painful Distress of mind, if my husband perceived me weeping he would revile me for it. At Length when he and his Friends
thought themselves too weak to over Set me (tho' I feared it was all ready done) he

18. *"the Divel . . . don't thee me"*: The Quaker use of *thee* and *thou*, though it now sounds formal,
was in this period more familiar, representing the singular rather than the plural "you" equivalent,
for example, to the French *tu*. The leveling of all such addresses to the personal form was the
Quakers' grammatical recognition of the "something of God" in all persons.

went to the Priest at Chester [Pennsylvania] to Advise what to Do with me. This man knew I was a member of the Church, for I had Shewn him my Certificate: his advice was to take me out of Pennsylvania, and find some place where there was no Quakers; and then it would wear off. To this my Husband Agreed saying he did not Care where he went, if he Could but restore me to that Livelyness of Temper I was naturally of, & to that Church of which I was a member. I on my Part had no Spirit to oppose the Proposal, neither much cared where I was, For I seemed to have nothing to hope for, but Dayly Expected to be made a Spectacle of Divine Wrath, & was Possessed with a Thought that it would be by Thunder ere long.

The time of Removal came, & I must go. I was not Suffered to go to bid my Relations farewell; my husband was Poor & kept no horse, so I must travel on foot; we came to Wilmington [Delaware] (fifteen Miles) thence to Philadelphia by Water; here he took me to a Tavern where I soon became the Spectacle & discourse of the Company. My Husband told them, "my wife is a Quaker," & that he Designed if Possible to find out some Place where there was none. "O," thought I, "I was once in a Condition deserving that name, but now it is over with me. O! that I might from a true hope once more have an Opportunity to Confess to the truth;" tho' I was Sure of Suffering all manner of Crueltys, I would not Regard it.

These were my Concerns while he was Entertaining the Company with my Story, in which he told them that I had been a good Dancer, but now he Could get me neither to Dance nor Sing, upon which one of the Company stands up saying, "I'll go fetch my Fiddle, & we'll have a Dance," at which my husband was much pleased. The fiddle came, the sight of which put me in a sad Condition for fear if I Refused my husband would be in a great Passion: however I took up this resolution, not to Comply whatever be the Consequence. He comes to me, takes me by the hand saying, "come my Dear, shake off that Gloom, & let's have a civil Dance; you would now and then when you was a good Churchwoman, & that's better than a Stiff Quaker." I trembling desired to be Excused; but he Insisted on it, and knowing his Temper to be exceeding Cholerick, durst not say much, yet did not Consent. He then pluck'd me round the Room till Tears affected my Eyes, at Sight whereof the Musician Stopt and said, "I'll play no more, Let your wife alone," of which I was Glad.

There was also a man in Company who came from Freehold in East Jersey: he said, "I see your Wife is a Quaker, but if you will take my advice you need not go so far (for my husband's design was for Staten Island); come & live amongst us, we'll soon cure her of her Quakerism, for we want a School Master & Mistress Too" (I followed the Same Business); to which he agreed, & a happy turn it was for me, as will be seen by and by: and the Wonderfull turn of Providence, who had not yet Abandoned me, but raised a glimmering hope, affording the Answer of peace in refusing to Dance, for which I was more rejoyced than to be made Mistress of much Riches; & in floods of Tears said, "Lord, I dread to ask and yet without thy gracious Pardon I'm Miserable; I therefore fall Down before thy Throne, imploring Mercy at thine hand. O Lord once more I beseech thee, try my Obedience, & then what soever thou Commands, I will Obey, & not fear to Confess thee before men."

Thus was my Soul Engaged before God in Sincerity & he in tender Mercy heard my cries, & in me has Shewn that he Delights not in the Death of a Sinner, for he again set my mind at Liberty to praise him & I longed for an Opportunity to Confess to his Truth, which he shewed me should come, but in what manner I did not see, but believed the word that I had heard, which in a little time was fulfilled to me. — My Husband as afforesaid agreed to go to Freehold, & in our way thither we came to Maidenhead, where I went to see the kind Dutchman before mentioned, who made us welcome & Invited us to stay a day or Two.

While we were here, there was held a great Meeting of the Presbyterians, not only for Worship but Business also: for one of their preachers being Charged with Drunkenness, was this day to have his Trial before a great number of their Priests, &c. We went to it, of which I was afterwards glad. Here I perceived great Divisions among the People about who Should be their Shepherd: I greatly Pitied their Condition, for I now saw beyond the Men made Ministers, & What they Preached for: and which those at this Meeting might have done had not the prejudice of Education, which is very prevalent, blinded their Eyes. Some Insisted to have the old Offender restored, some to have a young man they had upon trial some weeks, a third Party was for sending for one from New England. At length stood up one & Directing himself to the Chief Speaker said "Sir, when we have been at the Expence (which will be no Small Matter) of fetching this Gentleman from New England, may be he'll not stay with us." *Answer,* "don't you know how to make him stay? *Reply,* "no Sir." "I'll tell you then," said he (to which I gave good attention), "give him a good Salary & I'll Engage he'll Stay." "O" thought I, "these Mercenary creatures: they are all Actuated by one & the same thing, even the Love of Money, & not the regard of Souls." This (Called Reverend) Gentleman, whom these People almost adored, to my knowledge had left his flock on Long Island & moved to Philadelphia where he could get more money. I my self have heard some of them on the Island say that they almost Impoverished themselves to keep him, but not being able to Equal Philadelphia's Invitation he left them without a Shepherd. This man therefore, knowing their Ministry all proceeded from one Cause, might be purchased with the Same thing; surely these and Such like are the Shepherd that regards the fleece more than the flock, in whose mouths are Lies; saying the Lord had sent them, & that they were Christ's Ambassadors, whose Command to those he sent was, "Freely ye have receiv'd, freely give; & Blessed be his holy Name;"[19] so they do to this day.

I durst not say any Thing to my Husband of the Remarks I had made, but laid them up in my heart, & they Served to Strengthen me in my Resolution. Hence we

19. *"Freely ye have received . . . his holy Name":* Matthew 10:8.

set forward to Freehold, & Coming through Stony Brook [New Jersey] my Husband turned towards me tauntingly & Said, "Here's one of Satan's Synagogues, don't you want to be in it? O I hope to See you Cured of this New Religion." I made no answer but went on, and in a little time, we came to a large run of Water over which was no Bridge, & being Strangers knew no way to escape it, but thro' we must go: he Carried over our Clothes, which we had in Bundles. I took off my Shoes and waded over in my Stockings, which Served some what to prevent the Chill of the Water, being Very Cold & a fall of Snow in the 12 Mo.[20] My heart was Concerned in Prayer that the Lord would Sanctify all my Afflictions to me & give me Patience to bear whatsoever should be suffered to come upon me. We Walked the most part of a mile before we came to the first house, which was a sort of a Tavern. My husband Called for Some Spiritous Liquors, but I got some weakened Cider Mull'd,[21] which when I had Drank of (the Cold being struck to my heart) made me Extremely sick, in so much that when we were a Little past the house I expected I should have Fainted, & not being able to stand, fell Down under a Fence. My husband Observing, tauntingly said, "What's the Matter now; what, are you Drunk; where is your Religion now?" He knew better & at that time I believe he Pitied me, yet was Suffered grievously to Afflict me. In a Little time I grew Better, & going on We came to another Tavern, where we Lodged: the next Day I was Indifferent well, so proceeded, and as we Journeyed a young man Driving an Empty Cart overtook us. I desired my husband to ask the young man to Let us Ride; he did, twas readily granted.

I now thought my Self well off, & took it as a great favour, for my Proud heart was humbled, & I did not regard the Looks of it, tho' the time had been that I would not have been seen in one; this Cart belonged to a man at Shrewsbury [New Jersey] & was to go thro' the place we Designed for, so we rode on (but soon had the Care of the team to our Selves from a failure in the Driver) to the place where I was Intended to be made a prey of; but see how unforeseen things are brought to Pass, by a Providential hand. Tis said and answered, "shall we do Evil that good may Come?" God forbid, yet hence good came to me. Here my husband would have had me Stay while we went to see the Team Safe at home: I Told him, no, since he had led me thro' the Country like a Vagabond, I would not stay behind him, so went on, & Lodged that Night at the man's house who owned the Team. Next morning in our Return to Freehold, we met a man riding on full Speed, who Stopping said to my Husband, "Sir, are you a School Master?" *Answer,* "Yes." "I came to tell you," replied the Stranger, "of Two new School Houses, & want a Master in Each, & are two miles apart." How this Stranger came to hear of us, who

20. *in the 12 Mo.:* Quakers numbered the days of the week, beginning with Sunday, as well as the months of the year, in order to avoid giving even perfunctory honor to the pagan deities. After the Gregorian calendar reform of 1752, January rather than March became first month. Writing before that date, Elizabeth Ashbridge would have designated February as twelfth month.

21. *Cider Mull'd:* Mulled cider is heated, sweetened, and often spiced with cinnamon or cloves.

Came but the night before, I never knew, but I was glad he was not one Called a Quaker, Least my husband might have thought it had been a Plot; and then turning to my husband I said, "my Dear, look on me with Pity; if thou has any Affections left for me, which I hope thou hast, for I am not Conscious of having Done anything to Alienate them; here is (continued I) an Opportunity to Settle us both, for I am willing to do all in my Power towards getting an Honest Livelihood."

My Expressions took place, & after a Little Pause he consented, took the young man's Directions, & made towards the place, & in our way came to the house of a Worthy Friend, Whose wife was a Preacher, tho' we did not know it. I was Surprized to see the People so kind to us that were Strangers; we had not been long in the house till we were Invited to Lodge there that night, being the Last in the Week.—I said nothing but waited to hear my Master Speak; he soon Consented saying,"My wife has had a Tedious Travel & I pity her"; at which kind Expression I was Affected, for they Were now very Seldom Used to me. The friends' kindness could not proceed from my appearing in the Garb of a Quaker, for I had not yet altered my dress: The Woman of the house, after we had Concluded to Stay, fixed her Eyes upon me & Said, "I believe thou hast met with a deal of Trouble," to which I made but Little Answer. My husband, Observing they were of that sort of people he had so much Endeavoured to shun, would give us no Opportunity for any discourse that night, but the next morning I let the friend know a Little how it was with me. Meeting time came, to which I longed to go, but durst not ask my husband leave for fear of Disturbing him, till we were Settled, & then thought I, "if ever I am favoured to be in this Place, come Life or Death, I'll fight through, for my Salvation is at Stake." The Friend getting ready for Meeting, asked my husband if he would go, saying they knew who were to be his Employers, & if they were at Meeting would Speak to them. He then consented to go; then said the Woman Friend, "& wilt thou Let thy Wife go?," which he denied, making Several Objections, all which She answered so prudently that he Could not be angry, & at Last Consented; & with Joy I went, for I had not been at one for near four Months, & an Heavenly Meeting This was: I now renewed my Covenant & Saw the Word of the Lord made Good, that I should have another Opportunity to Confess his Name, for which my Spirit did rejoice in the God of my Salvation, who had brought Strange things to Pass: May I ever be preserved in Humility, never forgetting his tender Mercies to me.

Here According to my Desire we Settled; my husband got one School & I the Other, & took a Room at a Friend's house a Mile from Each School and Eight Miles from the Meeting House:—before next first day we were got to our new Settlement: & now Concluded to Let my husband to see I was determined to joyn with friends. When first day Came I directed my Self to him in this manner, "My Dear, art thou willing to let me go to a Meeting?," at which he flew into a rage, saying, "No you shan't." I then Drew up my resolution & told him as a Dutyfull Wife ought, So I was ready to obey all his Lawfull Commands, but where they

Imposed upon my Conscience, I no longer Durst: For I had already done it too Long, & wronged my Self by it, & tho' he was near & I loved him as a Wife ought, yet God was nearer than all the World to me, & had made me sensible this was the way I ought to go, the which I Assured him was no Small Cross to my own will, yet had Given up My heart, & hoped that he that Called for it would Enable me the residue of my Life to keep it steadyly devoted to him, whatever I Suffered for it, adding I hoped not to make him any the worse Wife for it. But all I could Say was in vain; he was Inflexible & Would not Consent.

I had now put my hand to the Plough, & resolved not to Look back, so went without Leave; but Expected to be immediately followed & forced back, but he did not: I went to one of the neighbours & got a Girl to Show me the way, then went on rejoicing & Praising God in my heart, who had thus far given me Power & another Opportunity to Confess to his Truth. Thus for some time I had to go Eight Miles on foot to Meetings, which I never thought hard; My Husband soon bought a Horse, but would not Let me ride him, neither when my Shoes were worn out would he Let me have a new Pair, thinking by that means to keep me from going to meetings, but this did not hinder me, for I have taken Strings & tyed round to keep them on.

He finding no hard Usage could alter my resolution, neither threatening to beat me, nor doing it, for he several times Struck me with sore Blows, which I Endeavoured to bear with Patience, believing the time would Come when he would see I was in the right (which he Accordingly Did), he once came up to me & took out his pen knife saying, "if you offer to go to Meeting tomorrow, with this knife I'll cripple you, for you shall not be a Quaker." I made him no Answer, but when Morning came, set out as Usual & he was not Suffered to hurt me. In Despair of recovering me himself, he now flew to the Priest for help and told him I had been a very Religious Woman in the way of the Church of England, was a member of it, & had a good Certificate from Long Island, but now was bewitched and turn'd Quaker, which almost broke his heart. He therefore Desired as he was one who had the Care of souls, he would Come and pay me a Visit and use his Endeavours to reclaim me & hoped by the Blessing of God it would be done. The Priest Consented to Come, the time was Set, which was to be that Day two Weeks, for he said he could not come Sooner. My Husband Came home extremely Pleased, & told me of it, at which I smiled Saying, "I hope to be Enabled to give him a reason for the hope that is in me," at the same time believing the Priest would never Trouble me (nor ever did).

Before his Appointed time came it was required of me in a more Publick manner to Confess to the world what I was and to give up in Prayer in a Meeting, the sight of which & the power that attended it made me Tremble, & I could not hold my Self still. I now again desired Death & would have freely given up my Natural Life a Ransom; & what made it harder to me I was not yet taken under the care of Friends, & what kept me from requesting it was for fear I might be overcome &

bring a Scandal on the Society. I begged to be Excused till I was joyned to Friends & then I would give up freely, to which I receiv'd this Answer, as tho' I had heard a Distinct Voice: "I am a Covenant keeping God, and the word that I spoke to thee when I found thee In Distress, even that I would never leave thee nor forsake thee If thou would be obedient to what I should make known to thee, I will Assuredly make good: but if thou refuse, my Spirit shall not always strive; fear not, I will make way for thee through all thy difficulties, which shall be many for my name's Sake, but be thou faithfull & I will give thee a Crown of Life." I being then Sure it was God that Spoke said, "thy will O God, be done, I am in thy hand; do with me according to thy Word," & gave up. But after it was over the Enemy came in like a flood, telling me I had done what I ought not, & Should now bring Dishonour to this People. This gave me a Little Shock, but it did not at this time Last Long.

This Day as Usual I had gone on foot. My Husband (as he afterwards told me) lying on the Bed at home, these Words ran thro' him, "Lord where shall I fly to shun thee &C.,"[22] upon which he arose and seeing it Rain got his horse and Came to fetch me; and Coming just as the Meeting broke up, I got on horseback as quick as possible, least he Should hear what had happened. Nevertheless he heard of it, and as soon as we were got into the woods he began, saying, "What do you mean thus to make my Life unhappy? What, could you not be a Quaker without turning fool after this manner?" I Answered in Tears saying, "my Dear, look on me with Pity, if thou hast any. Canst thou think, that I in the Bloom of my Days, would bear all that thou knowest of & a great deal more that thou knowest not of if I did not believe it to be my Duty?" This took hold of him, & taking my hand he said, "Well, I'll E'en give you up, for I see it don't avail to Strive. If it be of God I can't over throw it, & if it be of your self it will soon fall." I saw tears stand in his Eyes, at which my heart was overcome with Joy, and I would not have Changed Conditions with a Queen.

I already began to reap the fruits of my Obedience, but my Tryal Ended not here, the time being up that the Priest was to come; but no Priest Appeared. My Husband went to fetch him, but he would not come, saying he was busy; which so Displeased my husband, that he'd never go to hear him more, & for Some time went to no place of Worship.—Now the Unwearied adversary found out another Scheme, and with it wrought so Strong that I thought all I had gone through but a little to this: It came upon me in such an unexpected manner, in hearing a Woman relate a book she had read in which it was Asserted that Christ was not the son of God. As soon as She had Spoke these words, if a man had spoke I could not have more distinctly heard these words, "no more he is, it's all a fancy & the Contrivance of men," & an horrour of Great Darkness fell upon me, which Continued for three weeks.

The Exercise I was under I am not Able to Express, neither durst I let any know

22. ". . . to shun thee . . .": Psalms 139:7.

how it was with me. I again sought Desolate Places where I might make my moan, & have Lain whole nights, & don't know that my Eyes were Shut to Sleep. I again thought my self alone, but would not let go my Faith in him, often saying in my heart, "I'll believe till I Die," & kept a hope that he that had Delivered me out of the Paw of the Bear & out of the jaws of the Devouring Lion, would in his own time Deliver me out of his temptation also; which he in Mercy Did, and let me see that this was for my good, in order to Prepare me for future Service which he had for me to Do & that it was Necessary his Ministers should be dipt into all States, that thereby they might be able to Speak to all Conditions, for which my Soul was thankfull to him, the God of Mercies, who had at Several times redeemed me from great distress, & I found the truth of his Words, that all things should work together for good to those that Loved & feared him, which I did with my whole heart & hope ever shall while I have a being. This happened just after my first appearance, & Friends had not been to talk with me, nor did they know well what to do till I had appeared again, which was not for some time, when the Monthly Meeting appointed four Friends to give me a Visit, which I was Glad of; and gave them Such Satisfaction, that they left me well Satisfy'd. I then joyned with Friends.

My Husband still went to no place of Worship. One day he said, "I'd go to Meeting, only I am afraid I shall hear you Clack, which I cannot bear." I used no persuasions, yet when Meeting time Came, he got the horse, took me behind him & went to Meeting: but for several months if he saw me offer to rise, he would go out, till once I got up before he was aware and then (as he afterwards said) he was ashamed to go, & from that time never did, nor hindered me from going to Meetings. And tho' he (poor man) did not take up the Cross, yet his judgement was Convinced: & sometimes in a flood of tears would say, "My Dear, I have seen the Beauty there is in the Truth, & that thou art in the Right, and I Pray God Preserve thee in it. But as for me the Cross is too heavy, I cannot Bear it." I told him, I hoped he that had given me strength Would also favour him: "O!" said he, "I can't bear the Reproach thou Doest, to be Called turncoat & to become a Laughing Stock to the World; but I'll no Longer hinder thee," which I looked on as a great favour, that my way was thus far made easy, and a little hope remained that my Prayers would be heard on his account.

In this Place he had got linked in with some, that he was afraid would make game of him, which Indeed they already Did, asking him when he Designed to Commence Preacher, for that they saw he Intended to turn Quaker, & seemed to Love his Wife better since she did than before (we were now got to a little house by our Selves which tho' Mean, & little to put in it, our Bed no better than Chaff, yet I was truly Content & did not Envy the Rich their Riches; the only Desire I had now was my own preservation, & to be Bless'd with the Reformation of my husband). These men used to Come to our house & there Provoke my husband to Sit up and Drink, some times till near day, while I have been sorrowing in a Stable. As I once sat in this Condition I heard my husband say to his Company, "I can't bear any Longer to Afflict my Poor Wife in this manner, for whatever you may think of her,

I do believe she is a good Woman," upon which he came to me and said, "Come in, my Dear; God has Given thee a Deal of Patience. I'll put an End to this Practice;" and so he did, for this was the Last time they sat up at Night.

My Husband now thought that if he was in any Place where it was not known that he'd been so bitter against Friends, he Could do better than here. But I was much against his Moving; fearing it would tend to his hurt, having been for some months much Altered for the Better, & would often in a broken and Affectionate Manner condemn his bad Usage to me: I told him I hoped it had been for my Good, even to the Better Establishing me in the Truth, & therefore would not have him to be Afflicted about it, & According to the Measure of Grace received did what I could both by Example and advice for his good: & my Advice was for him to fight thro' here, fearing he would Grow Weaker and the Enemy Gain advantage over him, if he thus fled: but All I could say did not prevail against his Moving; & hearing of a place at Bordentown [New Jersey] went there, but that did not suit; he then Moved to Mount Holly [New Jersey] & there we Settled. He got a good School & So Did I.

Here we might have Done very well; we soon got our house Prettily furnished for Poor folks; I now began to think I wanted but one thing to complete my Happiness, Viz. the Reformation of my husband, which Alas! I had too much reason to Doubt; for it fell out according to my Fears, & he grew worse here, & took much to Drinking, so that it Seem'd as if my Life was to be a Continual scene of Sorrows & most Earnestly I Pray'd to Almighty God to Endue me with Patience to bear my Afflictions & submit to his Providence, which I can say in Truth I did without murmuring or ever uttering an unsavoury expression to the Best of my Knowledge; except once, my husband Coming home a little in drink (in which frame he was very fractious) & finding me at Work by a Candle, came to me, put it out & fetching me a box on the Ear said, "you don't Earn your light;" on which unkind Usage (for he had not struck me for Two Years so it went hard with me) I utter'd these Rash Expressions, "thou art a Vile Man," & was a little angry, but soon recovered & was Sorry for it; he struck me again, which I received without so much as a word in return, & that likewise Displeased him: so he went on in a Distracted like manner uttering Several Expressions that bespoke Despair, as that he now believed that he was predestinated to damnation, & he did not care how soon God would Strike him Dead, & the like. I durst say but Little; at Length in the Bitterness of my Soul, I Broke out in these Words, "Lord look Down on mine Afflictions and deliver me by some means or Other." I was answered, I Should Soon be, & so I was, but in such a manner, as I Verily thought It would have killed me. —In a little time he went to Burlington where he got in Drink, & Enlisted him Self to go a Common soldier to Cuba anno 1740.

I had drank many bitter Cups—but this Seemed to Exceed them all for indeed my very Senses Seemed Shaken; I now a Thousand times blamed my Self for making Such an unadvised request, fearing I had Displeased God in it, & tho' he had Granted it, it was in Displeasure, & Suffered to be in this manner to Punish me; Tho' I can truly say I never Desired his Death, no more than my own, nay not so much. I have since had cause to believe his mind was benefitted by the Undertaking, (which hope makes up for all I have Suffered from him) being Informed he did in the army what he Could not Do at home (Viz) Suffered for the Testimony of Truth. When they Came to prepare for an Engagement, he refused to fight; for which he was whipt and brought before the General, who asked him why he Enlisted if he would not fight; "I did it," said he, "in a drunken frolick, when the Divel had the Better of me, but my judgment is convinced that I ought not, neither will I whatever I Suffer; I have but one Life, & you may take that if you Please, but I'll never take up Arms."—They used him with much Cruelty to make him yield but Could not, by means whereof he was So Disabled that the General sent him to the Hospital at Chelsea,[23] where in Nine Months time he Died & I hope made a Good End, for which I prayed both night & Day, till I heard of his Death.

Thus I thought it my duty to say what I could in his Favour, as I have been obliged to say so much of his hard usage to me, all which I hope Did me good, & altho' he was so bad, yet had Several Good Properties, & I never thought him the Worst of Men. He was one I Lov'd & had he let Religion have its Perfect work, I should have thought my Self Happy in the Lowest State of Life; & I've Cause to bless God, who Enabled me in the Station of a Wife to Do my Duty & now a Widow to Submit to his Will, always believing everything he doeth to be right. May he in all Stations of Life so Preserve me by the arm of Divine Power, that I may never forget his tender mercies to me, the Rememberance whereof doth often Bow my Soul, in Humility before his Throne, saying, "Lord, what was I; that thou should have reveal'd to me the Knowledge of thy Truth, & do so much for me, who Deserved thy Displeasure rather, But in me hast thou shewn thy Long Suffering & tender Mercy; may thou O God be Glorifyed and I abased for it is thy own Works that praise thee, and of a Truth to the humble Soul thou Makest every bitter thing Sweet.—The End.—

THUS FAR WAS HER OWN WRITING THE OTHER SIDE WROTE BY HER HUSBAND & SENT WITH HERS —

Here Ends what was perfected by her Pen before she left home which was the 11th 5th mo 1753, tho' she had made some beginning & Several times expressed to me a

23. *the Hospital at Chelsea:* The Royal Hospital and military pensioners' hostel in Chelsea, now just south of Buckingham Palace, was founded by Charles II and completed in 1692 in the reign of William and Mary.

desire to commemorate the further gracious Dealings of Divine Providence with her & Leave some hints of her Experience for the Service of Such as should think worth while to Read what She Wrote; but a Concern for Visiting the Churches abroad Prevailing so weightily on her mind took the place of all Other Concerns.

Her Husband had been gone some two or three Years before she had a Certain Account of his Death; he left her near £80 in debt, for which by Law she was not Answerable, because without Effects; Yet as there were many Creditors who Complained, saying they would not have trusted him if it had not been for his Wife's Sake—she therefore (that truth might not Suffer) engaged to pay them all as fast as she Could; & as soon as Ability was Afforded settled to School keeping, whereby with her Needle she maintained her Self handsomely & by Degress paid off near all the said Debts in the time of her Widowhood, in which time she also traveled considerably in the Service of Truth.

In the 9 mo 1746 we were married at Burlington (West Jersey) in Indeared Affections, & the sense of truth greatly Prevailing at the time, which Blessing, thro' Mercy continuing, made our Company mutual, dear & agreeable, even to a wish, yet we must part.—Sufficiently Convinced that her Lord & Master called for her Service abroad, my Heart was Prepared and made willing to resign a Darling and worthy Object indeed of my Love & delight, & tho' it hath pleased the Lord (who is above all Worthy) to remove her without Indulging my Longing Desires of once more rejoycing with her in time, yet being fully satisfy'd that she is taken from the Troubles thereof to a Happy Eternity: I feel a good degree of Comfortable Composure & Resignation to the Divine Will; believing as she did that whatsoever He doth is right; never having once repented my giving her up to the Service of truth, in which she Died as Afforesaid.—

Aaron Ashbridge

A LAMENTATION ON THE DEATH OF ELIZABETH ASHBRIDGE.

The Dolour of my bleeding heart no Tongue nor Pen can declare; my hope, which alas, I thought well Grounded, being raised very high in Expectation of once more in time rejoicing with her my Dearly beloved in the fear of the Lord as we have often done with Inexpressable pleasure: the Strongest sacred Ties as well as the most tender Natural Affection, endearing, is even now all cut off quick and Vanished.—O! Lovely Creature; possessed of a more lovely mind; adorn'd with Grace and truth; exalted on the wings of ever Lasting Love, thou art fled to the Regions of Eternal Peace & rest: there always to Enjoy the full fruition of that divine Soul Melting pleasure which was thy Chief Concern to seek for thy Self and others Whilst on Earth.

O! that it had been my happy Lot to have gone with thee out of Time into Eternity, all this world if Ten times more worth & at my Command would I Gladly Give to be where thou art; even in perfect Peace, where no torments toucheth; I lament my loss & the Churches Loss of thee O annointed of the Lord & Noble Warrior—thou gave up thy Life in a glorious Cause. I bewail my Lonely Condition. I mourn as a Dove without his mate. I sorrow yet with hope that my Soul may also see an End of troubles, which I don't Expect in this World, having Nothing in it Left for which I even desire to live; therefore O Lord! do thou prepare & Let me go hence out of the Way of Temptations, which sorely beset: & yet thy Will be Done—Amen.

AARON ASHBRIDGE

Written next morning after the grievous account Came being the 12th of 8th mo 1755. [And sent to Susy Hatton a private Letter.]²⁴

The following was sent to me from Ireland signed by the clerk of the national meeting.   AA

SOME   ACCOUNT   OF   THE   LATTER   END OF   ELIZABETH   ASHBRIDGE,   WIFE   OF AARON   ASHBRIDGE   OF   GOSHEN   IN CHESTER   COUNTY,   PENNSYLVANIA.

In the year 1753, apprehending it required of her to Visit the Meeting of Friends in England and Ireland, she left her outward habitation with the consent of her Husband, and the Unity and Approbation of Friends (as appears by her Certificate) and performed a religious visit to many Meetings in this nation to the general satisfaction of friends. Wherein she endured so much bodily hardship in Traveling, and underwent so much Spiritual exercise in mind, that she fell dangerously ill at the city of Cork; and to those two causes she always imputed her disease. After recovering so much of her strength as to be able to proceed on her journey, she left Cork and came to Waterford, to the house of our friend John Hutchinson, where she remained very much Indisposed for the most part of Fourteen Weeks. And in

24.   The bracketed reference to Susy Hatton appears in the Boston Public Library copy. In the 1774 edition the same information is given with the title of the "Lamentation," and the name is spelled Susannah Hutton. The name appears as Susannah Hatton in Robson MS. 37 of the Friends Library, London, in a letter from her to Sarah Neal Stanton, near Philadelphia, dated December 1, 1760. The letter appears first in this copybook of correspondence, experiences, and testimonies, among them the elaborated version of the "Lamentation" described in the Note on the Text.

that Interval was at the Province Meeting of Clonmel, where she had Extraordinary Service; from thence got to the County of Carlow, and to the house of our Friend Robert Leckey.

Whilst there, some expressions which she uttered in an Affecting manner were taken down in writing and are as follows. The 7th 5 month 1755, Elizabeth Ashbridge being sorely afflicted with pain of body, express'd her fear of not being patient enough under it, but several times desired it saying, "Oh! dearest goodness grant me patience till my Change come, and then enable me; do not forsake me Lord of my Life." And speaking of what she had suffered, said, words could not express nor thought conceive what she had gone through these Seven Months; for what cause the Lord only knew. Altho' it had been so with her yet she would not have any be discouraged; for her Master (she said) was a good Master, and she did not grudge suffering for him; tho' he chastizes his children, 'tis for some good end; sometimes for their own, and sometimes for the good of others; and said she did not repent coming into this nation tho' she was so tired, being satisfied she was in her place and that it was the requirings of him who had supported her to a Miracle. And now it looked as if two poor weak women were sent to lay down their lives as a Sacrifice, while Strong Men could stay at home and be at ease; or to this purpose (her Companion Sarah Worrel having departed this life at the City of Cork a short time before). And as many faithful Servants had been sufferers in this land (they not being the first, nor she thought would not be the last), she mentioned something of its lying heavy on the Inhabitants of it, if there was not an amendment. But for those that had put their hands to the plough, she desired such might go on with Courage, and said God was on their side; and that it was happy for those who considered their Creator in the Days of their youth.

Another time when in extreme pain, cry'd out "Lord ! look down upon me," and Begged that patience (her old Companion) might not leave her, and said, altho' pain of body was her portion at present, through the Mercies of a gracious God, her mind was pretty Easy; tho' sometimes she feared that she was not quite fitted; but desired that his hand might not spare nor his eye pity, till she was wholly fitted for that glorious mansion which she aimed at, and into which nothing that's unholy can enter; yet had a hope that it was not in wrath she was chastized; for she had to acknowledge that she felt the Touches of Divine Love to her Soul; and said that she loved the Truth and that those that loved it was precious to her life, whether relations or not; and that she had sought it from her youth and was thankful for being preserved so as never to bring a blemish on it, since she had made profession thereof but had done what she could for it.

The 8th a friend taking leave of her, she told him, whether he heard of her life or Death, she hoped it would be well. The 9th some Friends being with her, she said something of the singularity of her tryals, but that the hand that permitted them had an indisputable right, to which she seemed resigned whether in life or Death, hoping it would be well. She said she loved the Truth and it had been her support, and desired those who had begun to walk in it, to keep close to it, and it would never leave them. She seemed thankful that the beauty of this world and the enjoyments of it, were stained in her view, and that she was made willing to give up all: the hardest was her dear husband, being so far from him, but even that was made easier than she could expect. Being wished a good night's rest, she said, that was what she did not expect, to be free from pain, but that every night that the Lord sent was good, and tho' uneasy hoped they would be all good nights, and when once the Gulf was shot she would have rest.

The 10th speaking to a Friend, she said, she endeavoured to live without a will, and that she hoped she had borne her afflictions with a degree of Christian Fortitude. Being in great pain and asked whether she would be settled, she said none could settle her but one, and in his own time she hoped he would. Then cried out, "Dearest Lord! Tho' thou slay me I'll die at thy Feet; for I have loved thee more than Life." The 12th she spoke affectionately to a Friend that visited her, gratefully acknowledging the care and tenderness shewn her and counted it a high favour, that the hearts and affections of her Friends were open to receive and sympathize with her. Having spoke something of the exercise of mind she went through before her convincement and of the time she got relief out of great distress, and was enabled to make covenant with the Lord; which time she still remembered, and hoped she would never forget it; being desirous often to return to Bethel,[25] and to remember the time of her espousals, she acknowledged the advantage there was in being deeply tried, and that it was the way to be able to speak comfortably to others.

Having grown weaker for several days, she departed this life in a quiet frame, the 16th of the 5 mo. 1755; and was so favour'd as to have her Senses continued to the End: and we hope and believe that she dyed in Peace with the Lord: for whose Sake she had been made willing to leave what was nearest to her in this Life & labour'd in the Work of the Gospel to the Edification of the Churches where her lot was cast. On the 19th her corpse, accompanied by many Friends, was conveyed in a solemn manner from our said Friend Robert Leckey's dwelling house (where she died) to Friends Burying Ground at Ballybrumhill[26] where several testimonies were borne to the Truth, in the service of which her Body was dissolved.

Thus our dear Friend finished her course: It remains briefly to add our Testimony concerning her. She was a woman of an excellent natural understanding: In

25. *to return to Bethel:* See Genesis 35:6–7. At God's command Jacob built an altar at Luza in Canaan, renaming it Bethel. To return to Bethel would be to keep fresh by remembering the experience of conversion, the Spirit's establishing of an altar within.

26. *Ballybrumhill:* The Ballybromhill burying ground still exists but has ceased to have any official affiliation with the Society of Friends. The plot is now known locally as "God's Acre," the title appearing on the modern entry gate, and lies near the village of Fennagh, County Carlow. Family papers relating to Robert Lecky of Kilnock (1700–1780) are on deposit in the Library of the Society of Friends, Dublin.

conversation cheerful, yet Grave and Instructive. She felt the affliction of others with a tender sympathy and bore her own with patience and resignation. As a Minister, she was deep in Travail, clear in her openings; plain and pertinent in her expressions; solid and awful in her deportment, and attended with that Baptizing power which is the evidence of a living Ministry; and which so eminently attended her in the last Testimony she bore in a publick Meeting, in great bodily weakness, that most or all present were reached and deeply affected thereby; and a young woman was Convinced of the Truth, to which she bore testimony, as a seal to the finishing of her Service in the Work of the Ministry, in which being so owned of her Master, we have no doubt but she now receives the reward of the Faithful Servant and is entered into the joy of her Lord.

JOHN GOUGH

TESTIMONY FROM WATERFORD

Elizabeth Ashbridge came to Waterford about the middle of the 12 mo 1755 to visit the church there, altho' under pain & bodily weakness; the desire of performing that service caused her to struggle hard with her disorder beyond what she could well bear, being desirous faithfully to do her great master's work. When she got to meetings & was therein publicly concerned she manifested the verity of that text of Scripture, if any man will do his will he shall know of the doctrine whether it be of God etc, for by certain experience heavenly doctrine was witnessed to be thro' her conveyed to the edification of the church and the solid comfort and refreshment of many poor souls. Her mien and deportment in the exercise of her gift was comely and reverent, her manner of expression free from any affectation, clear and strongly ingaging. Above all, the overflowings of divine goodness accompanying, manifested she had been baptized into Christ who under these ingagements furnished her with a good degree of his heart Searching convincing power, the great and awful sense of it wherewith she was clothed was visible in her appearances and shewed that she had not lightly entered upon or ingag'd in that service, but was well qualified for it and could readily distinguish twixt those who said they were Jews[27] & were not, and who presumed on the work of the ministry without being thereunto called—an instance of which was remarkable here.

Her conversation was an ornament to the profession she made, tending much to edification, her memory strong, her judgment clear and penetrating, nervous in Arguement, of an Affable, chearful & amiable temper, even in times of great weakness. Affectation & stiffness were opposite to her yet as occasion required she

27. *those who said they were Jews:* That is, those who were truly God's people.

was neither wanting or afraid to check that which tended to Evil, her Spirit humble tender & Simpathizing with the poor & afflicted & had a word of Comfort unto Such as Occasion.

That the dwelling of her Soul was near to the Spring of imortal goodness was Evident by the frequent inbreakings thereof. The Love that from it flowed to the bretheren was Strong, which drew her from a tender husband & outward Comforts over the mighty Ocean to distant regions & to travail hard inwardly & outwardly that Experimental knowledge might increase & Souls be brought back to their true rest & ever lasting Centre. This was her labour, this was her travail, this was the object of her desire, her joy & rejoycing to have it effected.

During her stay here she was ingaged to be at the province meeting at Clonmel & had extraordinary Service there tho' under great weakness & pain so that it was with great difficulty She got thither & back.

Whilst here her indisposition prevented her much getting to meetings—yet [she] was often visited & greatly beloved by friends & Some opportunities were laid hold of in [ms. torn] where she lodged, to the family whereof she was near & dear as well as to many more here. After a Stay of about 4 mos. under great infirmity & pain she was often pressing to get forward towards Dublin to be at the Ensuing national meeting, Accordingly set out hence and was accompanied by some friends to the house of Samuel Watson in the Co. Carlow.

J.G.   Testimony
Con: E. Ashbridge

Textual Variants

The variants among manuscript copies of Elizabeth Ashbridge's narrative are too numerous to be indicated here. Many of them, however, are minor. The variants given below are a selection from more significant differences among the manuscripts that have been used as a basis for this edition. These manuscripts are the two Bevan-Naish manuscripts 1172 and 2432 in the Woodbrooke Quaker Study Centre, Birmingham, England, which have been used as copy texts as described in the Note on the Text; two manuscripts held in the Friends Library, Dublin, abbreviated SR (for Samuel Russel, the apparent copyist) and Dub2; the manuscript in the Boston Public Library, abbreviated BPL; and the partial manuscript in the collection of the Friends Historical Library, Swarthmore College, abbreviated SW. Readings from the Nantwich first edition will be referred to by that edition's date, 1774. The adopted reading is given first, followed by variants.

p. 147   *Some Account.* Only SR provides an entirely different title, a traditional one for Quaker autobiography. The title page reads A / JOURNAL of THE LIFE / OF That Faithful Servant / OF Christ Jesus / Elizabeth Ashbridge / Psalms 112.6 The Righteous shall be had in Everlasting / Remembrance / DUBLIN / MDCCLXVII.

          I through disobedience: SR, Dub2, BPL. *I thought I by disobedience:* BN 2432. Not in 1774.

          To begin . . . beginning: SR, Dub2. *So I begin . . . beginning:* BN 2432. Not in BPL, 1774.

p. 151   *I was a Stranger . . . Land:* BN 1172, 2432, 1774. *in a Strange Land:* Not in SR, Dub2, BPL.

p. 152   *to go barefoot:* BN 2432, SR, Dub2, BPL, 1774. *to go on foot:* BN 1172.

          in my youth: BN 1172. *in my infancy:* BN 2432, SR, BPL. *in my childhood:* Dub2. *I having a different opinion of those sort of men than what I had in my youth:* 1774.

p. 153   *heard of my Father:* BN 1172, 1774. *heard of my parents:* BN 2432, SR, Dub2, BPL.

an Actress: BN 1172, Dub2, 1774. *an Actor:* BN 2432, SR, BPL.

p. 154   *I Passed . . . (as twas Called):* BN 1172, 1774. *I was confirmed by the Bishop:* BN 2432, SR, Dub2, BPL.

here I . . . before Baptism: BN 2432, SR, Dub2, BPL, 1774. Not in BN 1172.

But . . . as I Expected: Not in 1774.

Philadelphia: Dub2, 1774. *Fyal:* BN 1172. *Fial:* BN 2432. *Phial:* SR. *Phiall:* BPL.

p. 155   *but what to Do . . . Stranger:* BN 1172, BN 2432. *I was an utter stranger to:* SR. *I was entirely at a loss for:* Dub2. *I knew not:* BPL. *I seemed still an utter stranger to:* 1774.

p. 156   *the old Accuser:* The 1774 edition reads *the old amuser.*

p. 157   *that's full . . . forbearance:* Not in 1774.

p. 158   *full of Love:* Not in SR, 1774.

on Long Island: BN 1172 only.

In the interval: BN 1172 only.

Trenton: BN 1172, SW. *Trent Town:* BN 2432, SR, Dub2, BPL, 1774.

no other Bible: 1774 and all manuscripts but BN 1172, which reads *no other Book.*

Tears Issued from: BN 1172. *Tears came in:* BN 2432, SR, SW. *came from:* Dub2. *Came into:* 1774.

a little: not in BN 1172.

p. 159   *Give it out:* BN 1172, BN 2432, SW. *give it up:* SR, Dub2, BPL, 1774.

fully Suffered: only in BN 1172.

p. 160   *made me Esteem them:* BN 1172. *made me think they were:* BN 2432, SR, Dub2, BPL, SW, 1774.

Wm. Hammans: BN 2432, BPL. The name is so spelled in the epistle of 1752 from the Spring Meeting of Philadelphia area ministers and elders, of which Hammans and Elizabeth Ashbridge were signatories. *Hammond:* BN 1172, SR. *Hammocks:* Dub2. *Hammonds:* SW. *Hammons:* 1774.

about Baptism: All manuscripts. *about Babylon:* 1774.

p. 161   *the Divel:* This spelling of *devil* appears only in BN 1172.

p. 162   *gone . . . my Fast:* BN 2432, SR, BPL. *without breaking my fast:* Dub2, 1774. *fasted from Morning till Night:* BN 1172.

        Vaunt that . . . my youth: All manuscripts. *haunt the sins my youth were forgiven:* 1774.

        be in a great Passion: 1774 and all manuscripts but BN 1172, which reads *rage.*

        pluck'd: BN 1172. *pulled:* 1774 and all manuscripts. See p. 152 for a similar use of *pluck'd,* where it appears as *Pluckt.*

        before thy Throne, imploring: All manuscripts and 1774. *and Implore for:* BN 1172.

p. 164   *Proud heart:* All manuscripts and 1774. *Poor heart:* BN 1172.

        owned the Team: BN 1172. *owned the Cart:* All manuscripts and 1774.

p. 165   *in the house:* all manuscripts and 1774. SR adds *(Domus).*

p. 166   *under the care of:* 1774 and all manuscripts but BN 1172, which reads *under the Notice of.*

        requesting it: 1774 and all manuscripts but BN 1172, which reads *joyning with them fully.*

p. 167   *Distinct Voice:* SR, BPL, SW 1774. *Distant Voice:* BN 1172, BN 2432, Dub2.

        Words ran thro' him: 1774 and all manuscripts but BN 1172, which reads *Words Affected him.*

p. 168   *Paw of the Bear.* Only 1774 reads *Pay of the Bear.*

        in a flood of tears: BPL, 1774. *a flow of tears:* BN 1172. *floods of tears:* BN 2432, SR, SW.

        little house: 1774 and all manuscripts but BN 1172, which reads *little home.*

p. 169   *good woman:* 1774 and all manuscripts but BN 1172, which reads *Virtuous woman.*

        & would often . . . to the Better: not in 1774.

Earn your light: 1774 and all manuscripts but BN 1172, which reads *Earn The Candle.*

p. 170   *The End:* BN 1172 only.

Thus far . . . with hers: BN 2432. *Thus far was her own Acct. what follows was wrote by her last Husbd and sent with ye foregoing:* BPL. *The foregoing was her own account, what follows was wrote by her last husband, and sent over therewith:* 1774. Not in BN 1172, SR, Dub2.

Here ends . . . Other Concerns: This paragraph appears in BN 1172, in the two London Friends Library manuscripts, and partially in the SW fragment.

p. 171   *two or three Years:* BN 2432, SR, BPL, 1774. *more than two years:* BN 1172.

near 80 £: BN 2432, SR, BPL, 1774. *several score Pounds:* BN 1172.

near all the said Debts: BN 2432, SR, BPL, 1774. *near:* not in BN 1172.

The Travel Diary
of Elizabeth House Trist:
Philadelphia to Natchez, 1783–84

Edited, with an Introduction, by
ANNETTE KOLODNY

Introduction

I

In 1774 twenty-three-year-old Elizabeth House, daughter of Philadelphia Quakers, married a British officer stationed in the colonies, Nicholas Trist of County Devon, England. Elizabeth's widowed mother ran one of Philadelphia's finest boardinghouses, and the couple had met when Nicholas Trist's regiment was billeted in that city. As a fifth son in a family of landed gentry, Nicholas could not, under the law of primogeniture, inherit his family's estate.[1] Like so many young men of his class and situation, therefore, he sought a career in the military, joining the Eighteenth or "Royal Irish" Regiment of Foot and eventually found himself posted as a lieutenant to America.

It was clearly a love match, with the thirty-one-year-old lieutenant protesting bitterly when regimental business separated him from his wife. "A letter from you My Dear will decrease my anxiety," he wrote from New Jersey in September 1774, just months after their marriage.[2] Separations were similarly irksome to his "Dear Betsy," who followed her husband to New York in the winter of 1774 so that she might be with him for the birth of their son, Hore Browse Trist, on February 22, 1775.

By the time of his marriage, Nicholas Trist no longer wished to remain a soldier. Having traveled widely throughout the British holdings in North America, he had begun to purchase lands in Louisiana (then still a part of British West Florida) in the vicinity of Bayou Manchac, on the east bank of the Mississippi below Baton Rouge.[3] The "exercise" afforded him by the military was agreeable enough, Nicholas told his new bride, but "I only wish for the time to do it on my farm instead of in the King's high road."[4] Finally, having saved a sufficient sum to make good on his land investments, Nicholas Trist resigned his commission in Boston in 1775,

---

1. Dating back to feudal times, the English right of primogeniture declared that the succession of title and property passes to the eldest son. In this manner, large estates could be held intact from generation to generation.

2. Nicholas Trist to Mrs. Trist, September 15, 1774, Trist-Burke-Randolph Family Papers, Special Collections Department, University of Virginia Library, Charlottesville.

3. Fort Bute, at Manchac, had been a British frontier post until 1768, when General Thomas Gage ordered it abandoned in order to cut colonial defense expenditures. To protect the local inhabitants against raids, the British constructed a new fort at Manchac in 1778–79. It is possible that Nicholas Trist had earlier been stationed at Fort Bute.

4. Nicholas Trist to Mrs. Trist, September 15, 1774.

along with his close friend, Alexander Fowler. The year before, Fowler and his wife, Francis Elizabeth, had stood as godparents at the christening of Elizabeth and Nicholas Trist's son in New York. Now the two men looked to the American frontier to make their fortunes. But although Fowler would later venture only as far as the Ohio River, involving himself in trade and land speculation in and around Pittsburgh, Nicholas Trist once again made his way down the Mississippi to Natchez and the settlements that had fanned out around it.

Although Trist himself was no Loyalist—and had probably become a naturalized citizen of the new republic shortly after the outbreak of the revolutionary war—his investments prospered from the influx of settlers that followed upon the Revolution. A flood of Loyalists from the north brought rapid population expansion to the Louisiana Province settlements and quickly established the area as a rich site for the export of tobacco, lumber, and indigo. The richness of the land and the relative ease with which land grants could be obtained, however, were no compensation for the pain of yet another prolonged separation.

Both because of the dangers of travel during the revolutionary war years and because Philadelphia was considered a fitter place to raise and educate their son, Elizabeth House Trist had remained behind in Philadelphia, helping to run her mother's boardinghouse on Second Street. Mary House's was no ordinary establishment. With its Quaker leanings and its reputation for hospitality and superior fare, the boardinghouse attracted many of the most prominent delegates to the Continental Congress—Thomas Jefferson and James Madison among them. Jefferson was an especially frequent visitor, lured to Philadelphia not only by the Continental Congress but by meetings of the American Philosophical Society.[5] Even so, the heady blend of political debate and ardent discussions of *natural philosophy* circulating around the dinner table and in the parlor were not sufficient to blunt Trist's continued distress at her husband's absence.

Time and again Nicholas had written and "propos'd coming to you," but each plan fell through. Then, on September 15, 1780, in a letter posted from "River Mississippi 5 Leagues below Manchac," Nicholas Trist proposed an alternative. "In all of your Letters you complain of the disagreeable situation you are in," he reminded his wife, "and in the last you say that . . . You thought you had resolution enough to undertake the Journey." He therefore suggested that his wife "go to Fort Pit as soon as it is convenient and as Fowler has given you an Invitation remain with him untill he can provide a safe opportunity." The plan seemed reasonable, Nicholas continued, because "as genteel families are frequently coming

5.   Founded by Benjamin Franklin and based in Philadelphia, the American Philosophical Society provided a forum for the discussion of science, philosophy, agriculture, political theory, and the promotion of useful knowledge. Franklin was still president of the society when Governor Thomas Jefferson of Virginia was elected a member in 1780, along with François Marbois, George Washington, and James Madison. In 1781, Jefferson was elected a governing officer, or "councillor."

down perhaps you might get a passage with some or other of them." "I would not have you to venture by Your-Self," he made clear.

The conditions his wife might expect in Louisiana were primitive at best. "If you will be in want of a looking glass to dress your head," her husband warned, "you must bring one as I have nothing but a pail of water to shave by." And then in a postscript he added: "As flour sells for 20 Dollars a hundred I am oblig'd to eat Corn bread being not capable to give that price." These exigencies notwithstanding, Nicholas urged his wife to make the journey, concluding by "assuring you that every minute will be an age and that I shall not see an happy hour untill your arrival."[6] Not until 1783, however, with the signing of peace treaties that (temporarily) settled competing Spanish, British, and U.S. claims along the lower Mississippi, was it really safe for Trist to set out.

I I

In the years intervening, Trist's anticipation of her journey must have proven a subject of eager conversation with her mother's frequent boarder, Thomas Jefferson. For different reasons, each wanted to know more about the continent's western regions. For Elizabeth House Trist there was the prospect of permanent removal to her husband's holdings in Louisiana. For Jefferson there loomed the possibility of national expansion combined with his abiding fascination with the vast unknown continent.

Indeed, Jefferson considered himself something of a natural philosopher— what we might today term a scientific generalist—and had, since 1781, served as an officer of the American Philosophical Society. During the final years of the revolutionary war, in fact—in addition to his political responsibilities as the governor of Virginia— Jefferson had devoted himself to gathering the materials that would finally emerge as his *Notes on the State of Virginia,* a pioneer study of geography and natural history. Widely regarded as one of the most important scientific works yet compiled in America, *Notes on the State of Virginia* was composed as a response to a questionnaire about the New World and the new American states from the first secretary of the French legation, François Marbois. But the obligation to respond to a foreign diplomat's curiosity provided Jefferson with something more than an occasion to make a polite reply. The writing of the *Notes* was Jefferson's opportunity to organize materials he had been collecting for years, to speculate on his own scientific theories, and to hound his friends around the country for further infor-

6. From Nicholas Trist to Mrs. Trist, September 15, 1780, Trist-Burke-Randolph Family Papers.

mation. Among other things, Jefferson rebutted the Comte de Buffon's assertion that animal species in the New World were necessarily smaller and less vigorous than those in Europe. To demonstrate that the human species did not degenerate in America, Jefferson pointed to the physical prowess and oratorical powers of the Indian. To prove that the continent supported animal life of large proportions, he pointed to the recent discovery of fossilized mammoth bones in the Ohio Valley and pestered friends stationed in the West to secure for him "the different species of bones, teeth and tusks of the *Mammoth* as can now be found."[7]

The irony was that, although Jefferson speculated in the *Notes* about the sources of the Missouri and Mississippi rivers and postulated vast mineral deposits beyond the Ohio, he himself had never been farther west than Staunton, Virginia, just beyond the Blue Ridge Mountains. All his information had been gathered from books or piecemeal from friends. But Jefferson could not be satisfied with such evidence. Even as he sent the main text of his *Notes* to François Marbois in December 1781, he also began to press fellow members of the American Philosophical Society to sponsor a transcontinental exploration. As he wrote George Rogers Clark (the older brother of William Clark, who would later co-command the Lewis and Clark expedition) on December 4, 1783, "Some of us have been talking here in a feeble way of making the attempt to search that country . . . from the Mississippi to California."[8] Lack of funding relegated the idea to talk only.

Even so, when Jefferson drove his phaeton into Philadelphia in October 1783, before moving on to Annapolis to take up—for the last time—a seat in Congress, we may be sure that the idea of a transcontinental exploration was very much on his mind. For that reason, and for more personal ones, too, Jefferson again sought out his friend Elizabeth House Trist. He had in tow his eldest daughter, Martha (nicknamed Patsy), then just eleven years old. Still grieving over the loss of his wife, who had died a year earlier, Jefferson required companionship and guidance for the girl. Trist was then in the final stages of planning her own journey west and preparing her eight-year-old son for the imminent separation as best she could. Still, she managed to provide the attention Patsy's busy father could not, helping to supervise the girl's education and social life and acting almost as a second mother.

Before Jefferson left Philadelphia for Annapolis in the last week in November 1783, Trist helped him make more permanent arrangements for Patsy's care. Trist herself was about to depart on the first leg of her own journey, over the mountains to Pittsburgh. We will never know whether, compelled by his avid interest in western exploration, Jefferson then directly asked his friend to gather information for

7. Thomas Jefferson to George Rogers Clark, December 4, 1783, in *Letters of the Lewis and Clark Expedition with Related Documents, 1783–1854*, ed. Donald Jackson, 2nd ed., 2 vols. (Urbana: University of Illinois Press, 1978), 2:654.

8. Ibid., 654–55. George Rogers Clark (1752–1818) had been a revolutionary war general with extensive service on the Ohio frontier. His younger brother, William Clark (1770–1838), later joined Meriwether Lewis as a leader of the Lewis and Clark expedition to the Pacific in 1803.

him. More probably the idea was Trist's. Whatever the circumstances, the particularities of Jefferson's interests—his scientific fascination with fossil remains, his studies in botany, geography, and minerology, and his politician's interest in the future economic prospects of the western lands—all influenced the entries that Trist would make in her travel diary. As Trist wrote Jefferson in April 1784, near the end of her stay in Pittsburgh, "It would be one of the greatest pleasures of my life if I cou'd be one of your Company on such a tour." But as she knew "that will never happen," Trist contented herself with trying to record her journey for a mind like Jefferson's, confident that "a Philosophical mind like yours can gather information from all you see."[9]

To understand, then, that—whoever else might read it—Trist's diary was intended primarily for Thomas Jefferson is to understand some of its unique detail. The description of the coal deposits outside Pittsburgh, for example, was a response both to Jefferson's interest in geography and to his political interest in the potential economic resources of the western territories. With that same impulse, Trist described a shoreline seventy miles below the falls at Louisville with "a great quantity of stone that look like Iron ore," and regretted her inability to better observe the height of the timber along the banks. Aware of Jefferson's absorption in natural history, she lamented that she could not see firsthand the cache of "big bones . . . found three miles from this place back in the woods." But two weeks later, perhaps to compensate, the entry for June 10 offers lavish detail about the exploration of a limestone cave, "one of the most grand and beautiful natural structures and the greatest curiossity I ever beheld." Finally, on June 13, 1784, Trist paid a direct compliment to her intended reader, reminding him of the fort erected by American revolutionaries and "call'd after Governor Jefferson." "I wish'd to see the fort because it bore the name of my friend, but"—she continues apologetically—"I was dissuaided from making the attempt as it was not certain what Indians might be there."

Nineteen years later, in a communiqué dated June 20, 1803, to Captain Meriwether Lewis, President Thomas Jefferson officially charged the Lewis and Clark expedition to consider as "worthy of notice":

the soil & face of the country, it's growth & vegetable production, especially those not of the U.S.
the animals of the country generally, & especially those not known in the U.S.
the remains or accounts of any which may be deemed rare or extinct;
the mineral productions of every kind; but more particularly metals, limestone, pit coal, & saltpetre . . .

9. Eliza House Trist to Thomas Jefferson, April 13, 1784, quoted in Fawn M. Brodie, *Thomas Jefferson: An Intimate History* (New York: Norton, 1974), 177.

climate, as characterised by the thermometer, by the proportion of rainy, cloudy, & clear days, by lightning, hail, snow, ice, by the access & recess of frost, . . . the dates at which particular plants put forth or lose their flower, or leaf, times of appearance of particular birds, reptiles or insects.[10]

Behind many of Trist's entries, we can hear that same charge. Thus, long before the Louisiana Purchase empowered him to dispatch Lewis and Clark to the Pacific, Jefferson had already inspired one detailed report. It was what Elizabeth House Trist would modestly call "an account of my peregrination."[11]

I I I

To regard the travel diary of Elizabeth House Trist merely as an informational document written for Thomas Jefferson is to miss the source of its appeal. The entries are, at times, intensely personal. And, as the earliest extant diary by a white woman traveling downriver to frontier Natchez, the Trist manuscript offers a unique account of the conditions of frontier life in the years immediately following the Revolution.

Although the first two pages of the manuscript are now missing, it is clear that Trist set out from Philadelphia to Pittsburgh over what was then known as Forbes' Road. The route had originally been a buffalo trail used by the Indians. But during the years of the French and Indian Wars, when England and France fought over the dominance of the Ohio Valley, John Forbes had his men widen and improve the road so that it allowed the movement of troops and materiel to Fort Duquesne. There, in 1758, Forbes forced the French to evacuate and renamed their outpost Fort Pitt. Soon thereafter, Fort Pitt became the first British settlement west of the Alleghenies, a thriving community in its own right as well as a jumping-off place for travelers seeking access to the Ohio and the great natural transportation system of the Mississippi River.

With the surrender of General Cornwallis to George Washington in 1781 and the news of a peace treaty with Great Britain in the spring of 1783, a new wave of settlers pushed ever westward. Accompanied by Alexander Fowler, her husband's old friend from the Royal Irish, and by a female companion known only as Polly, Elizabeth House Trist traveled among them. But even though she followed a well-

10. See Donald Jackson, *Thomas Jefferson and the Stony Mountains: Exploring the West from Monticello* (Urbana: University of Illinois Press, 1981), 141.

11. Elizabeth House Trist to Thomas Jefferson, undated (received August 24, 1785), Trist-Burke-Randolph Family Papers.

established route across southern Pennsylvania and mentions some excellent inns and taverns, the journey was not an easy one. Repeatedly, she had to make do with cramped and uncomfortable quarters and with a lack of privacy that offended her middle-class sense of propriety. Despite these inconveniences, she acknowledges that her party was often "much better accommodated than we had a right to expect so far in the woods," and she quickly learned adaptations to frontier exigencies.

What really tested her determination were the treacherous mountain passes, swollen streams, and freezing temperatures of midwinter. On more than one occasion she notes that "this days journey has been as dangerous as any we have gone through." In early January 1784, for example, a sudden snowmelt rendered "the small runs as well as creeks . . . allmost impassible. The horses were frequently near swiming." The roads too were "very bad," so much so that "my horse cou'd scarcely keep his feet. He fell with me once." "Notwithstanding," she comments, "I did not feel much intimidated but plunged through with no other mishap than geting wet." Little wonder that Alexander Fowler "gave me credit for my good Horsemanship."[12]

When she finally arrived in Pittsburgh on January 9, 1784, she writes that she sighed in tribute to the revolutionary war soldiers who had lost their lives in the battle for Grant's Hill. And perhaps—though she does not say it—she also sighed in relief at having completed the first segment of her journey, itself a kind of victory in the battle against the elements. For the rest of the winter, at least, she and Polly would be lodged comfortably with the Fowlers.

Once arrived in Pittsburgh, Trist ceased to make daily entries in her diary, settling instead for lengthy summary passages. During her sojourn there she evidently changed her mind about the place. In one of the entries—probably penned in early spring—she confides that "I like the situation of Pittsburg mightily and was there good Society I shou'd be contented to end my days in the Western country." On May 20, by contrast, as she boarded a flatboat[13] to take her down the

12. Internal evidence within the diary suggests that Alexander Fowler had arranged for various goods and supplies to be brought back on packhorses; he was to meet the supply party en route. Fowler had thus probably made a business trip to the eastern seaboard which then permitted him to escort Trist on his return journey to Pittsburgh. Indeed, Fowler's business interests may have dictated the timing of the trip—so late in winter—when an earlier autumn passage over the mountains would have been less arduous.

13. Flat-bottomed boats were built in the vicinity of Pittsburgh, made of whipsawed and hewed timber. A flat, as it was commonly called, was constructed bottom-side up and turned over before it was launched. Oakum or old rope was driven into the cracks with a hammer. These boats were generally less than fifteen feet wide in order to negotiate the falls at Louisville, which had a fifteen-foot channel between the rocks. Fifty feet was a popular length, although Trist's flat may have been somewhat longer in order to accommodate the various supplies carried for trade or sale. Around the outside of the deck were upright posts about six feet high, and to these posts heavy planks were pinned as a protection against the fire of Indians or other attackers. Portholes for firing were cut into these planks, and flat crews regularly carried muskets and blunderbusses for protection. A roof often

Ohio, she writes that she "left Pittsburg with as little regret as I ever did any place that I had lived so long in." The kindness of the Fowlers and the occasional social "recreations" apparently could not compensate for the crudeness of frontier life.

Having officially been laid out as a town twenty years earlier, Pittsburgh in 1784 still had a feel of impermanence. Situated at the forks of the Ohio where the Monongahela and the Allegheny join, it provided the major gateway to the West. Trist comments on "the number of strangers resorting thither on their way to the Cumberland" and other newly opened frontier areas. As a result, despite its coal deposits, its orchards, its abundance of fish and maple trees, the town remained rough and unprepossessing. "There are about a hundred buildings," Trist observes, "all . . . built of logs and they in a very ruinous state."

With the spring thaws, she and Polly bade farewell to the Fowlers and looked forward to moving on. The journey down the Ohio and into the Mississippi had its own trials, however. To begin with, "the tardiness of the boat builder detain'd us till the river got so low" that navigation of the channels and sandbars was hazardous. Had they set out earlier, just after the thaws, the higher water levels would have rendered their passage both safer and swifter. Even so, at the outset, Trist consoled herself with the fact that "three days rain has swell'd the rivers and we have the flattering appearance of a speedy voyage." By the end of the month she was not so sanguine. "My mind was not at ease," she confides in the entry for May 28, because "the water of the river was every day decreasing and I was under great anxiety least we shou'd be detained till Autumn." About a half mile from Louisville, at Bear Grass Creek, the boat ran aground "fast on the Rocks," and the next day a river pilot hired to guide the boat over the falls at Louisville again ran "her on the Rocks." The boat had to be unloaded amid rapid currents, causing another eight-day delay.

Her accommodations on the flatboat "all things consider'd [are] not to be complain'd of"—even though she fell out of her berth the first night and bruised herself, and, during heavy downpours, "the roof let in the water in several places." What emerged as most tormenting during the Ohio passage were the gnats and mosquitoes that nightly disrupted the women's sleep and the malarial fevers that had begun to plague Polly on May 23.

Despite her eagerness to enter the waters of "the Grand Riviere," the transition from the Ohio to the Mississippi brought no relief. Narrow channels, sandbars, and masses of floating uprooted trees (called "sawyers" because of their apparent sawing motion within the river currents) rendered travel even more hazardous than on the Ohio. "I dont like this river," Trist concludes early on, because "the passage is attended with much more danger than I had any idea of." The mos-

---

covered part or all of the boat, thus protecting cargo and passengers from rain and sun. The flat bottom and the rectangular shape allowed the boats to glide on the water. Small canoes, for brief forays onshore or into narrow inlets, hung at the sides.

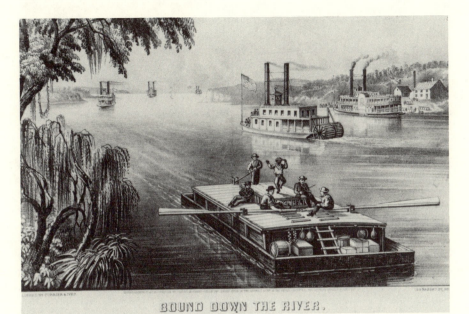

BOUND DOWN THE RIVER.

Figure 4.1 Even into the age of steam, flatboats continued to be a popular mode of river transportation, as illustrated by a Currier and Ives lithograph in 1870 showing steam-powered paddlewheelers and a flatboat on the Mississippi. (Courtesy Library of Congress.)

quitoes, too, were worse. Although she had "taken every precaution to guard against them," it was all "to very little purpose," Trist complains, "and I am in a continual fever with the effects of their venom." By June 18, her fifth day on the Mississippi, Trist was desolate: "My patience is allmost exausted. What with the Musquitos and the head winds I am allmost sick." Given these very real torments, it is all the more remarkable that Trist was able to maintain the discipline to make graphic and often moving daily entries.

I V

Because the only available passage downriver for a traveler like Trist was aboard one of the many flatboats that plied the Ohio and Mississippi for trade, the diarist enjoyed ample opportunities to view, firsthand, a frontier in transition. At settlements and private plantations the flat sold flour and other staples to a multiracial and international mix of settlers, especially along the Mississippi. On June 22, 1784, for example, several of the crew loaded the canoe and headed for a Spanish garrison where "the people . . . were in want of flour." On June 30, a stopover at a plantation engaged Trist in conversation with "a Mullato woman nam'd Nelly." Various parties of French and Canadians are also mentioned. Side by side with the tokens of obvious prosperity—Nelly supplied Trist and her company with watermelons, green corn, and apples—were also the signs of poverty, decay, and continuing political turmoil. Philip Alston had been forced to quit his "fine Plantation" because he was a key leader in an unsuccessful uprising in 1782 which contested Spanish rule along the Mississippi. The once elegant estate, as Trist notes, is now "quite abandon'd."

Whereas the mix of races and the ongoing competition between native peoples, English, French, Spanish, and "Americans" for dominance over the Ohio Valley and lower Mississippi are relatively familiar themes, the brutalizing poverty of the frontier has rarely been recorded. But Trist recorded everything. On June 15, some eighty miles below the Ohio, her flat docked at what was reputedly "the best hunting ground any where" on the Mississippi, and there she encountered "a poor family encamp'd at this place . . . . [who] had not a morsel of bread for the last three months." "The poor little children when they saw us," Trist writes, "cry'd for some bread." The family had already buried one of its sons "a little while before."

More than once in her diary Trist accounts herself fortunate because "the owners of the Boat seem to be well acquainted with the Rivers, this being the fifth time they have gone down the Ohio." Precisely because Trist traveled in the company of those best situated to recognize the magnitude of the changes taking place in the western lands, her diary provides a chilling—if inadvertent— exposé of Americans' blundering belief in a landscape of limitless resources. Despite their own observation of increasing human population, which thus required the flatboat's services for trade, the crew repeatedly set off on hunting expeditions as if the crush of emigration had not already taken its toll. Repeatedly, therefore, the "hunters return'd without any game." Even at "the best hunting ground any where on" the Mississippi, "the men return'd without even having fired a gun." Indeed, it was not until June 5, safely past the falls at Louisville, that one of the hunters finally returned "with a deer the first wild meat we have had." Apparently unprepared to contemplate the changes that they themselves had helped to effect, the flatboat's crew persisted in envisioning a pristine wilderness that no longer existed. The delusion is revealed as ludicrous on June 7 when the crew once again "went on shore to hunt," only to kill "a tame cow which they mistook for a Buffaloe." Never tempted by the appeal of a wilderness frontier, Trist saw what the flatboat crew could not: "There are such numbers of boats continually going down the river that all the game have left the shore."

Trist herself, of course, never lamented the passing of the raw frontier. Like most eighteenth-century women of her class, she preferred cultivated grounds and carefully designed open vistas to an apparently chaotic and untamed nature. Thus

she was always comparing the wild fruits and herbs she encountered to the cultivated varieties she knew in Philadelphia. Her eye for landscape, likewise, was an
eye to envision future settlements. In her view, the rolling hill country outside
Pittsburgh was merely "very extensive"—never beautiful—and only "if the country which is mountanous was clear'd . . . wou'd [it] be beyond discription beautifull." A visit to the fledgling Chartiers Town settlement sent Trist back to
Pittsburgh with a headache because of what she experienced as the oppressiveness
of "so much wood towering above me in every direction and such a continuance of
it." Similarly overwhelmed by the Chickasaw Bluffs on her passage down the Mississippi, Trist fancies that "there has been some great revolution in nature and this
great body of water has forced a passage where it was not intended and tore up all
before it." Beneath "ragged" banks fifty feet in height—as she had earlier been
oppressed by the "confined Prospect" in Chartiers Town—Trist confronted what
was, for her, a landscape "alltogether . . . awfull and Melancholy and some times
terrific."

The collusion of these two attitudes—the flat crew's inability to recognize
declining resources coupled with Trist's educated disdain for nature in the raw—
goes far to explain the waste and despoliation that marked even the earliest years of
frontier settlement. The resultant behavior is perhaps nowhere more graphically
rendered than in Trist's fascination with the killing of a North American white
pelican. Acknowledging that the birds "are very harmless and so tame that they
swim allmost in reach of our oars," nonetheless Trist accepts the bird as an oddity
for her amusement—or as another specimen for her intended reader. "I saw 14
quarts of water put into its mouth and it wou'd have held more." It is, she concludes, "the most curious bird I ever saw."

The Indian, too, figures for Trist as a frontier curiosity, but here her responses
are more complicated. Continued Indian resistance to white settlement along the
Ohio—what Nicholas Trist termed "the troublesomeness of the Savages"—had
been one of the elements preventing her husband's return to Philadelphia in 1780.[14]
But during the French and Indian Wars and, later, the War for Independence,
different tribes had aligned themselves with one or another of the warring European parties in a desperate effort to find allies who might protect their lands. Now
many of those tribes had treaty relations with the new nation, while others remained
in uneasy truce. The predominant characterization of the Indian, therefore, is as
an ever-present threat. Guns were readied on the flatboat on June 8 "for fear the
Indians shou'd attack us." In fact, however, Trist was never menaced by Indians
and, on the single occasion that she actually meets a group, she admits that "they
had all the appearance of friendship." She even managed her own gesture of

14.   "The News we have from the Ohio of the troublesomeness of the Savages," explained Nicholas Trist, writing from along the Mississippi below Manchac, "make it impossible to determine
when I shall come" (Nicholas Trist to Mrs. Trist, September 15, 1780).

friendship when she carried "the Squaw some bread" and offered a handkerchief to shade the Indian woman's infant from the sun. Even so, Trist cannot refrain from repeating the leader's reputation as a bad character. "They say he has plunderd several boats and murderd many people."

In a revealing entry dated June 11, 1784, Trist suggests the real source of her anxiety. Just as she had no sympathy for uncultivated nature, so too she feared the human form when it did not bear the familiar markings of Euro-American civilization. She was apparently not alone in this. The flatboat crew readied its blunderbuss and loaded the muskets at the approach of a canoe "which we supposed to be Indians." To everyone's relief, "they turn'd out to be some french men going to the Cumberland river to trade." What had alarmed everyone, of course, was that "their *appearance* was perfectly savage" (emphasis added). In short, they did not look like what Trist understood as *civilized*, "having little or no cloaths on and their hides quite as dark as the Indians." Like most Euro-Americans of the eighteenth and nineteenth centuries, Trist could neither empathize with the legitimate claims of the native peoples to their tribal lands nor accept the rich and diverse—albeit different—Indian cultures.

V

Trist's journey did not end as she had hoped. The husband who pleaded, in 1780, that "I shall not see an happy hour untill your arrival"[15] was never to greet her in Natchez. Nicholas Trist had died in the Manchac settlement on February 24, 1784, while his wife wintered in Pittsburgh.[16] Presumably the news reached Trist on July 1, when the boat docked a few days short of Natchez "to unload some flour"—and the diary abruptly breaks off. The separation that was to have been only temporary was now permanent.

Grief at her husband's death was only one of the young widow's burdens. As Nicholas had noted—all too prophetically—in that same letter in 1780, "if grim Death should overtake me before your arrival, in all probability you and my Child will lose the enjoyment of the little I am possessed."[17] The grieving widow therefore had to settle her husband's outstanding debts, sell his holdings, and do what she could to retrieve his investments. Her tasks were not made any easier by the

---

15. Ibid.

16. A British relative described the "circumstances" of Nicholas Trist's death as "deplorable": "He was seiz'd with a swelling in his stomach & head & died in a few days after" (Susanna Taylor to "My Dear Nieces," June 15, 1784, Trist-Burke-Randolph Family Papers).

17. Nicholas Trist to Mrs. Trist, September 15, 1780.

fact that "British" West Florida was now in Spanish hands, control having been ceded in the treaties between the United States and England and between England and Spain that concluded the Revolution.

Happily, Nicholas Trist's property was largely "unincumbered," but it was still "greatly lessened [in value] . . . owing to the change of government." The dons, moreover, had restricted the flow of currency and, in order to get her husband's remaining capital out of the country, Trist found herself "obliged to give twenty five per cent to get it exchanged into silver." "But," as she wrote her dear friend, Jefferson, "this loss I must submit to."

Although Trist did not find Louisiana an unattractive country, she did not relish being "separated any longer from my dear mother & child." The return to Philadelphia, however, proved every bit as lengthy—if not as physically arduous—as the trip to Natchez. For although the Anglo-American treaty, signed on September 3, 1783, reserved free navigation rights on the Mississippi for both British and American subjects, the Anglo-Spanish treaty, signed the same day, made no mention of Mississippi navigation. In 1784, hoping to thwart the south-westward advance of settlers from the United States, the dons closed the river to American navigation. As a result, Trist had no direct route home. Writing to Jefferson in the spring of 1785, she catalogued her various attempts to book passage on Spanish ships that would take her to Havana, Cuba, or even to Jamaica, from either of which, she hoped, she might "get a passage . . . to Philadelphia." "But if no immediate opportunity [to take passage to the Caribbean] should offer," Trist was also prepared to "go via the cape." The problem, she noted dismally, was that "there being no trade between the United States and this country, it seems almost impossible to get from here."

Finally, in the spring of 1785, Trist sailed for Jamaica and thence to Philadelphia, arriving home in early June. While en route, she wrote again to Jefferson, then ambassador to France, asking about his travels and wondering when his "embassy [would] be at an end." She was eager to compare travel notes with her old friend and, above all, she wanted "to give [him] an account of my peregrination."[18] That account is the diary that follows.

18. Stranded on the lower Mississippi for several months, Trist kept up a running letter to Jefferson, written in different places on different dates, with two segments prefaced as follows: Mississippi Acadian Coast, March 12, 1785, and "On board the Ship Matilda, Balise Mississippi," undated. A note in Trist's hand at the end of the concluding page reads "Letter to Mr. Jefferson. Recd by him Aug 24th." All quotations in the preceding paragraphs regarding Trist's handling of her husband's estate and her difficulty in returning to Philadelphia are from this lengthy segmented letter in the Trist-Burke-Randolph Family Papers.

V I

In the letter that Elizabeth House Trist wrote to Thomas Jefferson in the spring of 1785, she confided that should she "have the good fortune to get safe home, my desire for travelling will be fully satisfied."[19] Notwithstanding, Trist was to travel often throughout the rest of her life—though nothing would match the adventure or the perils of her journey to Natchez in 1783–84. On her return to Philadelphia, Trist devoted herself to looking after the welfare of her only child, Hore Browse Trist, but her financial independence was severely strained by the death of her mother in 1793. With the aid of Jefferson, she helped her son obtain a small inheritance from his paternal grandmother in England and, in 1798—again following Jefferson's advice—the young man purchased Birdwood Plantation adjacent to Monticello and removed there with his mother and his new wife, Mary. The period in Virginia resulted in intimate friendships between Trist and many of the more prominent families in nearby counties.

But the pleasant Virginia sojourn was relatively brief. In 1802 President Jefferson awarded Hore Browse Trist the lucrative position of Port Collector for the lower Mississippi River. Subsequent to the Louisiana Purchase the office was moved to New Orleans, and in 1804, after two years of separation, Trist, her daughter-in-law, and her two young grandsons left Virginia to join her son at his new post. But before the end of the year Hore Browse Trist died of yellow fever. His widow remarried in 1807 and, that same year, Elizabeth House Trist returned to Virginia—though not to Birdwood, which her son had sold at the time of the family's removal to New Orleans.

Without a permanent home or any large income to sustain her, Trist resided with relatives or with one or another of the families whose friendship she had earned during the years at Birdwood. From 1808 to 1823 she was, in effect, a welcome if perpetual houseguest. Among the places she was always to find a warm welcome was Monticello where, in 1823, she took up permanent residence. The lifelong friendship between Jefferson and her family was cemented the next year when her eldest grandson, Nicholas Philip Trist, married Virginia Randolph, Jefferson's granddaughter.

Trist ended her days at Monticello, outliving her friend Jefferson by two and a half years. The lucid and lively mind that had so easily charmed strangers into friends began to deteriorate, however. By 1824, a friend who attended her at Monticello informed Trist's grandson (then in Washington on diplomatic business) that his grandmother's memory "is utterly & absolutely gone, so much so, that not only from day to day, but from hour to hour, she forgets all that she saw, hears or reads." Worse, "she is conscious of this decay of memory & frequently speaks of

19. Ibid.

it"[20]—a sad fate for someone whose acute observations could have produced the travel diary. On December 9, 1828, at age seventy-seven, Elizabeth House Trist died in her sleep. As Virginia Randolph Trist reported to her husband, his grandmother had experienced difficulty in breathing, speaking, and swallowing the entire week before, and when she did attempt speech, "it was only to answer when spoken to, or to say 'O! dear, dear' or 'O! my' &c." Even so, Virginia continued, "the countenance of the corpse is placid."[21] So ended the life of a traveler who, nineteen years before Lewis and Clark, had composed for Jefferson a telling account of frontier America: a likable and warmhearted woman who, typical of her class and era, had asked for nothing more than "good Society . . . in the Western country."

A NOTE ON THE TEXT

I

In November 1952, John A. Kelly, a faculty member at Haverford College in Pennsylvania, made a gift of a typescript of a travel diary to the Southern Historical Collection at the University of North Carolina, Chapel Hill. Kelly had received the typescript in February of that year from Trist Wood of New Orleans. Long in family hands, the original manuscript diary was thought to be lost. The diary was by Elizabeth House Trist, and it recounted her grueling journey to frontier Natchez in 1783–84.

While doing preliminary research for a study of women on the frontiers, I came across the typescript in 1976. I immediately realized that it was the earliest extant diary by a white woman on the Ohio-Mississippi river frontier. And although I was then unable to locate more than a few additional letters by the author, I nonetheless discussed the diary—and Trist's responses to the frontier landscape—in *The Land Before Her: Fantasy and Experience of the American Frontiers, 1630–1860.*[22]

It was always my hope one day to publish the diary in its entirety, but I was reluctant to proceed without the original manuscript. The typescript at Chapel Hill, I suspected, included errors; and it indicated a number of missing pages. The staff at the Southern Historical Society, however, was unable to locate the original.

20. Ellen Wayles Randolph Coolidge to Nicholas Philip Trist, March 30, 1824, Papers of Nicholas P. Trist, Manuscript Division, Library of Congress, Washington D.C.

21. Virginia Randolph Trist to Nicholas P. Trist, Esq., December 10, 1828, Nicholas P. Trist Papers, Southern Historical Collection, University of North Carolina Library, Chapel Hill (transcribed from the MS by Jane F. Wells).

22. Chapel Hill: University of North Carolina Press, 1984.

And my efforts to track down family members and descendants over the next few years proved both frustrating and fruitless.

Then, in 1987, on a hunch, I called the archives at Monticello to see if the diary had surfaced amid Jefferson family papers. It had not, but an archivist there suggested I check the manuscripts collection in the Alderman Library at the University of Virginia. Less than two minutes into my conversation with Robert A. Hull, public services assistant in the Manuscripts Department, he revealed that the University of Virginia Library had received the original diary as part of a collection purchased from Holly Killebrew in 1982. There had been no apparent order or coherence to the collection when it was first accepted by the library, but by 1987 it had been organized into several chronological series, and Hull instantly recognized the diary I was seeking. By the end of July 1987, I had in hand a clear photocopy of the original, including pages apparently missing when the Chapel Hill typescript had been composed.

Almost simultaneously—on July 28—the reference archivist at the Southern Historical Collection, Richard A. Shrader, wrote to say that in 1982 Jane F. Wells had visited "to research the life of Elizabeth Trist" and had "mentioned to us that she intended to locate as much of Trist's correspondence as she could." And he kindly provided me with her address.

Jane Wells pointed me in some useful directions, even as my research assistant, Colleen O'Toole, helped me scour the Nicholas P. Trist Papers in the Library of Congress to flesh out a picture of Trist's life and her relationship to Jefferson. When the University of Virginia collection produced Trist's 1785 letter to Jefferson, my research was over and an early intuition confirmed. The diary was not intended solely as a private record. Nor did its wealth of detail suggest that it was for her husband—who had, after all, already made the journey more than once—or for her eight-year-old son. It was composed for Thomas Jefferson and thereby took on added historical interest.

The only mystery remaining in the diary is the identity of Polly, Trist's indefatigable travel companion. In *The Land Before Her,* I had tentatively identified Polly as a slave or personal servant. But more recent research reveals that Trist came from a Quaker family staunchly opposed to slavery; Trist's grandmother had manumitted her own slaves. More probably, therefore, Polly—a common eighteenth-century nickname for Mary—was a younger relative or family friend who joined Trist to provide companionship and for her own motives as well. Polly may also have had relatives she sought to visit in British West Florida; or perhaps the sheer adventure of the journey lured her. In any event, each woman made the other's trip possible as propriety decreed that middle-class white women did not travel alone to the frontier.

In Trist's 1785 letter to Jefferson, she wrote "Poly joins me in affectionate love to [Jefferson's daughter] Patsy," who was then resident in France with her father. Presumably, despite the minor change in spelling from the diary, this is the same

Polly—a woman known also to Jefferson and his daughter, and now accompanying Trist on the difficult return passage to Philadelphia.

II

   Although the original pages measure a little less than 6 by 8½ inches and Trist's handwriting is sometimes small and cramped, the diary is nevertheless a readable text—despite its missing and torn pages. When Trist was rushed she resorted to abbreviations, but even these are easily comprehensible to a modern reader: *y^{ds}* for yards, for example, or *pr* for per. What will be less familiar are the run-on sentences, the inconsistencies in spelling and punctuation, and the occasional employment of words and phrases no longer in common usage. As was the habit of her day, Trist repeatedly reverses *of* and *off,* employs *least* for *lest,* and writes *were* when we would expect *where.* Because it was not until the nineteenth century that English codified the rules of grammar, spelling, and punctuation, Trist freely strung together as many clauses as she chose, spelled the same word differently from page to page, and used dashes, periods, and commas almost interchangeably. A capital letter does not always open a sentence, though generally Trist observed this rule, whereas a capital within a sentence more often denotes an emphasized word than a place-name or nationality. The question of punctuation is further complicated by the age and decay of the original manuscript and by the conditions under which Trist was forced to scribble. It is not always clear, in short, whether an ink mark is meant to be a comma or a period, or whether a period was intended but a slip of the hand on board a rocking flatboat produced a dash instead.

   To make the text as accessible as possible, I have silently modernized Trist's punctuation, while leaving her original spelling and abbreviations intact. Where her usage is archaic, I have provided glosses in footnotes to the text.

   Despite the peculiarities in spelling, and despite the rare instances of changes in place-names, Trist's route is easy to follow on any good map of the United States. The modern reader need only be careful not to confuse what Trist terms "the last war" with "this war." Traveling as she was through a landscape dotted with military forts, Trist refers to the French and Indian War of 1754–63 when she designates a site as belonging to "the last war." "This war" means the Revolution, whose recent conclusion had permitted her journey.

ACKNOWLEDGMENTS

The travel diary of Elizabeth House Trist is part of the Trist-Burke-Randolph Collection (Ms. 10,487), Manuscripts Division, Special Collections Department, University of Virginia Library, and is published by permission. Among those who helped with the research at Monticello were Sondy M. Sanford, formerly assistant curator, and Susan R. Stein, Curator. Ms. Sanford provided information on Birdwood and Monticello, including a copy of the letter relating the circumstances of Trist's death at Monticello, while curator Stein gave me a guided tour of the second-floor bedrooms where Trist spent her last days. The extraordinary concentration of my research assistant, Colleen O'Toole, allowed me to proofread my typescript of the diary against photocopies of the original manuscript. Ms. O'Toole was also tireless in checking the contents of several microfilm reels of the Papers of Nicholas P. Trist from the Library of Congress. Dávid and Erno Kolodny-Nagy helped me locate illustrative materials at the Library of Congress. And Susan Bouldin, assistant to the dean at the University of Arizona, helped me prepare the final version of the introduction. Finally, I wish to express my gratitude to Barbara Hanrahan, humanities editor at the University of Wisconsin Press, whose confidence in the project allowed her to wait patiently for its conclusion.

The Travel Diary
of Elizabeth House Trist:
Philadelphia to Natchez, 1783–84

[The first two pages of the diary are missing; the third page is badly torn along the right margin, and several lines along the bottom are missing.]

3

[December 23, 1783] dinner and at 6 O Clock PM arrived at Lancaster. Put up at *Steel's* tavern, a very good House. For tea I went to visit my old friend Mrs. James [last name missing], who received me with her usual kindness. She urged me to accept of a bed, but as we intended to set out early in the Morning, I declined accepting her kind offer. 24th [December 24, 1783] Arose very early with an intention to set of before Breakfast, but it set in to snow very fast which detained us till 10 O' clock; we rode some distance before we baited[1] our Horses, the roads beyond description bad: we cou'd get no further that day than Elizabeth Town, which is 18 miles from Lancaster; had very good entertainment at the Sign of the Bear. On the 25th [December 25, 1783] left it before Breakfast. The weather's moderated a little but very ruff roades. Cross'd a beautifull creek about a mile beyond [page torn] . . . town call'd Swatana. It takes [Bottom third of page is missing.]

4

We scarse go out of a walk, which makes our journey tedious. We arrived at Chambers' ferry on the Susquehanna at 3 O Clock PM but found it impassable, such quantity of Ice running. None wou'd attempt to put us over. We were under necessity of staying at the ferry House all night. People uncommonly obligeing, but the House very bad for the winter season, not being finished. Were obliged to Sleep in the same room with Mr. Fowler and another man. Not being accustom'd to such inconveniences, I slept but little. On the 26th [December 26, 1783] Mr. Chambers got several more hands and with great exertions put us over. The boat being full of Horses and the rapidity of the current, together with the Ice, made it

---

1. *baited:* Fed.

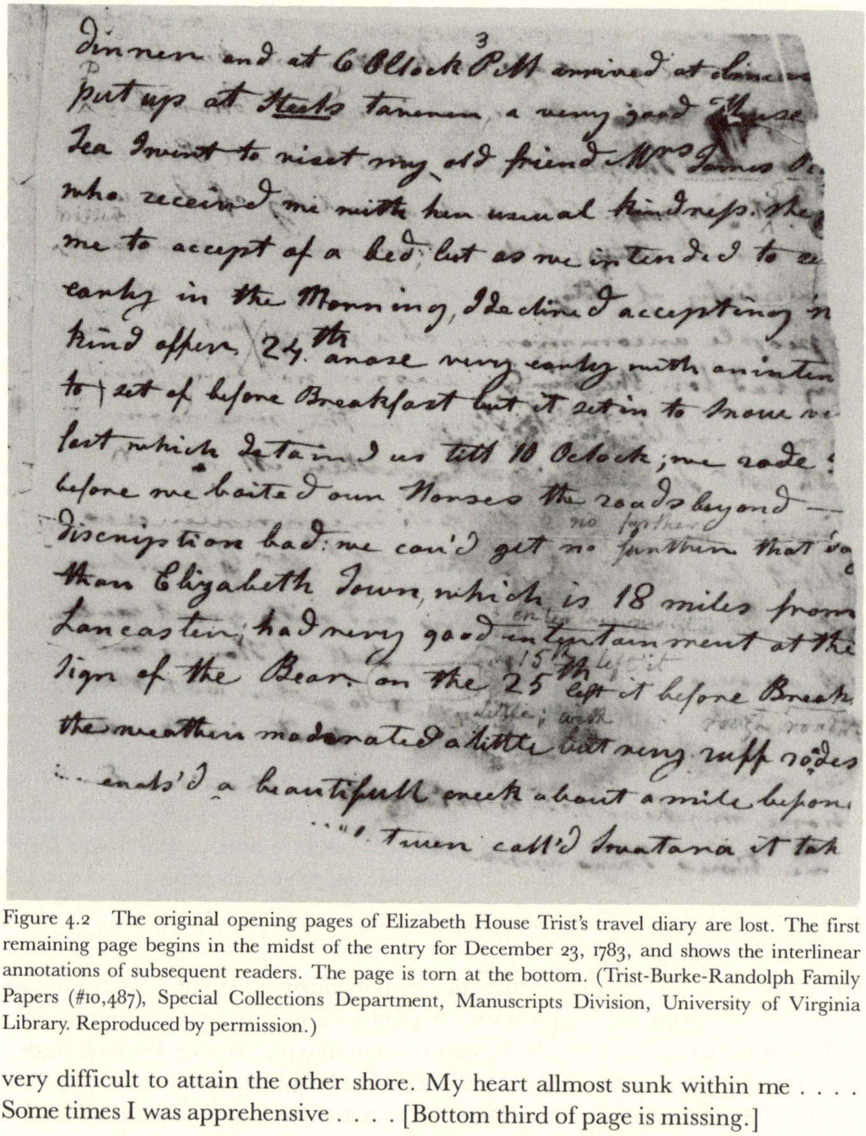

Figure 4.2   The original opening pages of Elizabeth House Trist's travel diary are lost. The first remaining page begins in the midst of the entry for December 23, 1783, and shows the interlinear annotations of subsequent readers. The page is torn at the bottom. (Trist-Burke-Randolph Family Papers (#10,487), Special Collections Department, Manuscripts Division, University of Virginia Library. Reproduced by permission.)

very difficult to attain the other shore. My heart allmost sunk within me . . . . Some times I was apprehensive . . . . [Bottom third of page is missing.]

5

about a mile from the landing, happen'd to row down to the shore. (He was the Gentleman that sent me my Marching orders from Mr. Trist.)[2] His Surprise was

2.   *He was . . . from Mr. Trist:* Captain Simpson was probably known to Nicholas Trist from his service in the British army. Before the federal postal system was established, mail to and from the

great at seeing me at such a season travelling. He insisted on our going to his House, where we were kindly and Hospitably entertaind by himself and wife, to whom he had been but lately married. She seems a very good Woman and has a fine Plantation. We had every thing good and comfortable with a hearty Welcome. 27th [December 27, 1783] After breakfast we left Capt. Simpson and cross'd a very pretty creek call'd Yellow Breeches; this part of the country affords many delightfull prospects.

At ½ Past 4 OClock we arriv'd at Carlisle. Put up at Mr. Pollock's³ tavern, a very genteel House. He a very facetious⁴ old Gentleman and his Wife a very kind Woman. The town much larger than I expected to see at

6

such a distance from navagation. It was too cold for to walk after we allighted; therefore I only judge what presented it self to me as I pass'd. I was surprised on entering the town to see such fine buildings. It seems they were erected at the Publick expence for barracks and stores, at present unoccupied. On the 28th [December 28, 1783] after Breakfast we set off. We had the pleasure of a fine clear cold day. Went about 14 miles, put up at McCracken's tavern. As Mr. Fowler had business in the Neighborhood, we staid the remainder of the day and night; the House tolerable. 29th [December 29, 1783] After breakfast we proceeded; the weather extremely cold all the morng but Soften'd Towards the middle of the day. We arrived at Quigleys before [name obscured because of torn page], the person who had Mr. Fowler's goods in possession: we were under the necessity of staying all night, waiting to see the Pack horse men. This place is situated on the . . . . a very pretty . . . . [Page torn at bottom.]

7

the Mountains and discharges it self in to the Susquehanna. This country, the last war,⁵ was the frontier. The old people of the House entertain'd us with an account of their former sufferings, being continually harrass'd by the Indians; but they

---

frontiers was conveyed by private individuals, often travelers and tavern keepers, and sometimes by friends of the sender or recipient. Hence, Elizabeth House Trist probably received her "Marching orders" in a letter conveyed to her through Simpson, then resident on a major road connecting Philadelphia and the western frontiers.

3. *Mr. Pollock's:* Presumably this is the same Pollock mentioned in Nicholas Trist's letter of September 16, 1780, to his wife: "You [may] draw on me at sight for the Hundred Dollars or if any person will lend you that sum I will repay it to Mr. Pollock or any other person" (Trist-Burke-Randolph Family Papers, Special Collections Department, University of Virginia Library, Charlottesville). Clearly, Nicholas Trist was telling his wife how to raise funds for her trip and, at the same time, reassuring any lender of payment.

4. *facetious:* Witty, mirthful.

5. *the last war:* That is, the French and Indian War, 1754–63.

have lived to see an end to them.[6] They are upwards of eighty, and the old woman told me she coul'd ride a 100 miles in one day without being fatigued if she cou'd get a horse that wou'd carry so far. They have but one Son who is married and has a house full of children. They have given all up to this son and have a room in the House; he maintains them. It gave me plesure to see so much harmony subsist among them. The son's wife told me they had lived together fourteen years, and she never saw the old people out of temper. They are very religious presbeterians; prayers before every meal and after; but their conversation chearfull and happy. I believe if there are good

8

people in the world, they are to be found at this place. My heart over flow'd with benevolence, for it cou'd not be envy to see an old couple that had live'd Sixty years together endeavoring to please each other and to make every one as happy as themselves. A true picture of rural felicity: God continue to grant you his blessing, my worthy old man and Woman. 30th [December 30, 1783] The Pack Horse men did not arrive; as the snow began to fall, we concluded it best not to wait least we shou'd lose the path over the Mountain. After being kindly entertaind we proceeded on our journey. The Snow still falling very thick, we were obliged to push on for want of a place to stop at that was fit for a christian. At one House we stayed to feed our horses, the family was large—a good farm and a Mill, the buildings good; but every thing was so dirty that I would rather have slept out of doors. I dont believe any of the children had been washed since they were born; one of the Girls was

9

allmost a woman. I had no Idea that there were such beings upon this earth. We began to assend the blue Mountain at Clark's gapp. It look'd a litle tremendious as we had no guide, and the snow fell so fast that Mr. Fowler was uneasy least he shou'd lose the path. But thank God we pass'd it with out any mishap, tho we found it difficult to accomplish: the assent more gradual than the decent. We arrived at Mr. Elliotts in the Path Vally in the evening, having rode 25 miles—a good days journey, all things considerd. A good supper of Partrages and good Beds made some amends for the fatigue of the day.

[December 31, 1783]—After having had a good nights rest, on the 31st we set off; the Snow up to the Horses bellies. After rideing 2 miles we began to ascend the Tuscarora Mountain. Found it as Steep as the one we cross'd the day before, but not quite so bad as some horses had broke the

6. *an end to them:* That is, an end to their sufferings.

I O

road a little. Upon the Summit of the Mountain, my saddle turn'd. It was with great difficulty I cou'd stick upon the Horse. Mr. Fowler got down to assist me and was up to his middle in the Snow. Had I dismounted, I believe I must have Perished for I cou'd not have mounted again; and I am certain I cou'd not have walk'd 2 or 3 miles through the snow, it was so deep. On one side of me was a thicket and on the other a precipice. The cattle in the vally look'd no larger than dogs. We suffered another inconvenience for want of a breast plate to our saddles, for some places that we had to ascend where[7] allmost perpendicular, and our saddles slip'd so that we cou'd scarcely keep our selves on by holding the main.[8] We were Six hours going 10 miles to fort Lyttleton, so call'd from a fort having been erected there last war for the Protection of the frontiers; but at present, there is nothing of it to be seen. What was much more agreeable, we found

I I

good entertainment. The House is kept by one Bird, who had been a Capt. in the continental Service and knew how to live better than the generallity of back woods men. [January 1, 1784] We left fort Lyttleton on Newyears day. Rode 19 miles. Came to the Juniatta in the evening, found a difficulty in crossing, it being very deep and full of Ice. We were obliged to put up at the first House we came to, which is not a licensed tavern; but for want of such, travillers are under the necessity of putting up there. The Man of the House is a Magistrate, and the laws of Pennsylvania prohibits such great men from retailing spiritous liquors; therefore, he only *cou'd make out the bill, and his Wife received the Money.* Our entertainment the worst we had met with, notwithstanding the Man was a Colonel in the Militia. The whole House consisted of two rooms: the private room was occupied

I 2

by the Colonel, his lady and children. The other, which serv'd as kitchen, cellar, and Hall, had two dirty beds. The one occupied by Polly and my self was up in a dark corner surrounded by pickling tubs which did not yield the most agreeable smell in the world; the other by Mr. Fowler and a Lawyer Hamilton (who came after us) on his way to the court at Hannas Town. A Hog driver, his Son and daughter, a Negro wench, and two or three children had the floor for their birth.[9] For my part, I kept my cloaths on, to keep my self from the dirt off the bed cloaths. Neither cou'd I sleep for the crying of the children and the novelty of my situation.

7. *where:* Were.
8. *the main:* The horse's mane.
9. *birth: Berth.*

[January 2, 1784] We arose very early and after paying our bill—which came to three dollars for a supper of cold pork and a bowl of Gin Grogg[10] and some sour buckweed bread—we left the banks of the Juniatta with as little reluctance as any place we parted from, tho the situation is very pretty.

1 3

I was much pleased with the prospect of the country—which is Mountanious— and the river Juniatta running through these Mountains for a 100 miles: a clear beautifull Stream, but only navagable for rafts and that only in the time of the freshes. It affords fine fish and, from its being shaded with evergreens, its beauty was much heighten'd at this season. I cou'd not but figure to my self that this must be the Lethe, tho the fields were not Elysium.[11]

[January 2, 1784] We arrived at Bedford time enough for Breakfast on the 2d, which is 15 miles from Colo[nel] Martin's. This Village consists of about a 100 Houses, some of them very good. It is built in a Vally, partly Surrounded by a pretty Stream, a Branch of the Juniatta call'd Rhea Stone. The country looks Beautifull, even in this dreary Season. There is something enlivening and de- lightfull

1 4

in the situation of this Town which seems in the center of a bason[12] form'd by the surrounding Hills. We were so pleased with our entertainment that we did not set off till noon on the 3d. [January 3, 1784] For my part, I cou'd with pleasure have staid longer. We went no further than 13 miles. Stop'd at a little Hut Kept by one Ryan. The neatness of the place and the attention of the man made us as happy as if we had been in a palace—if we cou'd have been accomodated with a chamber to our selves, but that was impossible. The whole House was but one room built with logs, no floor or windows. A good fire served to give light to the house as well as to Warm it. We had a little particion run along the side of our bed, and we hung our great coats up at the foot, which made our birth very private. Mr. Fowler and Mr. Hamilton retired to the Kitchen for us to go to bed; and I made it a rule to get up be- fore day light that I might not see anybody nor they [see] me dress. It is so customary

1 5

for the Men and Women to sleep in the same room that some of the Women look upon a Woman as affected that makes any objection to it. One told me that I talk'd

10. *Gin Grogg:* Gin in hot water with spices.
11. *Lethe . . . Elysium:* In Greek mythology, Lethe is the river in the underworld of Hades which produces forgetfulness of the past; Elysium is the abode of the blessed after death, a place of ideal happiness.
12. *bason:* Basin.

to upon the subject that she thought a Woman must be very inecure in her self that was afraid to sleep in the room with a strange man. For her part, she saw nothing indelicate in the matter, and no man wou'd take a liberty with a woman unless he saw a disposition in her to encourage him. Our entertainment was as good as if in a city. The Man and his Wife had formerly kept a Tavern in the city of Dublin, and are very assiduous and obligeing. The woman went on before us to a House she had about Twenty miles off, to prepare for our accomodation the next day. 4th [January 4, 1784] After Breakfast, we set out on our journey and soon began to assend—the Allegany Mountain it is call'd. Three miles to the summit. We found no difficulty, the ascent being gradual.

1 6

We pass'd over some very poor barren land where there was plenty of game. But the land on the Mountain, in general, seems to appear very good. We stop'd at a farm house to feed our Horses. The people were most all sick. In the winter season, the Woman inform'd that all ways some or other of the family were sick. There is allways a mist which freezes as it falls and adds greatly to the beauty of the trees, but I fancy the moisture of the air makes it unhealthy. In the afternoon, we arrived at Stoney Creek, which is another beautifull Stream as wide as the Juniatta.— Mrs. Ryan prepared for our reception. The House had been good but was allmost gone to decay, having been deserted all the war as the Indians had murdered many families in the Neighborhood. We had a private room, and in every respect much better accomodated than we had a right to expect so far in the woods upon a road that no person traviled during the war.[13]

[January 5, 1784] We left Stony creek on the Morng of the 5th.

1 7

This days journey very tiresome, there being no house for us to bait our Horses at. We found the roads very indifferent. We cross'd a fine creek call'd Quimahone before we came to the Laurel Hill and arrived at Fort Ligonier in the evening, after having rode 21 miles. The weather warm and a drisley rain through the whole day and night. 6th [January 6, 1784] Was waked in the Morning by a pretty severe Thunder Storm and a very great fall of rain, which had melted all the Snow and obliged us to proceed on our journey—tho the rain still continued—for fear the creeks riseing shou'd detain us for several days; which we were given to understand frequently happen'd in great freshes, there being no Bridges on the West side of the Mountains. Before our departure, I visited the fort, it being esteem'd the best Stockade in the Western Country. There is about a Dozn log huts erected

13. *the war:* That is, the revolutionary war.

within the fort, which the families in the Neighbourhood resorted to when ever
they apprehended danger from the Savages. After Breakfast we set off. Ligonier is
situated upon a creek call'd Loyalhanna. There are

1 8

two or three dwellings besides those in the fort—one of which General Sinclair[14]
formerly lived in, at present unoccupied. We found very good entertainment at
one Mr. Galbreath's. The land in this Neighbourhood is very fertile, and the country seems pleasant. We found the Loyalhanna very rapid and allmost too high to
pass with safety, occasion'd by the melting of so great a quantity of snow. Indeed,
this days journey has been as dangerous as any we have gone through. The small
runs as well as creeks were all most impassible. The Horses were frequently near
swiming. Notwithstanding, I did not feel much intimidated but plunged through
with no other mishap than geting wet; the roads very bad. My Horse cou'd
scarcely keep his feet. He fell with me once, but I was so lucky as to keep my
saddle. Mr. Fowler gave me credit for my good Horsemanship. We were emersed
in difficulties several times, particularly geting through a Swamp about 9 miles
from Ligonier. Our horses were up to their bellies and cou'd not move one foot,
which obliged us to dismount. Not being quite as heavy as our Cavilry,[15] and
picking our way, we got out without sinking higher

1 9

than our knees in the mud. We arrived at Hannas Town in the evening, after
having rode 21 miles and a very disagreeable ride it was. The town consists of a
Dozn log huts; it had been before the War much larger. A party of Brittish and
Indians surprised the town, murdered several, and carried of several families captives to Detroit. Some of the inhabitants saved themselves by taking refuge in a
little Stockade and defended themselves with only fifteen muskets against 300
Indians and Brittish who signalized themselves[16] by taking the Women and children and burning the town. The courts are held at this Place and, unfortunately for
us, are siting at this time. We found a difficulty in geting a place of Shelter, such a
number of people being assembled to attend the court. Mr. Orr, the Sheriff, was so
kind as to give us a bed at his House, which only consisted of one room and that, on
acct of his business, as Publick as the Bar room of a tavern. His Wife had a bed in

---

14. *General Sinclair:* General Arthur St. Clair (1743–1818) led American forces against the Indians
in the Ohio Valley, suffering several defeats in the 1780s. He would later be named the first governor of
the Northwest Territory (1787–1802).

15. *Cavilry:* That is, horses.

16. *signalized themselves:* Made themselves noteworthy or notorious.

one corner of the room; we occupied the other. The poor Woman had been lately brought to bed and was very Ill. She appeared to be a very delicate good Woman and had been comfortably situated

2 0

before the place was burnt. I did not know what to do about going to bed, there being no curtains to screen us from the sight of every one that came. At last, we had recourse to our cloaks and blankets, which answered the purpose very well. [January 7, 1784] The Wind changed in the night to the NW, and in the morng of 7th the whole earth appeared like Glass and so cold that we hardly had resolution to set out. But necessity obliged us to proceed, which we did after Breakfast. The roads were so slippery that it made it very dangerous rideing. We concluded to go about two Mile out of the way to get over. Horses frosted, the cold so intense that I was allmost dead. We found it impossible to get to the next stage which is 20 miles. Therefore, hired a guide to conduct us to a good farm house, which was but 10 mile, where we were inform'd we cou'd be provided with beds. We stop'd at a litle cabbin about half way to warm our selves and got a very good dinner. It was evening before we got to Waltowers, the name of the owner of the farm. We found a comfortable room, warm with a stove. I felt quite happy for we were allmost

2 1

frozen. We had a good comfortable supper of fat bacon fried and some Coffee. I eat it with a mighty good appetite. We met Mr. Irwin, a Gentleman from Pittsburg at this House. Old Mr. Waltowers and Mr. Irwin had one of the beds, Polly and myself the other—but we found no difficulty in being private, having good worsted curtains round the bed. We allways made it a practise to dress and undress behind the curtain. Therefore, found no difficulty, notwithstanding there were Six or 7 men in the room. Mr. Fowler and the rest of the people had some clean straw spread on the floor. I must confess I never slept better. [January 8, 1784] In the Morng of the 8th, after breakfast, we set of; the weather still excessive cold. Our Horses scarse able to keep their feet. We stoped at a little cabbin to warm our-selves, being allmost frozen riding only 5 mile. After geting a little thaw'd, we again proceeded on our journey. Our difficulties seem'd to increase. We were obliged to dismount at every hill or run the risk of breaking our necks. Some times our Horses wou'd tumble, and some times

2 2

our selves. I had one tumble that hurt me a good deal: decending a very steep hill, at the foot of which runs Turky Creek, which is 12 miles from Pitts-g. We found the creek so full of Ice as to make it at that place impassible. For my part, I wou'd rather have run the risk than assend the hill again, notwithstanding the Man who lived on the other side call'd to us not to attempt it unless we ment to lose our lives. We were obliged to go up the hill and ride a mile further up the Creek before we cou'd attempt to cross. At last we got through, but not without being in great danger. We got some dinner at the Widow Myers and set of in hopes to get in to Pittsburg before bedtime. We met with an inhabitant of that place at Waltowers. Polly's Horse being in better Spirits than mine, she push'd on in Company with this man. I cou'd not get my Horse out of a walk, and every step his feet allmost sliping from under him, at last down we came; but lucky enough to receive no damage.

2 3

Only it made his cowardise increase and added nothing to my courage. Poor beast, he trembled every step he took after that. Night came on and, for the first time since I left home, my Spirits forsook me. I began to prepare my self for the other world, for I expected every moment when my neck wou'd be broke. I cou'd not help crying. Mr. Fowler kept before me and, it being dark, I did not expose my weakness. Some times I wish'd he wou'd ride on and leave me [so] that I might get down and *die.*—At last we came to the Bullock Pens, a farm belonging to Mr. Eliott. I was allmost overcome with cold and fatigue, having been on Horseback 3 hours and only rode 6 miles. We concluded to stay till Morning. It was a bitter night and a very bad house. Mrs. Elliott was so kind as to part beds from her husband, on our account. She wedged me in with her self and child in a miserable dirty place, she having

2 4

resign'd her birth to Mr. Fowler. I never lay so uncomfortable in my life. The people were civil and did us a kindness by affording us a Shelter and put themselves to some inconvenience to accomodate us, or I cou'd say a great deal more in dispraise of our entertainment. [January 9, 1784] We got into Pittsburg time enough for dinner on the 9th of January.—About 3 miles before you enter the town, there are two roads. The one to the right is call'd the Allegany, from its vicinity to a River of that name. The other is call'd the Monongahala, lying to the left, which likewise takes its name from a river. We took the right hand road and, notwithstanding the intence cold, I was pleased with its beauty, being situated on the banks of the river and that river had as Majestick an appearance as tho it was near the Ocean. It was quite unexpected to me to behold so large a body of water such a distance from the Sea.

Figure 4.3   A late eighteenth-century view of Pittsburgh at the forks of the Ohio, with a flatboat in the river foreground. The flag flies atop Fort Pitt. (Georges Henri Victor Collot, *Voyage dans L'Amèrique septentrionale, ou Description des pays arrosés par le Mississippi, l'Ohio, le Missouri et autres rivières affluentes* [Paris: Arthus Bertrand, Libraire, 1826]; plate 5. Courtesy Library of Congress, Geography and Map Division.) (See figure 4.6, p. 219.)

2 5

Just as we enter the *town,* Grants Hill presents itself on our left hand. It appears to be about 100 feet in height. A sigh escaped me as a tribute to the Memory of those poor fellows that were slain in battle at that place.

> A heap of dust alone remains of thee
> Tis what thou art and what the proud shall be.[17]

Fort Pitt is situated upon a point of land form'd by the junction of the two rivers

17.   Quoted from Alexander Pope's "Epistle to Robert, Earl of Oxford," 1721. The original lines read:

> A heap of dust alone remains of thee:
> 'Tis all thou art, and all the proud shall be!

with the Ohio, for the Ohio appears to me to be a continuation of the Monongahala; but the Allegany meeting here with the Monongahala take their course
together and forms the source of the Ohio. Both rivers are about half a mile wide,
and the banks are in most places about 60 feet high. On the Monongahala, where
the town is chiefly built, there are about a Hundred buildings; all (except one [of]
stone and one or two frame) are built of logs and they in a very

2 6

ruinous state. The Allegany is a fine, clear, cold water. The banks are not as high
as the other river; neither is there any declivity which makes the land fall away in
the time of the freshes. There is a fine orchard belonging to the Garrison. A
number of trees have fallen that were planted near the water side. About 12 feet was
carried away this Spring—but the other shore receives it, which is call'd the Indian
side. The land is exceeding rich and abounds with an abundance of maple trees,
from which they make quantitys of sugar. I pd[18] a visit to their camps in the time of
their sugar harvest, which is as soon as the sap begins to rise, and was much
pleased with the excursion. The vegetation, being much quicker on that side of the
river, presented to our view a beautifull verder,[19] a sight that we had been a
stranger to for some time. The low land, lying between the river and the

2 7

high lands or hills, is call'd bottoms, and nothing can exceed the quallity of those
grounds. In the month of May they look like a garden, such a number of beautifull
flowers and shrubs. There are several wild vegetables that I wou'd give the preference to[20] those that are cultivated: Wild Asparagus, Indian hemp, shepherd
sprouts, lambs quarters, &cc—besides great abundance of Ginsang, Gentian and
many other aromatick. On the other side of the Monongahala, the land is amaizing
lofty. Tis supposed that the whole body of it is cole and goes by the name of the cole
Hill. At one side it has been open'd to supply the inhabitants with fuel. It is equeal
in quallity to the N'castle[21] or any other I ever saw. The Hill is seven Hundred feet
perpendicular, and on the top is a settlement. The land is fertile and capable of
raising all kinds of grain. The timber is very large, and the shrubbery pretty much
the same as is produced

18. *pd.:* Paid.
19. *verder:* Verdure or greenness.
20. *preference to:* Preference over?
21. *N'castle:* Newcastle-upon-Tyne, the capital of Northumberland, England, was famed as a
coal-mining center.

2 8

in the bottoms. The prospect from this Hill is very extensive; and if the country which is mountanous was cleard, it wou'd be beyond discription beautifull. Grants Hill is a delightfull situation. I think I wou'd give the preference for to live on [the hill] as you are more in the World. The river is more confin'd, but the Objects are not so deminitive below you. The fort is situated upon the point or near it. Formerly it was a very elegant fortification, but the English—when they abandon'd the port in 73—destroy'd it, and the present one is built out of the ruins. The Barracks are of Brick, but poor patch'd up things. The Gates, ramparts &cc. seem to be sufficiently strong to answer their intended purpose as a protection against the Indians. There are so many hills that command it that, [even] if it was much stronger, I fancy it cou'd not make any great resistance

2 9

against a few good pieces of Artillery. In the spring of the year, the rivers abound with very fine fish, some of them exceeding good—particularly the Pike, which greatly exceed those that are caught below the Mountains in flavor and size, some of them weighing thirty pounds. The cat fish are enormous; some of them are obliged to be carried by 2 Men. The perch are commonly about the size of Sheep heads, but they have been caught that weigh'd 20 pound. There are several other kind—such as herring, &c—but different from ours. The bass look more like our Sea perch, only much larger, and I give them the preference to all the rest for their delicacy of flavor. Upon the whole, I like the situation of Pittsburg mightily and, was there good Society, I shou'd be contented to end my days in the Western country. I made an excursion over the Monongahala to the Cherties settlement,[22] about ten miles from Pittsburg, where Mr. Fowler has a fine tract of land laid out in farms.

3 0

The Cherties Creek is the most serpentine of any I ever saw. In the course of ten miles, we had to cross it five or six times. Here and there a farm wou'd present it self to our view with a few acres around it clear'd. But the country is yet in a very rude state or else it wou'd afford many beautifull prospects—it being Hilly and the land of a superior quallity. For my part, I felt oppress'd with so much wood towering above me in every direction and such a continuance of it. A little opening now and then, but a very confined Prospect: nothing but the Heavens above and the

22. *the Cherties settlement:* Now Chartiers Town, Pennsylvania.

earth beneath, and a pretty spring bubbling every here and there out of the side of a Hill.

I began at last to conceit[23] myself Attlass with the whole World upon my shoulders.[24] My spirits were condenc'd to nothing. My head began to ach[e], and I returnd to town quite sick.—

May^ye 20th [May 20, 1784] Left Pittsburg with as little regret as I ever did any place that I had lived so long in. Mr. & Mrs. Fowler treated us with every possible attention, and from the number of strangers resorting thither on their way

3 1

to the Cumberland &cc made the winter pass a way much more agreeable than it otherwise wou'd. We where at several dances at which there wou'd be fifteen or twenty ladies and as many Gentlemen. If there had not been those little recreations, I shou'd certainly have been very miserable. The tardiness of the boat builder detain'd us till the river got so low that I was in great trepedation least our passage wou'd be stop'd. But good fortune has attended us. Three days rain has swell'd the rivers, and we have the flattering appearance of a speedy voyage. Our accomodations, all things consider'd, not to be complain'd off. The weather pleasant and every thing wears a smiling aspect. We soon came to Mackees Island, 4 miles from Pittsburg. It appears to be about a mile in length and very fertile, as is most of the land in this country. About three miles further is another fine Island nam'd Montiers; seven miles long, it is a very fine tract of land. I am inform'd *Montier* has sold it to several people at different times. This Montier is the descendent of a frenchman

3 2

and Indian. He has nothing but the external politesse of the former; his habits and dispossission bespeak his origin from the Mother, [he] being a savage in every sense of the word. The Ohio is full of small Islands; therefore must omit particularizing, not being acquainted with their names—if any they have. We arrived at dark at fort McIntosh, having come 30 miles. It was noon when we left Pittsburg. There is a Sergeants guard kept at this place, but the night is too far advanc'd for us to see what kind of a place it is. We had a comfortable dish of tea at about 9 OClock. In preparing for bed, I unfortunately fell from my birth backwards; bruisd my head and shoulder and otherwise hurt myself sufficient to make me a litle more carefull in future. However, I got a pretty good nights rest and, in the morng of the 21st [May 21, 1784], we were Eighty miles on our way. At noon we

23. *to conceit:* To imagine.
24. *Attlas . . . my shoulders:* Atlas was a Greek god who held up the pillars of the universe.

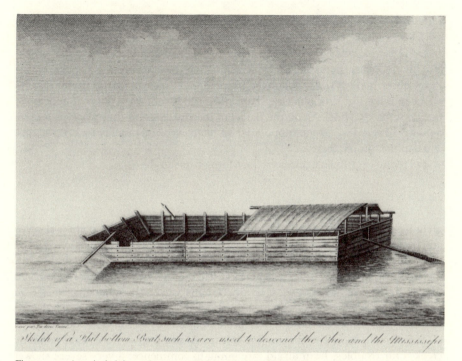

Figure 4.4   A typical eighteenth-century flatboat, designed for hauling goods and people on the Ohio and Mississippi rivers. Generally built in the vicinity of Pittsburgh, "flats" were constructed of whip-sawed and hewed timber. Fifty feet was a popular length; the width rarely exceeded fifteen feet, in order to permit passage through the narrow channel at Louisville. Around the outside of the deck were upright posts about six feet high, and to these posts heavy planks were pinned as a protection against the fire of Indians or other attackers. Not shown are the portholes for firing that were generally cut into the planks. At the time Trist made her journey, flat crews regularly carried muskets and blunderbusses. Passengers' sleeping quarters were located beneath the covered shelter. (Georges Henri Victor Collot, *Voyage dans L'Amèrique septentrionale, ou Description des pays arrosés par le Mississippi, l'Ohio, le Missouri et autres rivières affluentes* [Paris: Arthus Bertrand, Libraire, 1826], plate 7. Courtesy Library of Congress, Geography and Map Division.) (See figure 4.6, p. 219.)

reach'd Wheeling, which is a Hundred miles from Pittsburg. We went a shore for milk. There is the remains of a stockade and a few log Houses: one of them a very good one occupied by

3 3

a Mr. Tane, who owns a good deal of land in this Neighbourhood, which is very rich and the situation very high. Yet the people seem to have caught the infection of the country, a desire for the Kentucki. I am allmost in extacy at the Magnificence of the display of nature. The trees are deck'd all in their gay attire, and the earth in its richest verdure. So much for blooming May.

22d [May 22, 1784] After a good nights rest we arose, had a comfortable breakfast. By 9 Oclock got as far as the Muskingum, 171 miles from Pittsburg: a fine River about 300 y^{ds} wide, about 200 miles in length, takes its rise from a swamp about 40 miles this side lake Erie. Passd the little Kanhawa at noon; it appears to be about 150 y^{ds} wide. Along the banks of the river, just at that place, is a great quantity of very large stone supposed to be of an excellent quallity for mills stones, equal to the french Burrs.

23d [May 23, 1784] 9 O clock in the Morng came to the

3 4

great Kanhawa or new river, a beautiful situation for a town. The point is clear'd, and the banks are high. There was a very pretty fort at this place, till about 4 years ago. It was destroy'd by the savages. The land is the property of General Washington.[25] We came a 100 miles in 21 hours and drifted all the way. 1 O clock PM passd the Guyandat. We have not yet seen any Indians, but tis thought dangerous to go on shore as they have been seen lurking about this part of the river. We have not seen any wild beasts till today a bear presented himself to our view; but he made off before our people cou'd get a fire at him. At sun set, we were as far as sandy creek. Our troubles, I am afraid, are going to commence: a very severe shower that has wet our beding. Polly taken very unwell with a fever and bad headach, which alarms me least it may continue. This evening has all the appearance of rain.

24th [May 24, 1784] A very fine morng after a very dreadfull night. Thunder and severe lightning and exceeding

3 5

heavy rain. Our birth made very disagreeable: the roof let in the water in several places—

We pass'd an Indian camp in the night. We cou'd hear them yell, but it was too dark for us to see them. 8 o Clock in the morng pass'd the Lioto. It appears to be a very pretty little river. One can hardly be a judge of what width the rivers are, for they are so shaded with large trees that the view is contracted. The Wind against us and very high, which obliges us to make fast to the shore for the first time. I amused myself gathering wild ginger, which grows in great abundance along the banks. The wind has abated a little, and we are enabled to proceed on our voyage,

25. *property of General Washington:* George Washington, like many other southern planters, had been speculating in western lands since before the Revolution.

only hav^g laid by one hour. Pollys fever returned towards eveng; however, we had a tollerable good night.

25th [May 25, 1784] The morning clear, but the wind against us, which impedes our going very much. We passd the little Miami after dark, 126 miles from the Lioto, and [we passed] licking creek at 11 O clock.

3 6

26th [May 26, 1784] A fine clear cold morning, the wind in our favor. At 7 O clock pass'd the big Miami. It is a fine river, the banks much higher and more clear'd than any of the rivers I have seen, except the big Kanhawa. There are numbers of creeks continually presenting themselves, and some of them very large. And what is extraordanary—when ever you see a creek on one shore, there is allways another directly opposite. Noon came to limestone creek. The big bones are found three miles from this place, back in the woods.—The difficulty attending my getting there, for want of a guide and other obstacles, obliges me to give up all thoughts of satisfying my curiossity; tho we shall stop to wait for some of our people who have been out to hunt for several hours. The wind being so much in our favor, our boat makes so much way that we are apprehensive they will not be able to come up with us. After regaling

3 7

our selves with a walk on the shore for half an hour, our hunters return'd without any game, which was a disappointment as we expected to have had some fresh meat for dinner. There are such numbers of boats continually going down the river that all the game have left the shore.

Pass'd the Kentucke 11 O clock at night. Had not the opportunity to see it, but am told it is about the size of the great Kanhawa. There are no settlements upon the river, which surprised me. Such a number of people having gone to that country, I expected to have seen the lands about here well inhabited. But it seems they go up the river Kentucke about a 100 miles before they come to the settlements.

27th [May 27, 1784] Arrived at bear grass creek six o clock in the evening, about a half a mile from Louisville. The great number of boats that lay up the creek and several families that were encamp'd at that place made me think I had

3 8

got into the world of spirits.[26] We were met by several Gentlemen, that I had the

26. *The great number . . . spirits:* Another reference to the River Lethe of Greek mythology, on whose banks the dead drink of forgetfullness of the past and wait their turn to pass over into Hades, the underworld.

View of the Rapids of the Ohio and of Louisville taken from the village of Clarkesville

Figure 4.5   At the time of Trist's journey, river pilots were regularly employed to help guide boats through the treacherous rapids of the Ohio at Louisville. A contemporary sketch of the rapids shows two flatboats. (Georges Henri Victor Collot, *Voyage dans L'Amèrique septentrionale, ou Description des pays arrosés par le Mississippi, l'Ohio, le Missouri et autres rivières affluentes* [Paris: Arthus Bertrand, Libraire, 1826], plate 18. Courtesy Library of Congress, Geography and Map Division.) (See figure 4.6, p. 219.)

pleasure of being acquainted with, who conducted us to the fort where Mr. Taylors family reside for the present.[27] Our accomodation not the most desireable in point of elegance, being an old log hut. Mrs. Taylor has four daughters. Polly and myself occupy this place as a chamber. We spread our beds at night and, in the Morning by rolling them up, they serve as seats. An old barrell with a board on top is our table. And this is comfortable to what many are obliged to put up with.— The polite attention of the Gentlemen to serve us renders our situation as agreeable and more so than we have any reason to expect. The Fort has been a very good one but is now out of repair. There are 12 habitations within the enclosear. The Town is laid out in lots, but not many buildings erected. What there is, hardly

27.   *the fort . . . present:* Captain Edmund Taylor, from Orange County, Virginia, had been an officer in the Continental Army and was now settled with his family in Louisville, Kentucky; by 1780 he was a town trustee. Fort Nelson, where the Taylor family temporarily resided in 1784, stood at the corner of present-day Seventh and Main streets in Louisville. Colonel Richard Taylor followed his cousin in resettling his family from Virginia to Louisville, bringing with him in 1786 the infant Zachary Taylor (1785–1850), who would become the twelfth president of the United States.

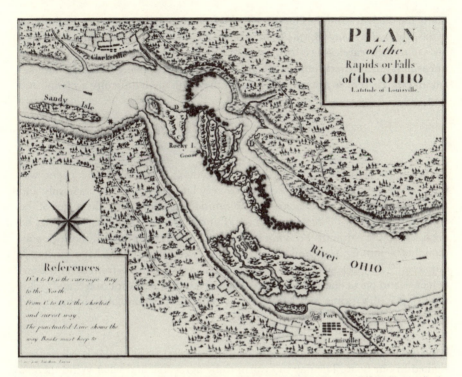

Figure 4.6   A contemporary map of the rapids and falls on the Ohio River at Louisville details the difficult and narrow passage through which Trist's flatboat had to maneuver. The map also locates the fort at which Trist briefly resided. (Georges Henri Victor Collot, *Voyage dans L'Amèrique septentrionale, ou Description Des Pays arrosés par le Mississippi, l'Ohio, le Missouri et autres rivières affluentes* [Paris: Arthus Bertrand, Libraire, 1826], plate 17. Courtesy Library of Congress, Geography and Map Division.)

deserving the name of Houses. But so necessary is a shelter that a little cabin about 12 feet square lets for six and eight Dollars per month. The situation

39

of this place is very pretty: the bank high and commands a view of the falls and Islands. At any other time, I shou'd take much more satisfaction in examining the beauties of this place, but my mind is at present not in a very tranquil state. Our boat is fast on the Rocks, and it is doubted whether she will be got off. This spot is reckon'd unhealthy, owing to the springs which are impregnated with copperness;[28] yet the inhabitants are so perverse that they will use this water because it is cold, in preference to the river. I observ'd some ponds of stagnated water—partic-

28.   *copperness:* Copperas, an iron sulphate that tinges the water green.

ularly the ditch around the Garrison—which must contribute to the unhealthiness of the place. 28th [May 28, 1784] Our boat took a pilot to go over the falls, but either his villinay or carelessness run her on the Rocks—which occasion'd *us* great uneasiness, the owners and people great fatigue, [they] being obliged to unload her and the current so amaizing rapid that they with great difficulty accomplish'd it in

4 0

the space of eight days. The expence attending this unfortunate event was upwards of fifty Pounds. We were treated very kindly by Mr. Taylors family and indeed by every one in the place. But my mind was not at ease: the water of the river was every day decreasing, and I was under great anxiety least we shoud be detained till the Autumn. I did my endeavour towards disappateing those gloomy thoughts by joining in several little dances that were made on the Miss Taylors & our accts.[29] I experienc'd the greatest attention and politeness from several Gentlemen—and particular marks of friendship from Colonel Anderson[30] and Colonel Lewis[31] of Virginia and Mr. Trant, a young Gentleman lately from Ireland and has lately open'd a store at this place.

Nine o clock in the morning 5th of June [June 5, 1784] we left the falls, all matters righted in our boat. The day too warm to be agreeable and what Wind there is against us. The river appears to more advantage this side

4 1

the falls than above. The shore seems clearer and in many places, for about a mile in length, there is a regular Wall to support the bank, as if built of the finest hewn stone. One of our men went on shore to hunt and, being gone several hours, returnd with a deer the first wild meat we have had. Sun sets. Pass'd salt river which runs up in the Kentucke settlements, as they are call'd.

I am inform'd there are a number of good Plantations up on this river. At 10 oClock made fast to the shore for the night for fear of geting aground, as there are many sand bars in the course of a few mile. The river is low which will lengthen our voyage very much. We go but 30 mile in a day, and above the Falls we went 50—

29. *accts:* Accounts.

30. *Colonel Anderson:* Colonel Richard Clough Anderson of Hanover County, Virginia, was the father of Charles Anderson, later governor of Ohio.

31. *Colonel Lewis:* Probably a relative of Meriwether Lewis (1774–1809), also of Virginia, who would lead the Lewis and Clark expedition, 1803–1806.

6th [June 6, 1784] After a disagreeable night tormented with Gnats and Musquitos, we left our moorings at the dawn of day; very severe

4 2

thunder gusts all the Morning. In the afternoon we went on shore in the canoe at
the Point of an island to hunt for turtle eggs. This island is of a sandy soil and
abounds with grape vines— which they say are very luscious when ripe. We did
not succeed in getting eggs, but caught a fine Gosling. Along the shore there is a
great quantity of stone that look like Iron ore. I dont think the land very remarkable from the falls to this place, which is about 70 miles: the timber not very large,
at least upon the water side, and I have no oppertunity of seeing any other. Heavy
rain all night.—We pass'd the Green river about two oClock in the Morning of the
7th [June 7, 1784]. About nine it began to clear, and our people went on shore to
hunt and kill'd a tame cow which they mistook for a Buffaloe. However, it turned
out very good Beef. They

4 3

employ'd all the rest of the day jerkin it to preserve it, which is done by cutting it
into small thin pieces and running them on sticks, lay them on a scaffold; under-
neath they make a small fire and a great smoke, which in a few hours drys [the beef
strips] so as to keep a long time.

8th [June 8, 1784] In the Morng rain but cleard up. Warm and continued so all
the day. Nothing remarkable but passing a great many Islands and geting into
very shoal water on a sand bar. We were very apprehensive our boat woud ground,
but with great care we got clear.—

We pass'd a fine large river about Sun set, which I conclude to be the Buffaloe.
None of our people even rememberd to have seen it before, having I suppose gone
by it in the night. The owners of the Boat seem to be well acquainted with the
Rivers, this being the fifth time they have gone down the Ohio. 'Tis the largest
river between this and the Allegany. I was alarm'd about noon, seeing our boats
were geting their guns in order—for fear the Indians shou'd

4 4

attack us—several of them being encamp'd on the Shore, and our boat was under
the necessity of making fast directly opposite to them. The Wind being high made
the river so ruff that our boat cou'd not stem the waves. I must confess I was well
pleased when we again put of, which we did in about an hour. The weather a little
moderated.

This part of the river is thought to be the most dangerous. The Indians keep along here more than any where else, but we have been very lucky as yet, not having seen any to be certain off till today.

9th [June 9, 1784] A bad night on account of the Musquitoes not to be borne. Employed ourselves in making a Pavilion[32] out of some course gauze I bought for that purpose at Pittsburg. Am in hopes this night will be something better than the last, as we shall be able to keep of our teasing visitants—for they have allmost done for me allready.

4 5

10th [June 10, 1784] Just before sun rise we pass'd the Wabash, a very fine river which runs 500 miles in to country. There are very fine french settlements upon this river—one about 180 miles up call'd the O Post. I am inform'd the country is very healthy and the land very fertile, and that it is a place of considerable trade. About 8 oClock we observed two canoes with Indians making towards us. We were prepared for their reception if their intentions had been hostile. The boat in company hail'd them and invited them to come on board. One of the canoes accepted the invitation. Two Indians and a very handsome squaw with a young child. They had formerly been of the Delaware tribe, but a number of them had left that Nation about fourteen years ago and went to live up the Wabash. They have been our very great enemies this War.[33] One of the

4 6

fellows calls himself James Dickison. He is one of their chiefs, and a sensible fierce looking fellow, but his character is very bad. They say he has plunderd several boats and murderd many people that have been going down this river. My curiossity led me to visit them, as they had all the appearance of friendship. They eat and drank and smoked the calmut.[34] As it is good to have friends at court, I carried the Squaw some bread; and as her Infant was exposed to the sun, I gave her my Hankerchief to shade it, for which she seem'd very thankfull. Mr. McFarlane gave them some flour and meat and a bottle of Whisky, *to make glad come.* After honoring us with their company for about an hour they wish'd us well and left us in great good humour. We arrived at the Big Cave early in the evening and went on shore to see it.

32. *Pavilion:* Tent.

33. *this war:* That is, the revolutionary war.

34. *calmut:* Calumet, a clay-bowled, reed-stemmed tobacco pipe, traditionally an Indian symbol of peace.

4 7

I lament that we had not a little more day light that I might examine it more minutely. When the river is high, it stands directly on the waters edge. But that happens not to be the case [now], which embellishes the Prospect much, by presenting us with a fine flight of steps of white stone that has the appearance of marble, clean and elegant, directly in front of the Cave which appears to be about forty feet high and sixty in width and resembles an old castle. The entrance is as large as a common door to house. A grape vine runs up on each side, and a tree juts over the top, which adds to its beauty. It was so dark that we were obliged to set fire to some light wood to see our way into the cave. The upper part of the passage is about four feet wide, but near the earth the rocks jut out so as to make the path only a foot and a half. I was disappointed not finding

4 8

more room, as the passage indicated something capacious; but the widest part does not exceed seven foot. The driping of the water form'd some petrefactions[35] that resembled columns. We soon hurried out, for the dampness made it disagreeable. Upon the whole, I think it one of the most grand and beautifull natural structures and the greatest curiossity I ever beheld. There is a fine smooth perpendicular rock for about a quarter of a mile [that] nearly joins the Cave, which looks as if it was built for a garden Wall. It appears to be about 20 feet high. After we got into the canoe to go on board the flat, by one of the people extending his voice, we observed that there was an amaizing echo. We diverted our selves for some time; every word that was spoken was repeated as distinctly as if a little girl on shore was mocking us. For my part, I cou'd hardly be persuaded but what

4 9

some people had encamped on the shore after we got to the boat. The wind began to blow which obliged us to make fast to the shore for the night, which was so fine and rocky that we were not troubled as heretofore with Musquitos.

11th [June 11, 1784] The wind lull'd, but the weather very warm. About 10 oClock was alarm'd by a canoe making for our boat, which we supposed to be Indians. The blunderbuss was mounted, the Muskets loaded, and every matter properly arrainged for fighting. My self disposed of between the flour barrels. But to my great satisfaction they turn'd out to be some french men going to the Cumberland river to trade. Their appearance was perfectly savage, having little or no cloaths on

35. *petrefactions:* Petrifications in the form of stalactites or stalagmites.

and their hides quite as dark as the Indians. They had come from O Post. At 9 oClock in the evening we reach'd as far as the Shawanoe or Cumberland river. It is

50

a large river and runs a great way in to the country. I am inform'd that it takes its rise from the Allegany Mountain in Washington county, Virginia. The meandering of the river makes it above two thousand mile to its source. We pass'd the Chinokee river in the night.

12th [June 12, 1784] A fine Breeze but the wind as usual contrary, which makes our passage tedious. In the morning we came to the Massac, a place where formerly there had been a fort and was evacuated by the french in the year [17]58. The land is remarkable good about here and very fine hunting grounds. Our people went on shore to hunt, but coming to an Indian camp where there was some squaws, they did not think it prudent to fire—tho they saw a drove of Buffaloe and two deer. About noon a heavy cloud that portended a storm made our Gentlemen think it prudent to

51

put to shore and very lucky for us we did—for in all probability our boat woud have stove or [been] greatly damaged, for a more violent wind I never heard. The trees crack'd about us, and it thunder'd, lightned and rain'd as if heaven and earth were coming together. For an hour after which, all was again calm, and we proceeded on our voyage but very slow, the current very dead. Supposed to be the back waters of the Mississippi. Made fast to the shore for the night as it is thought unsafe to enter the Mississippi in the dark.

13th [June 13, 1784] After a pleasant cool night [with] very few Musquitoes to trouble us, I arose in expectation of seeing the Grand Riviere but had not that satisfaction till four Oclock in the afternoon. The day pleasant and the wind in our favor. Upon any other occasion, I shou'd be sorry for the exchange— the

52

Water of the Mississippi uncommonly low so as to discover a large sand bar near the junction of the two rivers—but the current is much stronger than the Ohio. About 3 miles below the mouth of the Ohio, there is a fort or, rather, the remains of one which was erected by the Americans this War and call'd after Governor Jefferson. I was inform'd it at present was occupied by a Nation of Indians call'd the Taumas who have been nutaral,[36] notwithstanding the English took great pains to

36. *nutaral:* Neutral.

make them take up the hatchet against us. To avoid their snares, they abandon'd their grounds on the Miami, about 60 mile from Detroit, and came down to this part of the coountry. Mr. Bevird and two of the men went on shore in hopes to get a hunter.[37] I was eager to accompany them. I wish'd to see the fort because it bore the name of my friend, but I was dissuaided from making the attempt as it was not certain what Indians

5 3

might be there. They returned unsuccesfull and gave me a very unfavorable account of the place, which they found totally abandon'd and the worst situation of any upon the river, the land very low. We anchor'd about 7 miles below the Ohio. The evening cool but no comfort till we got under our *bear*[38] for the Musquitos. The navagation of this river is renderd dangerous by a number of logs that are fix'd by one end at the bottom of the river, and the other end is about two feet above the water. Many boats are lost by running upon these logs and the greatest attention is necessary to avoid them. However we are happy in being with carefull good men, well acquainted with the river.

14th [June 14, 1784] At dawn of day we left the shore and soon came in sight of the Iron bank; a great quantity of ore may be picked up on the surface

5 4

of the earth. It is 16 miles from the Ohio, a fine high situation. And I am told there is to be a town laid out here very soon. At ten oClock we pass'd Reed creek 12 mile from the Iron banks. We saw some elk on a sand bar. Our men went on shore and pursued them in to the thicket and kill'd two of them, but it detain them so long that they had to row 30 miles before they reach'd the flat. In the afternoon we got among the Canadian Islands. There are nine of them, and are so call'd from a number of poeple on their way from Canada down this river having stop'd there for some time. The last Island we came to we observed the channel on both sides to be bad on account of the fallen timber which rear their heads above water and some of them being less steady than others. The force of the current makes them bow, which has fix'd upon

37. *a hunter:* Perhaps an Indian hunter to help the boatmen locate game.
38. *bear:* probably a bearskin cover.

5 5

them the name of Sawyers.[39] We got in the midst of them, and I have not words to
express the horrors of our situation. For my part, I resign'd my self up, expecting
our boat wou'd be tore to pieces—but with great exertion we got through them.
We stood in great need of the two hands that went on shore to hunt, our boat being
but weakly man'd. I dont like this river. The passage is attended with much more
danger that I had any Idea of. We are obliged to make fast every night; and the
banks are so high, the current so rapid, and the river close to the shore so fill'd with
fallen timber and brush, that it is attended with great difficulty to accomplish.
They were several hours before they cou'd make fast for the night, and at last we
were obliged to tye the boat to some floating wood in eddy water. As it happen'd to
be a calm night, we lay very well till morning.

5 6

15th [June 15, 1784] Shifted our quarters to a more secure haven. The place we
were at is call'd Loncela Greece, the best hunting ground any where on the river.
As our provisions are allmost ex'austed, tis agreed to lay by for this day in hopes of
killg some deer. The men returnd without even having fired a gun. I lament the
loss of this day as the wind wou'd have been in our favor. The river is riseing,
which affords us some satisfaction. Every one thinks their troubles the greatest, but
I have seen so many poor creatures since I left home who's situation has been so
wretched, that I shall begin to consider my self as a favord child of fortune. Here is
a poor family encamp'd at this place. A Man and his Wife, their father and
Mother, and five children, left the Natchez seven months ago on their way to
cumberland river and had not a morsel of bread for the last three months. They
had buried one of the oldest of

5 7

their sons a little while before. The poor little children, when they saw us, cry'd for
some bread. Our Gent. gave them some flour—and I had the pleasure to contribute to the happiness of the Women by giving them some tea and sugar, which was
more acceptable to them than diamonds or pearls.—16th [June 16, 1784] Left Lance
La greece, which is 80 miles from the Ohio. The river has risen 3 feet which makes
us go briskly. We pass'd two Glades, the only clear land I have seen except where
some person had been living. We made fast at sun set, after having gone 80
miles.—17th [June 17, 1784] After going 20 miles, we were obliged to make fast to

39. *Sawyers:* An American colloquialism referring to the up-and-down sawing motion of
uprooted trees floating or stranded in a river.

the shore. The wind contrary and very high. It happen'd to be a clear good bank which enabled us to go on shore. Had the pleasure to see the wind favord some, tho not kind to us, for a large boat with all her sails set, with a Dozn men at the oars, came up the river quite fast. They left N Orleans

5 8

3 months ago, bound to Illinois. One Oclock P.M. The wind died away, and we push'd our luck again. The Musquitos bite and tease me so much that my life is allmost a burthen to me. I do sincerely think that all the wealth of the Indias wou'd not induce me to live in a Musquitoe country. I had no Idea they cou'd possibly be so intolerable. We did not go more than 15 miles before we were obliged to make fast to the shore for the night.

18th [June 18, 1784] The wind still against us. We came to the first of the Chickasaw Bluffs about Seven o clock in the morng, which is 201 miles from the Ohio. My patience is allmost exausted. What with the Musquitos and head winds, I am allmost sick. The passage early in the Spring wou'd be pleasant, but at present there is nothing but trouble. I have various Ideas about this river:—[I] some times conceit—I am got to the fag end[40] of the world; or rather that it is the last of Gods creation and the Seventh

5 9

day came before it was quite finnish'd. At other times, I fancy there has been some great revolution in nature, and this great body of water has forced a passage were[41] it was not intended and tore up all before it. The banks are now about 50 feet high, very ragged, and every here and there great pieces of the earth tumbling in to the water. Often great trees go with it, which fill the river with logs. Some places along shore there will be great rafts of fallen timber. The water is as muddy as a pond that has been frequently visited by the Hogs. Alltogether its appearance is awfull and Melancholy and some times terrific. One oClock P.M. came to more of the Bluffs, 12 mile from the first we pass'd. They are high red banks and look as if the earth was impregnated with copper ore. The Chickasaw Indians are settled back of this place. They, in company with

6 o

some refugees, robed several boats at this place. We came in sight of the last of the Bluffs at sun down, which is 45 mile from the first, and made fast for the night.

40. *fag end:* That is, extreme end.
41. *were:* Where.

19th [June 19, 1784] The wind so high and against us that we cou'd not attempt going till noon when the wind greatly moderated. We found a difficulty in passing the Bluff. A point of an Island made the channel very narrow and look'd as if two waters met, which caus'd a whirlpool. Our boat went round like a top and alarm'd me a good deel, a litle while before having been inform'd that last year a Mr Lankasang lost a boat at this very spot with 600 barrells flour on board. She dash'd against some raft wood that happend to be lodged there at that time and sunk directly. But fortunately for us, the coast was pretty

6 1

clear. We went about 30 miles when we were obliged to lay by an hour sooner than we woud have done—some heavy clouds appearing that indicated a storm—but its progress was not so rapid as was expected. This is a Passionate sort of a climate, quickly raised but soon blows over. However, this [storm] was not so easily appeased. It began about 10 oClock and seem'd to vent its utmost fury the whole night. In all my days I never saw such a continuance of severe lightning and heavy rain, a most uncomfortable night. I am so stung with the Musquitos that I look as if I was in the hight of the small pox. I have taken every precaution to guard against them to very litle purpose, and I am in a continual fever with the effects of their venom.

20th [June 20, 1784] No rain but cloudy and warm. At noon we found ourselves a little mistaken in our reckoning.

6 2

We came to the last Bluff and we thought we pass'd it the day before. Our progress very slow. A week this day since we enterd the Mississippi and have not got 300 mile.

21st [June 21, 1784] We went very well till noon when we were obliged to lay by for a couple of hours for a storm of wind and rain. After it abated, we again set of. Sun set, as usual made fast to a fine high sand bar, the most agreeable mooring we have had: no bushes to harbour the Mosquitos. We were not troubled quite so much.

22d [June 22, 1784] Pass'd the river St Francis 6 oClock in the morng, which is 75 mile below the lower Bluff. About 10 came to a very pretty glade full of fine ripe plumbs. There are great quantitys of them growing in this country, but I dont think they are as large as those that grow in Pennsylvania. In

6 3

the Evening Mr Gibson and Mr McFarlane, with three of the hands, set of for Noahs ark, a spanish fort about 12 leagues up the white river, as they had heard that the people of that Garrison were in want of flour.

23d [June 23, 1784] About sun set we arrived at white river and made fast to an Island to wait the return of our canoe. This day very pleasant and fewer Mosquitos.

24th [June 24, 1784] A very long day waiting the return of our people. This Island is full of young willow trees, which smell very fragrant. A large boat from the Illinois, encamp'd on this Island for the night. They are going down the river to take off some people who lost their boat three month ago.

25 [June 25, 1784] About 10 oClock in the morng our people return'd, having sold 100 barrells

6 4

at 17 Dollars pr[42] barrell. They got unloaded by noon and we again proceeded on our voyage. There are a great many Pelican about here, the first we have seen. They are a fine Majestick looking bird and at a distance resemble the swan. One of our people kill'd one and brought it on board the boat. They are all white, except the wings which are tinged with black. It measured ten feet from the tip end of one wing to the other. The Bill is about an inch wide and a foot in length. The under jaw or bottom of the bill resembles white leather and expands in an extraordanary manner. I saw 14 quarts of water put into its mouth, and it wou'd have held more. I can not comprehand what use they make of this amaizing pouch, unless to scoop up the little fish. They are very harmless and so tame that they swim allmost in reach of our oars. The most curious bird I ever

6 5

saw. We pass'd the Arkanza about 5 oClock in the evening. Went about seven mile before we lay by for the night, which made our days journey 25 mile. An extremely warm day and night, allmost coddled.[43]

26th [June 26, 1784] The weather the same. I can hardly keep my self alive. The river has risen three feet, which is a cordial to my spirits as it facilitates our going.

27th [June 27, 1784] So eager are every one to proceed that we left our moorings so early that we went 7 or 8 mile round an Island when we might have saved so much by waiting till day light. The weather exceeding warm. About 5 oclock in the afternoon came to the great Cut point. The water, by frequently over flowing the land here, has made a channell.

42. *pr:* Per.
43. *coddled:* Parboiled or stewed; thus, very hot.

6 6

There appears to be several of them. With in a few years [the water] has made a passage through a point of land of a few hundred yds,[44] which cut of 30 mile. Here we saw the poor french men who had their boat sunk. We gave them the good news of their boat being near at hand.

28th [June 28, 1784] The wind in our favor, very reviveing to me for I am every day more anxious to be at the end of my journey or voyage. In the afternoon, our boat—by the violence of the current—was drove against a large tree that was about 20 yds from the shore. It held us by the roof, notwithstanding the water run so rapid as to carry every thing before it. If the boat had not been very strong, we shou'd certainly been cast away. They were obliged to cut away part of the roof before we cou'd get disengaged. For my part, I gave my self up. I did not even

6 7

see a probability of saving my life— for the other boat was some miles a head of us, and I thought the canoe crush'd to pieces. But that was not the case. She weathered the encounter.

We met some french going [N]oahs Ark.

29th [June 29, 1784] At 8 oClock in the morning we came to the Yasow, a long river that makes at the back of an Island. The passage is difficult at this place. There is another cut of, and the water is allways very ruff in that case and requires great exertions to keep in the right channel. This cut of is 90 mile from the great cut point, which is 108 mile from the Arkanza. We stoped at an Island for the night, and I lost my poor little Dog, Fawnis.[45]

6 8

Tis supposed the Allegator got him as one was seen swiming about the boat in the evening— poor little fellow.

30th [June 30, 1784] at 10 oClock came to the great Gulph, which is 75 mile from the Yasow. This is the first settlement we saw on the river. Tis the property of Capt Barber, at present occupied by a Mullato Woman nam'd Nelly. She was exceeding kind to us, gave us water mellons, green corn, apples—in short, everything that she had was at our service. Her conversation favord rather more the Masculine than was agreeable. Yet I cou'd not help likeing the creature, she was so hospitable. She gave us the history of her life. She may be entitled to merit from some of her actions. But chastity is not among the number of her virtues.

44. *yds.:* Yards.
45. *little Dog, Fawnis:* This is the first mention of the dog. Presumably Trist did not begin such a journey with a pet in tow. She may therefore have acquired the dog as a gift during her stopover in Pittsburgh, Louisville, or elsewhere.

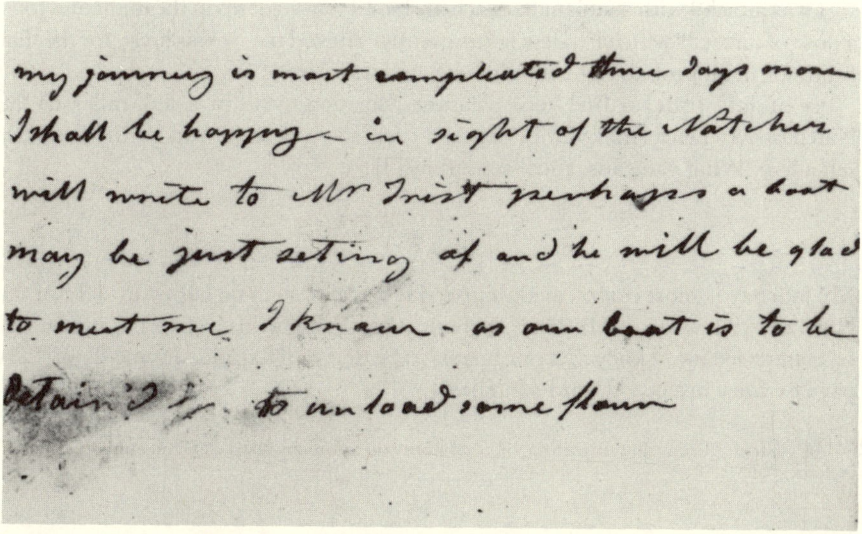

Figure 4.7   Written on July 1, 1784, the final entry in Elizabeth House Trist's travel diary breaks off toward the top of the page in mid-sentence. Because there are also smudge marks and attempted corrections in the final line, this fact may indicate some sudden agitation or interruption. (Trist-Burke-Randolph Family Papers (#10,487), Special Collections Department, Manuscripts Division, University of Virginia Library. Reproduced by permission.)

6 9

After spending a couple of hours with Mrs Nelly we took our departure, and in the afternoon came to the little gulph, 18 miles below the G[reat] Gulph. There was a fine Plantation at this place belonging to Phil Allston; but at present it is quite abandon'd.[46] He, being concern'd in the revolt at the Natchez, was obliged to fly the country. The imprudent conduct of a few designing men has allmost broke up the Natchez Settlement and ruind many that were elegantly settled.[47] We went 15 mile before night.

46.   In 1781, following a brief attempt on the part of the British to regain the fort, the Spanish once again took control of Natchez and most of what had been British West Florida. This reassertion of authority provoked one final uprising along the Mississippi north to Natchez. Led by James Colbert, a roving band of six hundred whites and Chickasaw ambushed Spanish travelers through most of the year 1782. Colbert's key lieutenants included John and Philip Alston, who had also been involved in the conspiracy against Spanish rule in 1781. With news of the peace treaty of 1783, the uprising subsided, Spain took firm control of the lower Mississippi, and those who had openly opposed Spanish rule—like the Alstons—fled the area.

47.   By 1783, Natchez was a rural community numbering perhaps five hundred residents, most of them living along Second and St. Catherine's creeks. Unlike New Orleans (which then boasted more than four thousand inhabitants and a thriving economy), Natchez had not prospered under either French or British rule. As part of French Louisiana and British West Florida, it was viewed as an isolated frontier wilderness, and neither Paris nor London adequately promoted the cultivation of a staple crop for export, so necessary for economic growth in the era of mercantile colonialism.

I was attackd with a violent headach and so Ill that I got up in the night and took a dose of tarter,[48] which in a few hours greatly relieved me. It was lucky for me that I did, for in all probability I shou'd have had a violent fever.

1st of July [1784] a fine cool pleasant Morning. Within a few miles of the Natchez. My heart sinks within me, and I feel so weak that I can hardly keep my self a live. What can cause these sensations[?]

7 0

My journey is most compleated. Three days more I shall be happy in sight of the Natchez. Will write to Mr Trist. Perhaps a boat may be just seting of, and he will be glad to see me, I know. As our boat is to be detain'd to unload some flour [Last page of diary breaks off, mid-sentence.]

48. *Tarter:* Tartar, double tartrate of potassium and antimony, used as an emetic or purgative.